MODERN AMERICA

by

John Vick

UNWIN HYMAN

Published by Unwin Hyman Ltd
15-17 Broadwick Street
London W1V 1FP

First published in 1985 by University Tutorial Press Ltd.
Reprinted 1988
© John Vick 1985
ISBN 0 7231 0885 4
Printed and bound in Great Britain by
Scotprint Ltd, Musselburgh, Scotland.

Acknowledgements

The author and publisher are grateful to the following for permission to use photographs and line illustrations:

The Associated Press Ltd. (p. 178); Auckland Collection (p. 85); The Batemann Archive, BBC Hulton Picture Library (pp. 30, 59 bottom, 125, 130, 148, 152, 155, 189, 193); Camera Press Agency (pp. 11, 73, 107, 110, 136 top and bottom, 138, 181, 182, 186, 197, 198, 200, 201); Central Press Photos Ltd. (p. 161); Embassy of Viet Cong (p. 173); Imperial War Museum (pp. 90, 96); Janine Wiedel Photo Library (p. 164); John Hillelson Agency Ltd. (p. 150); The Photo Source (pp. 21, 74); The Mansell Collection (p. 1); National Archives (p. 87 bottom); National Film Archive London © Raymond Rohauer, (p. 26 bottom); Naval History Photographs (p. 89); Peter Newark's Western Americana (pp. 18, 20, 23, 26 top, 31, 34, 37, 39, 41, 46, 49, 50, 52, 57, 59 top, 77, 98, 120, 123, 132, 145, 176); Popperfoto (p. 190, 202); United States Department of the Interior National Park Service (p. 4); United States Naval Photographic Centre, Washington (pp. 78, 91, 141, 177); Ford of Europe Incorporated (p. 27); American History Picture Library (p. 158).

Cover: Courtesy of the New York Convention and Visitors Bureau.

Despite every effort, the publishers have been unsuccessful in seeking permission to reproduce the following photographs: pp. 9, 86, 87 and 110. They ask the copyright holders or their agents to contact them about this should this book succeed in coming into their hands.

Contents

Introduction

The history of any country is always controversial. There is rarely a universally accepted version of events. The bias of the historian, the information available to him at a particular time and the skill with which he evaluates it, will all produce a variety of interpretations of the past. This diversity is certainly available in the history of twentieth century America. This book points to some of the areas where there is active debate. Contrasting opinions are offered in the text and documentary material to assist the reader to come to independent judgements. All students must be prepared to question facts and conclusions. They should read widely to find alternative interpretations and additional evidence.

The main focus of this book is the political history of America as seen through events at Washington D.C. Other important areas of study such as economic, social and cultural trends mainly receive attention when they have a bearing on this principal theme.

Unnecessary confusion can be caused in deciding how to name this country. As a general rule this book has used 'the United States' when it is clear that it is the government that is referred to. When the nation as a whole is considered, 'America' is more appropriate. In practice, most writers find these terms interchangeable.

In writing this book I have benefited from the help and encouragement of many people. In particular, I would like to thank David Warnes who made valuable suggestions about the structure and contents of the book, and Ernest Thomas, whose considerable patience, stylistic criticisms and meticulous typing immeasurably improved the end product.

1 America in the twentieth century

E Pluribus Unum

The motto of the United States *E Pluribus Unum* – Out of Many, One – could hardly be more appropriate to the American nation which entered the twentieth century. It was originally intended to refer to the coming together of many separate states (there are now fifty) to form one United States of America. The motto was given added meaning by the massive settlement of immigrants in the nineteenth and early twentieth centuries (see page 3). In 1800 most Americans were of British origin; by 1900 about half were people with roots in non-English speaking areas such as Russia, Poland, Germany and Italy. Since 1945 in particular a large number of immigrants have come from Spanish-speaking Central American countries and from South-East Asia. The country can truly be described as a 'melting pot' in which a bewildering variety of races, nationalities, cultures and languages have been transformed, sometimes painfully, into 'Americans'.

This diversity is further emphasised by the vastness of America and the geographical and economic variations this creates. In the early years of this century the rapidly growing industrial cities of the North and East which were making America one of the wealthiest nations in the world, attracted large numbers of new immigrants in search of work. The poorer agricultural communities of the Midwest and South were more likely to be dominated by 'native born' White Anglo Saxon Protestants (WASPs) who were often deeply suspicious of the new arrivals in the cities. The situation in the South was further complicated by the fact that America's blacks (a tenth of the total population) were concentrated in the region. They usually lived in considerable poverty and under the domination of the whites.

1.1 Entering a new world. Russian Jewish refugees entering New York harbour in 1892.

The American Constitution

To govern a nation as complex as America is no easy task. Nonetheless, the American Constitution (system of government) written in 1787 has been remarkably successful, requiring very few amendments (changes). The two most important features of this Constitution are 'federalism' and the 'separation of powers'.

Federalism

Federalism means there are two distinct layers of government. The 'Federal Government' in Washington D.C. is responsible for issues affecting the whole United States, such as defence, economic policy or commerce between the states. All matters not clearly allocated to Washington are left to the government of the individual states to decide for themselves.

The separation of powers

The Constitution is designed to make it impossible for any person or group to totally dominate the country. It does this by completely separating the various areas of government, President, Congress and Supreme Court, and allowing each one to balance or obstruct the activities of the others if it is thought necessary. The diagram on page 5 outlines some of the major powers possessed by the branches of government, and indicates ways in which each one can restrict the others. If there are any disputes about the operation or meaning of this written Constitution, the Supreme Court makes a judgement. This power can be crucial under some circumstances.

Despite the intentions of the 'Founding Fathers' in the eighteenth century, the modern President is undoubtedly the most important element in the Federal Government. It must be realised, however, that in many vital ways he is less powerful than a British Prime Minister. For example, he has very little direct control over what laws are passed because he is obliged to enter into a process of bargaining with

1.2 The expansion of the United States.

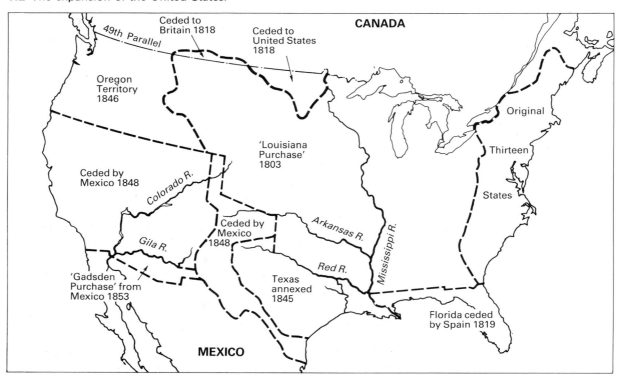

Population of the United States (millions)

1800	5.3
1850	23.2
1900	76.1
1910	92.4
1920	106.5
1930	123.1
1940	132.6
1950	152.3
1960	180.7
1970	205.1
1980	227.7

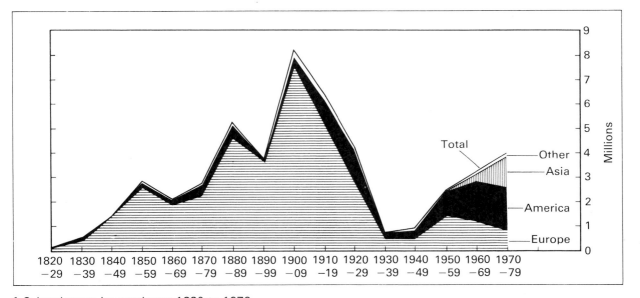

1.3 Immigrants by continent: 1820 to 1979.

Source
U.S. Bureau of the Census.

Congress if he is to get what he wants. He is by no means always able to win his battles in this respect. This is often because one or both houses of Congress may well not be dominated by his own political party.

Negotiation and compromise are also of great importance inside Congress. The procedure for turning a bill (the proposed law) into an act (final law) is very complex. At each stage there is the possibility that small groups or individuals will be able to block further progress. If the bill is to advance at all an enormous amount of behind-the-scenes bargaining is required. Lyndon Johnson was a master of the art of 'wheeler-dealing' as is described on page 6.

Political parties

Unlike the British Parliament, where all MPs can usually be relied upon to vote with

1.4 Ellis Island in New York harbour where all immigrants reported.
Between 1892 and 1954 12 million immigrants passed through Ellis Island.

1.5 The United States of America (not including Hawaii and Alaska).

1	New Hampshire	5	Rhode Island
2	Vermont	6	New Jersey
3	Massachusetts	7	Delaware
4	Connecticut	8	Maryland

their own party, American politicians are much more independent and vote as individuals on most issues. There are two major parties, the Republicans and Democrats, to which most politicians belong, but it sometimes appears very difficult to distinguish between them. The Republicans usually seem to appeal to conservatives, the wealthy, big business, and those who distrust government interference in their way of life. The Democrats generally obtain more support from liberals, racial minorities, big cities, the poor and those who believe government should be more active in solving problems. There are enormous numbers of exceptions to these 'rules', the most striking of which are the white Southern Democrats who in the past have been noted for their oppression of the blacks and their dislike of Federal Government interference in their affairs. The 1970s saw the start of a process which will probably produce a clearer distinction between the two parties as the Republicans attract most conservatives and the Democrats appeal more strongly to liberals. Throughout most of the period covered by this book, however, generalised ideas and philosophies matter less than personalities and particular issues in influencing American political loyalty.

Americanism

More important to most Americans are not the ideas which divide them, but the ideas which bind them together. This rather vague philosophy is known as 'Americanism' and emphasises equality, democracy and freedom. All Americans, regardless of race, religion or political views are promised equal opportunities to make the most of their talents. Freedom of speech and the press are greatly valued as essential features of the

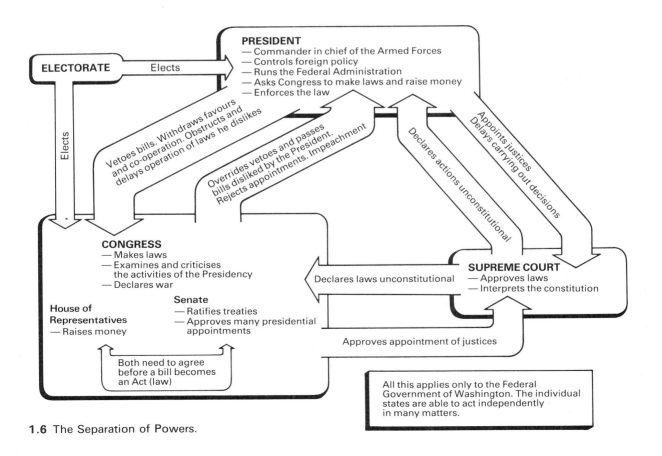

1.6 The Separation of Powers.

The Johnson Treatment

Both as Democratic leader in the Senate and as President, one of Johnson's greatest assets was his ability to manipulate and persuade other people to vote as he wanted. Few other politicians could match his skill. He played on the fact that all members of Congress were insecure, anxious to please their constituents and afraid of the next election, which was rarely far away. His interviews with reluctant allies were legendary. Two journalists describe the 'Johnson Treatment':

It 'could last ten minutes or four hours. ... Its tone could be supplication, accusation, cajolery, exuberance, scorn, tears, complaint, the hint of threat. ... It ran the gamut of human emotions. ... Interjections from the target were rare. Johnson anticipated them before they could be spoken. ... The Treatment was an almost hypnotic experience and rendered the target stunned and helpless.'

Source
Evans, R. and Novak, R., *Lyndon B. Johnson,* New York: New American Library, 1966.

American democratic system of government which is regarded as an example for the whole world to follow. It is assumed that this political freedom is impossible without economic freedom. This has meant that attempts by governments to interfere in the affairs of private businesses, for whatever reasons, have usually been strongly resisted. Most Americans believe that virtue and hard work should be rewarded, and that freedom of economic enterprise is the best way to make sure that this happens. The assumption that any American can 'get on' is illustrated by the number of Presidents who have talked with pride of their progress from 'log cabin to the White House'. It is no accident that the typical American hero is the cowboy who by his own struggles against evil and nature is able to make a life in the wilderness for himself and his family with no help from anyone else. He stands or falls by his own efforts. This philosophy is frequently referred to as 'rugged individualism'. The fact that the reality of life for many Americans in no way matches up to this ideal does not make it a less powerful sentiment. Americanism has helped to forge a nation which is remarkably united despite the striking contrasts within it.

Timeline

America since 1775

1775	Britain's thirteen colonies in North America begin their armed rebellion.
1776	Declaration of Independence by the thirteen colonies.
1783	Britain is forced to accept the independence of her former colonies. These are now known as the United States.
1787	The Constitution of the United States of America is ratified.
1803	The territory of the United States is doubled by the 'Louisiana Purchase' from France.
1812–14	The United States goes to war with Britain because her ships are being forcibly prevented from trading with Britain's enemy, France.
1819	Florida is ceded by Spain to the United States.
1823	The 'Monroe Doctrine' warns European powers to avoid intervening in the affairs of the American continent.
1845	The formerly independent Texas is annexed by the United States.
1846	The United States and Britain agree that the line of latitude 49° North is the frontier with Canada westwards to the Pacific. This followed a similar agreement in 1818.
1846–48	Victory in the war with Mexico brings vast territories, including California, to the United States.
1853	The 'Gadsden Purchase' of further territory from Mexico.
1860	Abraham Lincoln elected President.
1861	The American Civil War starts after eleven southern states form the Confederacy and attempt to leave the United States.
1863	Lincoln's Emancipation Declaration proclaims all slaves to be free.
1865	The Confederates surrender. Lincoln is assassinated.

1865–77	'Reconstruction' of the former Confederate States in order to readmit them to the Union.
1867	Alaska is purchased from Russia. Midway Island is annexed.
1898	After the victory in the war with Spain the United States gains the Philippines, Guam and Puerto Rico. Wake Island and Hawaii are annexed.
1900	Parts of Samoa are annexed.
1901	Theodore Roosevelt becomes President.
1903	A ten mile wide zone across Panama is obtained for the United States to build a canal connecting the Pacific and the Caribbean.
1909	Taft becomes President.
1913	Wilson becomes President.

2 Defining America's world role

The end of war and the making of peace 1918–20

On 11 November 1918 an armistice came into force to end the First World War. At the time the United States had an army of 2 million soldiers in France holding a fifth of the Allied front line against Germany. The war had had a considerable impact in America, although nothing like as drastic as the effect on other participants. Fifty thousand died on the battlefield, and the cost was $50 million a day by the end. The American economy prospered, as the demand for food, raw materials and manufactured goods of all kinds soared.

The United States had declared war on Germany in April 1917 because German submarines had attacked American ships trading with Germany's enemies. President Woodrow Wilson had insisted that Americans, as neutrals in this war, had the right to trade with any nation in the world. This trade happened to be vital to the war effort of Britain and France, as well as being enormously profitable to American farmers and businessmen, so for many Americans the principle of 'neutral rights' and private profit fortunately coincided.

2.1 American troops leaving New York for the war in Europe.

President Wilson and the Paris Peace Conference

Wilson saw the war purely as a struggle between Right and Wrong; profit did not come into it. He believed Americans should be fighting to enforce the principles of justice in the world which Germany's undemocratic, military government was endangering. When the war was over he wanted 'Peace without Victory'. He did not want the winners to humiliate the losers by forcing them to accept unfair conditions to end the fighting, which would merely cause further wars. Wilson outlined the United States' war aims in his 'Fourteen Points' in January 1918 (see page 11) which gave details of the type of world he hoped to build, with particular emphasis on freedom of trade, disarmament, and autonomy or self determination (the rights of nations to rule themselves). Most important for him was the creation of a 'League of Nations' to help keep the peace in the future. These idealistic

2.2 Europe in 1914.

2.3 Europe in 1919.

schemes, often vague, misunderstood, or difficult to put into practice, were the basis on which Wilson negotiated at the 1919 Paris Peace Conference.

Wilson's passionate concern for this conference can be seen by the fact that he was there himself for most of the period from December 1918 to July 1919, an unusual, and much criticised absence from his other duties. His efforts were only partly rewarded by the terms of the Treaty of Versailles, the most important of the treaties which were eventually signed in Paris. He faced strong and bitter challenges from Britain and France in particular, who were determined to punish Germany and prevent her threatening their security again. Their ideas of 'justice' were very different from Wilson's. He was obliged to give way on important issues such as the reparations to be paid by Germany for the cost of war damage, and the one-sided disarmament of Germany but not of her enemies. He was able to stop France from breaking up Germany into several smaller states, and in line with his ideas on autonomy, several new nations were created out of the ruins of the

2.4 Woodrow Wilson, President 1913–21.

President Wilson's 'Fourteen Points' (*extracts*) 'Program of the World's Peace'

1 'Open covenants of peace, openly arrived at', with diplomacy to proceed frankly and openly thereafter;

2 freedom of the seas in peace and in war;

3 the removal insofar as practical of barriers to the equitable flow of trade and access to markets;

4 reduction of armaments to the lowest level consistent with national security;

5 an adjustment of colonial claims based on the interests of the colonial peoples involved as well as the interests of the claimant power;

6 evacuation of Russian territory and co-operation to permit Russia 'the independent determination of her own political development and national policy';

8 all French territory 'should be freed' and invaded portions restored;

10 autonomy for the peoples of the Austro-Hungarian empire;

12 autonomous development for the peoples of the Turkish empire;

13 an independent Poland comprising territories inhabited by indisputably Polish people;

14 'A general association of nations must be formed under specific covenants for the purpose of affording mutual guarantees of political independence and territorial integrity to great and small states alike.'

Source
Congressional Record, 65th Congress, 2nd Session, Volume 56, pp. 680–681

Questions

(1) What is the meaning of 'autonomy'? What practical problems were involved in putting this principle into practice in regions such as the Austro-Hungarian empire or Poland?

(2) What is meant by 'barriers to the equitable flow of trade and access to markets' (Point 3)?

(3) Which point would Britain and France probably be least willing to accept? Explain your answer.

(4) Why was it necessary to evacuate Russian territory (Point 6)? It would be helpful to consult Chapter 7.

(5) What name is given to the organisation described in Point 14? For what reasons did Wilson's critics oppose America's entry into this body?

(6) A cynic might argue that some of these principles happen to fortunately coincide with America's self-interest. Which points might be used to support this idea? Explain your reasons in each case.

German, Austro-Hungarian, Russian and Turkish Empires. Most important of all he succeeded in making the League of Nations an inseparable part of the treaty. This gave Wilson the hope that any faults in the treaty could eventually be put right by negotiation, and peace might be kept by nations joining together under the principle of 'collective security' to act against any other nation which threatened war. It was this part of the treaty that caused the greatest controversy at home.

The struggle to ratify the treaty

The American Constitution demands that all treaties signed by the President must be approved (ratified) by two-thirds of the Senate before they can come into effect. If the vote had been taken in early 1919 it would probably have been clearly in favour of ratification. This situation changed during the year.

The traditional attitude of a large section of American opinion to foreign policy was

An isolationist view of the league

Senator Henry Cabot Lodge of Massachusetts, chairman of the very influential Senate Foreign Relations Committee, was one of the most skilful and determined opponents of the league and Wilson personally. In this speech to the Senate in August 1919 he stated some of his objections:

1   'I object in the strongest possible way to having the United States agree, directly or indirectly, to be controlled by a league which may at any time ... be drawn in to deal with internal conflicts in other countries, no matter what those conflicts may be.... It must be
5   made perfectly clear that no American soldiers ... can ever be engaged in war or ordered anywhere except by the constitutional authorities of the United States.'

Source
Congressional Record, 66th Congress, 2nd Session, Volume 58, pp. 3778–3784. Quoted in Smith, D. M. *The Great Departure: The United States and World War I 1914–1920*, John Wiley and Sons, Inc., New York, London, 1965, pp. 184–185

Questions
(1) Why was the Senate's opinion of the Treaty of Versailles so important?

(2) Lodge feared that the league might force the United States to deal with the internal conflicts of another nation (line 3). Was this a real danger? (It might help to re-read point 14 on page 12.)

(3) What decision was eventually reached concerning American involvement in the league?

that the United States should avoid all foreign entanglements except in extraordinary circumstances, such as 1917. The United States could look after her own and the world's interests best by avoiding overseas obligations. 'Moral influence' should be used instead of military power, economic aid, or any other device. This 'isolationist' outlook was still strong, particularly in the Mid-West where the Republicans gained much of their support. Republican opposition to Wilson and the

---

A disillusioned liberal reflects on the Treaty of Versailles

William Allen White was a very influential Republican newspaperman from Kansas whose views were representative of liberals disappointed by the treaty's failures:

1   'I cannot feel that the President is to be blamed .... I have seen day by day his struggle .... He was bound to the rocks with the vulture forever at his entrails. But they have – those damned vultures – taken the heart out of the peace, taken the joy out of
5   (the) great enterprise of the war, and have made it a sordid malicious miserable thing like all the other wars in the world .... We had such high hopes of this adventure; we believed God called us, and now at the end we are put to doing hell's dirtiest work, starving people, grabbing territory – or helping to grab it for our friends;
10   standing by while the grand gesture of revenge and humiliation links this war up with the interminable chain of wars that run back to Cain. It was not for this that Americans died – clean beautiful great visioned men who came seeking the Grail.'

Source
William Allen White to Ray Stannard Baker, 3 June 1919, Box 125, *Baker Papers*. Quoted in Noggle, B. *Into the Twenties*, University of Illinois Press, 1974, pp. 136–137

Questions
(1) Who was the President referred to in line 1? To which political party did he belong?

(2) White writes in lines 4–5 about the 'joy' behind the 'great enterprise of the war'. What principles does he think America was, or should have been, fighting for in 1917–18 to make the enterprise joyful?

(3) Who were the 'vultures' whom he blamed for this disappointing treaty?

(4) Give precise details of what he described as 'hell's dirtiest work' (line 8).

Democrats had been increasing since 1918 and was given a boost by the issue of the treaty, particularly the matter of the league, and any possible commitments this might mean for the United States. Isolationists joined forces with many liberals, who although they often disagreed with each other on virtually everything else, both disliked the treaty. Liberals criticised it for maintaining the 'old order' in Europe, for example, by not breaking up the British and French Empires. In addition, many 'hyphenates' (Irish-Americans, German-Americans, Italian-Americans and other groups) were unhappy at the failure of Wilson to satisfy their 'home countries'' national demands. These groups traditionally voted Democrat but now opposed Wilson. Others were totally uninterested in such a remote issue and failed to back Wilson.

The debate in the Senate became very bitter and personal, often losing sight of the issues altogether. In September Wilson started an exhausting nationwide tour to campaign for support for the league. This broke his health and he suffered a stroke which left him an invalid until he left the White House. The Senate finally rejected the treaty and league in March 1920 when the vote was seven short of the necessary two-thirds majority, with forty-nine in favour and thirty-five against.

Wilson tried unsuccessfully to make the 1920 presidential election into a vote effectively for or against the treaty. The Democratic candidate James M. Cox backed the league. The Republican Warren G. Harding's attitude was less clear. He certainly did not back the league, but he kept his options open for some future world role for the United States. He said he wanted the nations of the world to be 'associated together in justice, but it will be an association which surrenders nothing of American freedom'. Harding won decisively, backed by the isolationists, with 16 152 200 against Cox's 9 147 353. This meant that the league died as an issue in America and the United States entered upon a period when foreign policy was supposedly 'isolationist'. The United States signed a separate peace

treaty with Germany in 1921 which meant she had no formal part to play in the rebuilding of Europe in the 1920s.

Republican foreign policy 1921–32

Despite the apparent verdict of the voters in the 1920 presidential election, after Harding became President in 1921 and under Coolidge in 1923 and Hoover in 1929, the United States was still involved in the affairs of other countries. No country with the wealth of America, whose economy was so important to the prosperity of the whole world, could realistically cut herself off from all entanglements. If she did serious problems might be created for America and the world. The United States, despite not being a member, worked with the league particularly on humanitarian projects. In addition, in 1928 Secretary of State Frank B. Kellogg co-operated with French Foreign Minister Briand to produce a Peace Pact which aimed to outlaw the use of war as a way of solving disputes. This pact was eventually signed by sixty-four nations.

Repayment of war debts

The most pressing problem in the early 1920s was that of repayment of debts arising from the war. The United States had lent $10.3 billion during and after the war to her friends, nine-tenths of which had been to buy American goods. Most Americans expected early repayment with normal interest charges, but America's debtors were having severe economic problems and were reluctant to pay unless Germany first paid her reparations to them. This sum had been fixed by the Reparations Commission in 1921 at $33 billion, a crippling burden for the weakened and unwilling Germany to pay. When Germany announced in 1923 that she could no longer pay, France and Belgium occupied Germany's major industrial area, the Ruhr, and started to take the goods they felt were theirs by right. The result for Germany was political and

America's mission in the world

Theodore Roosevelt, a Republican, was President from 1901–09. He was determined to ensure that the United States took a leading part in world affairs, as he explains here:
    'The United States has not the option as to whether it will or will not play a great part in the world. It *must* play a great part. All that it can decide is whether it will play that part well or badly.'

Question
What economic and technical changes had taken place since the nineteenth century to convince people like Theodore Roosevelt that the United States must abandon her traditional isolationism? (Think carefully about what sort of contacts America had with other countries and how events in other parts of the world might affect her vital interests.)

economic chaos, notably enormous inflation in which the mark became worthless. This affected America as well.

The United States co-operated with the Reparations Commission by nominating an American banker Charles Dawes to head a committee to investigate the crisis. The Dawes Plan of 1924 arranged for an international loan to Germany, a reorganised Reichsbank, a new Reichsmark to replace the old currency, and reparations were reduced to more manageable amounts. Reparations were further reduced by the Young Plan in 1929, again backed by the United States. From 1924 the role of the United States government and private individuals and businesses in the German economy was vital. Large sums of money were lent or invested in Germany which enabled her to recover effectively from the despair of 1924. In the years 1924–29 Germany received more in loans, often from America, than she paid out in reparations. This was a vital contribution to European recovery.

When depression ravaged the world economy after 1929, and especially after the international financial crisis of 1931 ('the Hoover Moratorium'), the United States again attempted to contribute towards recovery. Most significant was Hoover's proposal in 1931 (the 'Hoover Morarorium') for a year's postponement of the repayments of all international debts. The results of this were slight however. The situation needed more radical solutions by this time.

1922 Washington Conference on the Limitation of Armament

The United States wanted to take a lead in the direction of disarmament, not only to keep the peace, but also to keep government expenditure, and therefore taxes, low in accordance with her economic policies. (See Chapter 3.) An area where this was of major concern was the Pacific and East Asia.

In the years leading to the First World War the United States became a major imperialist power and gained territory in the Caribbean (see Chapter 7) and the Pacific. By the 1920s she had colonies in the Philippines, Wake Island, Guam and many other Pacific islands. This gave her a considerable strategic interest in a region where Americans were also traditionally very involved as businessmen and Christian missionaries. Throughout this century many Americans have felt a closer emotional attachment to this area than to Europe and there have been frequent disagreements about where America's vital interests really lie. (See, for example, Chapters 8 and 10.)

In the 1920s the United States' position seemed to be threatened by an increasingly powerful and restless Japan. The possibility of a dangerous and costly arms race appeared to be avoided at the 1922 Washington Naval Conference. The major powers in the region, the United States, Britain, Japan, France and Italy, agreed to limit their tonnage of warships to a ratio of 5:5:3:1.75:1.75 respectively. In fact, the United States did not even build ships to the limits allowed by the treaty resulting from the conference and in effect stepped down from any appearance of world leadership after 1922.

Japan was not pleased by the outcome of the conference, even though there was no interference with her special privileges in China. These dated from 1915 and included the stationing of troops in Manchuria.

Japanese-American relations were also made worse by the very restrictive and discriminatory Immigration Act of 1924 which reduced the number of immigrants into America from over 700 000 in 1924 to about 50 000 each year after 1930. Japanese, who had earlier been a large proportion of immigrants, were virtually excluded.

The Japanese invasion of Manchuria in 1931 brought about a further worsening of relations with the United States. Hoover who, as a Quaker strongly disapproved of the use of force, was only prepared to use moral condemnation of this act of aggression, and did not even approve of the use of economic sanctions on Japan. This policy was followed by the rest of the world. Japan formally abandoned the Washington Naval Treaty in 1934, and appeared to be intent on further expansion in Eastern Asia. This was to play an important part in drawing the United States into a more active world role, and a final realisation that isolationism, whatever its merits in the nineteenth century, was not a practical or wise policy for the twentieth century.

3 The New Economic Era

The decade before 1929 is famous as a period of previously undreamt of prosperity and glamour. The writer F. Scott Fitzgerald called the 1920s 'The Jazz Age', but was very disillusioned with what he thought was a trivial, shallow, thoughtless way of life which turned away from the important problems of the age. Those who were more enthusiastic about these years called them 'The Roaring Twenties'. The Republicans, who dominated government at this time, believed they had created a 'New Economic Era' when all economic problems either had been, or were about to be solved. They claimed that the good things of life were to be made permanently available to all Americans.

3.1 King Oliver's Creole Jazz Band of 1920, with Louis Armstrong on trumpet and Lil Hardin on piano; King Oliver kneeling with trombone.

Timeline

America at home 1919–40

1919   Eighteenth Amendment ratified. Prohibition starts 1920.

1920   Senate rejects League of Nations (March).
Harding elected President (November).

1922   Fordney–McCumber tariff approved.

1923   Harding dies and is succeeded by Coolidge.

1924   Coolidge re-elected President.

1928   Hoover elected President.

1929   Wall Street Crash and the start of Depression.

1930   Hawley–Smoot tariff approved.

1932   Reconstruction Finance Corporation formed.
Bonus March (July).
Roosevelt elected President (November).

1933   The New Deal launched in the 'Hundred Days' (March).
Prohibition ends (March).

1935   WPA, Social Security Act, Wagner Act.

1936   Roosevelt elected for second term of office.

1937   Controversy over 'Packing the Court' (February).
Roosevelt briefly cuts government spending which leads to sharp recession 1937–38 (June).

1938   Roosevelt loses support for New Deal in mid-term elections.

1940   Roosevelt elected for third term in office.

The economics of Republicanism

The First World War on the whole had a beneficial impact on the lives of those Americans who did not actually have to fight. The years 1914–18 saw a considerable economic boom, but many feared that peace would bring hard times as the government stopped spending the vast sums of money needed to fight the war, and European countries recovered and began to compete with American producers. Wilson had no clear plan for reconstructing America at home to cope with the problems of peace; he was too concerned by events in Paris, and so important decisions were either not taken, or left to the Republicans who dominated Congress after 1918, and ran the Presidency from 1921.

Most Republicans believed that governments should be involved as little as possible in the day-to-day running of the economy. If businessmen were left alone to make their own decisions they thought that high profits, more jobs, and good wages would be the result. This policy is often known as *laissez-faire*. The only role for the government is to help business when requested.

Presidents Harding (1921–23) and Coolidge (1923–29) both followed policies which largely gave business what it wanted. Both men chose cabinets mostly composed of millionaires who could be expected to

3.2 *The New York Times,* 13th June 1920, reports the nominations of Harding and Coolidge by the Republicans for the presidential elections of that year.

sympathise with any difficulties facing businessmen.

'Restoring' free enterprise

During the war the government had felt it necessary to become involved in the running of many different areas of economic activity in order to produce an efficient war effort. Government either owned, managed or regulated industries such as shipping, railroads, food production and munitions. With the coming of peace the Republicans were determined to 'return to normalcy' and end this unwelcome and, as they believed, damaging interference in free enterprise. Some of this government activity could have had a valuable part to play in the future, but by 1920 Congress had ensured that free enterprise was fully restored.

Balancing the budget

When Harding, an easy-going man of very limited ability, came to power he was faced by the much feared collapse of the wartime

3.3 Warren Harding, President 1921–3, greeting Babe Ruth, the legendary baseball star.

boom. Unemployment rose sharply to reach a peak of over 10% of the workforce in 1921. His major remedy for this was to 'balance the budget'; that is, to make government spending as low as possible, and to make it equal the amount raised in revenue as taxes. It was believed to be essential that spending, and particularly taxes, should be as low as possible in order to give encouragement to everyone to work harder, and thus earn more money which could be kept and spent, rather than given to the taxman. Taxes were reduced throughout the 1920s, especially for business and those who earned the highest salaries. The poor hardly benefited at all.

Protecting the American economy

Most farmers and businessmen believed that they should be protected from foreign competition by imposing high tariffs (taxes) on all goods entering America, thus making them more expensive than American produced goods. In 1922 the Fordney–McCumber Act increased tariffs to record levels to satisfy this demand, but the results were in fact damaging, although this was not widely believed at the time. It meant that other nations were prevented from selling their goods in America, and so they could not earn enough money to buy American goods themselves. Also other countries retaliated by imposing their own tariffs on American goods in a 'trade war'. The overall result was a level of world trade lower than it might otherwise have been.

Curbing the power of 'Labor'

For several years after the war there was a series of bitter strikes as employers tried to cut their costs by reducing wages and increasing hours. Labour unions found it very difficult to operate in the face of often violent, strike breaking employers and unsympathetic laws. The government encouraged employers in their attempts to break the power of unions as they believed they interfered with the free enterprise

system. The government did nothing to prevent the exploitation of weak groups of workers such as women, children and old people, and the notorious 'yellow dog' contracts (whereby employers would not hire anyone who belonged to a union) were allowed to continue. The result was that union membership fell from 5 million in 1920 to 3.4 million in 1929 and the number of strikes declined in the late 1920s. Prosperity affected most of those who had a job, but their wages did not increase as quickly as company profits. Hours of work remained high, not surprisingly if the views of the President of the National Association of Manufacturers in 1929 were widely shared: 'Nothing breeds radicalism more quickly than unhappiness unless it is leisure.' Even where unions were strong, their leaders were not prepared to challenge the system. For example, John L. Lewis, aggressive leader of the United Mineworkers, was a strong supporter of the Republicans.

Anti-union feeling often went alongside hostility to 'socialism'. The end of the war saw a change of target from enemies abroad to enemies at home. The Russian Revolution of 1917 scared many into believing that these events could be repeated in America. Socialists of any sort were scarce in America but a 'Red Scare' nevertheless soon reached fever pitch. Socialism was often identified with immigrant groups, and so there were demands for tests of '100% Americanism' on a wide variety of individuals and organisations. Immigrants were a clearly visible and easily attacked 'un-American' group and the 1918 Alien Act gave wide powers to the government to deport 'subversive aliens'. A bombing wave in 1919 increased the hysteria. In 1920 one Democratic candidate fought on the slogan 'SOS – ship or shoot'. In the same year Attorney-General Palmer ordered the arrest of nearly 6000 people of whom 1000 were deported, usually on the basis of flimsy evidence.

The most notorious example of this hostility, which continued throughout the 1920s, was the Sacco and Vanzetti case. These two Italian immigrants, who spoke

3.4 The alleged anarchists, Sacco and Vanzetti, entering the court house during their trial, 1921–7. They were sent to the electric chair.

little English, but were self-confessed anarchists and draft dodgers, were arrested on a charge of murder and convicted in 1921, despite there being little evidence against them. Their trial and lengthy appeals gained massive international publicity and appeared to show that the American system of justice was in fact far from just. They were eventually electrocuted in 1927.

Corruption in the White House

By 1923 the post-war depression had ended with unemployment now around 3%, but different problems arose for Harding. Several of his friends and colleagues had a reputation for business practices of questionable legality and this spread to their behaviour in government. The worst example was the 'Teapot Dome Scandal' which exposed Albert B. Fall, Secretary of the Interior, who had received large payments from companies to whom he had agreed to lease the highly profitable United States Navy oil reserves at Teapot Dome and elsewhere. Fall escaped with a modest $100 000 fine and a year in prison.

It is probable that Harding did not know of these dealings, but his administration's reputation suffered badly in later years. The 'inside story' on page 25 was typical of many revelations of behaviour unsuited to the White House. He did not have to deal with the situation himself because his health collapsed and he died suddenly in August 1923 as the scandals in the White House were becoming public. Vice-President Calvin Coolidge, much to his surprise, was sworn in as the new President. Coolidge was an honest but rather uninspiring President. One biographer described him as a 'Puritan in Babylon', while the humourist Dorothy Parker, on being told that Coolidge was dead, wondered, 'How could they tell'?

'Bargain day in Washington'

Study this cartoon and answer the questions which follow:

Source
Ellison Hoover in *Life*, March 6, 1924 in Hofstadter, Miller and Aaron, *The American Republic,* Volume 2, Prentice and Hall, Inc., 1970

Questions
(1) a   In what year did the events satirised in this cartoon take place?
 b   What name is usually given to the episode upon which this cartoon is commenting?
 c   What is this cartoon trying to say about American government at this time?

(2) a   Find out the identity of the items bearing the 'SOLD' signs. Where are they all to be found?
 b   Explain the slogan 'Navy Slightly S-oiled'.

(3) a   Who was the President at this time, and to which political party did he belong?
 b   Describe this party's economic policies. Why do you think critics argued that these policies were in many ways responsible for the events shown in the cartoon?

At home with the Hardings

Alice Roosevelt Longworth was a relative of President Theodore Roosevelt and very active in Washington's social and political world. Her memoirs reveal with some relish, but also distaste, some of the disreputable aspects of life in the White House under Harding:

'Though violation of the Eighteenth Amendment was a matter of course in Washington, it was rather shocking to see the way Harding disregarded the Constitution he was sworn to uphold. Though nothing to drink was served downstairs, there were always, at least before the unofficial dinners, cocktails in the upstairs hall outside the President's room and guests were shown up there instead of waiting below for the President. While the big official receptions were going on, I don't think the people had any idea what was taking place in the rooms above. One evening while one was in progress, a friend of the Hardings asked me if I would like to go up to the study ... (It) was filled with cronies ..., the air was heavy with tobacco smoke, trays with bottles containing every imaginable brand of whisky stood about, cards and poker chips ready at hand – a general atmosphere of waistcoat unbuttoned, feet on the desk, and the spittoon alongside ... I think everyone must feel that the brevity of his tenure of office was a mercy to him and to the country. Harding was not a bad man. He was just a slob.'

Source
Longworth, A. R., *Crowded Hours*, Charles Scribner's Sons, 1933, pp. 324–5

1924 presidential election

Coolidge was able to clean up the mess quickly and effectively, and restored the tarnished image of the Presidency in time for the 1924 presidential election.

The Republicans' task at this time was made easier by the fact that the Democrats were hopelessly divided and chose John W. Davis, a weak compromise candidate who pleased very few people. The Progressives, a radical offshoot from the Republicans, nominated La Follette, but his chances were slim. Most electors responded to Coolidge's promise of stability and continued prosperity under the Republicans. 'Keep Cool With Coolidge' was the slogan which typified his campaign. The result was a landslide for Coolidge with 15 275 003 votes, to Davis'

8 385 586, and La Follette's 4 826 471. Republicans also had large majorities in both houses of Congress.

Economic boom

In 1928 when Coolidge surveyed the State of the Union he said: 'No Congress of the United States ever assembled ... has met with a more pleasing prospect than that which appears at the present time. In the domestic field there is tranquility and contentment ... and the highest record of years of prosperity'. Few would have denied this. Government policies did little to help this boom though; in fact, high tariffs and balanced budgets could have hindered prosperity. More important was the advance

3.5 President Calvin Coolidge. Official portrait by Charles S. Hopkinson.

The introduction of electric power transformed the lives of millions of people, particularly in towns and cities. Electric power was used extensively in industry and the home for the first time. New mass entertainments were created, notably cinema and the radio. By 1929 the cinema was an industry worth $1.5 billion per year with attendances of 110 million people per week. By 1930 40% of all families owned a radio set to listen to the 612 broadcasting stations. The influence of all this on the population's lives can only be guessed at. Certainly popular entertainment was closely connected to big business as advertisers spent vast sums of money, often through the radio and cinema, to persuade people to buy the vast range of customer goods available for the first time.

Amid all this glitter and prosperity America also had some seamier aspects to its way of life which governments either would not, or could not, control.

of science and technology resulting in improvements in efficiency, and the growth of whole new industries.

The most important new industry was the manufacturing of automobiles. The big three manufacturers, Ford, Chrysler and General Motors, were able to mass produce cars, at a price which actually fell throughout the 1920s, and so could be bought by a large proportion of the population. By 1928 there was one car for every six Americans compared with one for every sixteen in 1919. In 1929 automobiles accounted for 12.7% of the value of all American manufactures and employed 7.1% of all factory workers. This industry also stimulated many others such as steel, glass, rubber, oil, road construction and tourism. The impact on the American way of life was striking, perhaps most obviously in the growth of suburbs as people were able to live further away from their places of work. A profitable building boom was the result.

3.6 The movie star, Rudolph Valentino, in a still from the silent film 'The Sheik'.   (© Raymond Rohauer)

3.7 An early example of a Model 'T' Ford mass production line at Highland Park, Michigan, U.S.A.

Prohibition

In 1919 the Eighteenth Amendment to the Constitution of the United States was ratified. This, together with the Volstead Act which actually enforced the amendment, made the manufacture, sale and transportation (but not purchase) of intoxicating beverages illegal. Prohibition was nothing new. Before 1919 thirty-five states had some sort of prohibition, but only thirteen were 'bone dry'. 'Drys' were typically WASPs (White Anglo-Saxon Protestant) from somewhat backward, conservative small towns and farming areas who were unhappy at the direction America appeared to be taking. Organisations such as the Anti-Saloon League of America pointed out the severe damage done to family life, morals, health and the economy. Their particular targets were the rapidly expanding cities, the homes of new immigrants, whose traditions seemed to be totally alien to the 'dry' version of the American way of life. The views of some preachers, like Billy Sunday on page 28, gained support during

A vision of America without alcohol

Billy Sunday was an evangelical preacher whose radio broadcasts attracted massive audiences. His optimistic forecasts on the effects of prohibition were shared by millions:

'Slums will soon be only a memory. We will turn our prisons into factories and our jails into storehouses and corncribs. Men will walk upright now, women will smile, and the children will laugh. Hell will be forever for rent.'

Questions
(1) Explain why Billy Sunday and many others believed all these things would happen.
(2) Describe a 'typical Prohibitionist'. You might include information on occupation, religion, regional and national origin.

A record of the first official efforts at enforcement of Prohibition in 1920

January 16th: The law took effect.

January 31st: Congress was informed that wholesale smuggling of liquor was in progress on the borders.... The director of the Customs Service reported that only 'an infinitesimal quantity' of this liquor was being seized, (and) advised Congress that it had not adequately prepared to meet the problem....

February 19th: Two agents of the Internal Revenue Department engaged in prohibition work were arrested at Baltimore on charges of corruption.

February 28th: Two carloads of patent medicine containing 55% of alcohol were seized in Chicago by government officials.

March 10th: Federal agents in Brooklyn began a round up of druggists accused of selling whisky without a prescription from a doctor.

May 8th: The federal prohibition office in New York City complained: 'We are making a great many arrests, but the co-operation of the local authorities is absolutely necessary. We don't get that co-operation.'

May 24th: Dr Charles W. Eliot of Harvard University declared in an address at Boston that people with money and social position were helping to defeat the law.

June 6th: The special train of the Massachusetts delegation to the Republican National Convention was raided by prohibition agents who seized its stock of liquor.

July 2nd: Jail sentences aggregating fifty-nine months and fines totaling $85 000 were imposed on officials of two companies in New York City, found guilty of withdrawing 25 000 gallons of industrial alcohol which were diverted to beverage purposes.

Source
Merz Charles, *The Dry Decade,* University of Washington Press, pp. 57–60

Arrests and seizures made by Federal Prohibition Agents

	1921	*1925*	*1929*
Illegal distilleries seized	9 746	12 023	15 794
Gallons of distilled spirits seized	414 000	1 103 000	1 186 000
Number of persons arrested	34 175	62 747	66 878

In 1929 prohibition prosecutions accounted for 75% of all criminal prosecutions in the federal courts.

The mounting number of arrests and seizures could be interpreted as a sign of more effective enforcement of the law. Give a more convincing theory together with the reasons for it.

the war when many believed that grain made into alcohol could be better used for bread. Also some people were hostile to the brewers because large numbers were of German origin.

Although every state voted for prohibition in 1919 it was never successfully put into practice even at the start, as the diary on page 28 suggests. Congress never gave enough money to pay for the enforcement of this law, which was probably unenforceable anyway, and so illegal drinking was very common. The liquor trade soon passed into the hands of gangsters, who were often able to dominate police and local governments. Chicago's mayor 'Big Bill' Thompson was

3.8 Victims of the Saint Valentine's Day Massacre in Chicago, 1929.

clearly associated with gangsters such as Al Capone. Their activities soon spread from 'bootlegging' to narcotics, gambling and prostitution.

Most people recognised that prohibition was a disaster, but few ambitious politicians dared openly oppose it because the 'drys' were so influential in many areas. It was not until 1932 that the Democratic Party became 'wet' and voted to end it, but even then it came after a debate more bitter than that over the misery caused by the economic depression of that year. President Roosevelt finally obtained the end of prohibition in 1933 amid considerable rejoicing.

Ku Klux Klan

The sinister, but very powerful, KKK was founded in 1915 and expanded rapidly, especially in the South, during the 1920s. It aimed to protect what it believed was the 'American way of life' from all that was alien. Their view of a good 'American' was a 'WASP'. Particular targets were negroes, Catholics, Jews and other racial minorities. The KKK had an elaborate and bizarre organisation with mysterious rituals and a secret language. They were responsible for murders, beatings, mutilations, arson and a general reign of terror in many areas. Often they controlled local government and the police force, as the experiences of Robert Coughlan confirms on page 32. By 1930 the KKK's power was broken by internal feuds, and only continued as isolated groups of fanatics.

Agricultural depression

While life for the majority of Americans had never been better, some groups suffered real poverty. Many workers in textile factories and coal mines received very low wages and were lucky actually to have a job. Worst off were those who depended on agriculture for a living, a very large proportion of the population, for whom survival was a severe struggle. During the war agriculture had prospered as demand from Europe forced food prices and farmers' profits up. As European food production recovered after 1918 American farmers started to suffer. The statistics on page 66 show that prices fell sharply and did not recover until the late 1930s. Although prices were below pre-war levels, farmers' problems perhaps appeared worse than they were. The fact that wartime prices were so high made their collapse after 1918 all the more shocking. The truth was that the 1920s saw a return to near 'normality'.

The major problem facing farmers was that their production was always greater than the demand, not just in America, but in the whole world, so surpluses could not easily be exported. This situation was complicated by the fact that American patterns of food consumption were changing, damaging cereal farmers in particular. For example,

3.9 A Ku Klux Klan ceremony. The fiery cross and hooded costumes have always been part of the sinister Ku Klux Klan ritual.

'Konklave in Kokomo'

Robert Coughlan was a Catholic brought up in the town of Kokomo, Indiana, which was dominated by the Ku Klux Klan. Here he recounts his experiences:

'... the Catholic Church very easily assumed, in the minds of the ignorant majority, the proportions of a vast, immoral, foreign conspiracy against Protestant America.... Not all Catholics were in on the plot: for example, the Catholics you knew. These were well meaning dupes whom one might hope to save from their blindness.

... Literally half the town belonged to the Klan when I was a boy.... With this strength the Klan was able to dominate local politics. In 1924 it elected the mayor ... and swept the lists for city councilmen. It packed the police and fire departments with its own people, with the result that on parade nights the traffic patrolmen disappeared, and traffic control was taken over by sheeted figures whose size and shape resembled those of the vanished patrolmen.

... The Klan first appealed to the ignorant, the slightly unbalanced, and the venal; but by the time the enlightened elements realised the danger it was already on top of them.

... Indianapolis ... was dominated almost as completely as Kokomo ... the Grand Dragon had his headquarters there ... and from there he ran the state government. "I am the law in Indiana", he said, and there was no doubt about it.'

Source
Coughlan, Robert, 'Konklave in Kokomo' in Leighton, I. (ed.) *The Aspirin Age,* Simon and Schuster, 1968, pp. 114–116

Questions
(1) In the early twentieth century why might Catholics be disliked in Indiana for reasons other than their religious views? Think about where Catholics might have come from and how the local population might be affected by their arrival.

(2) What other groups did the KKK persecute?

(3) What acronym (a word composed of the initial letters of other words) describes the supposedly ideal American? What do these initials mean?

consumption of barley for beer fell by 90% due to prohibition, and demand for wheat fell by 25% in the years 1900–25, as an increasingly prosperous population preferred more luxurious foods. But, although incomes fell, costs such as taxes, wages, fuel and transport prices all stayed high.

Many farmers ran into crippling debt and were forced to sell up. There were one million fewer farms at the end of the decade than at the beginning. Many of those who remained were still unable to enjoy what were becoming 'essential' facilities: in the mid 1920s a mere 7% of farms had gas or electric light, and just 10% had piped water.

The only real solution to the problem was co-operation by all farmers, combined with government planning to end surpluses by bringing production down to equal demand. This idea was bitterly opposed by most farmers who hated the thought of government interference. Instead they sought higher tariffs, but these would have done nothing to help even if they had been accepted. Most farmers tried to make the most of what they had by increasing production through using more machinery and expanding the acreage they cultivated. This, of course, made the overall situation even worse.

Those who lived in towns and ran the government were generally content to ignore these problems. This was short sighted. Cheap food is good for the urban consumer in the short term, but in the long run industry too suffered, because rural poverty meant that those in the countryside could not afford to buy the goods produced on such an enormous scale in the towns. The fragile prosperity of the New Economic Era was suddenly shattered in 1929, and the plight of the farmers soon spread to the whole nation.

4 The Wall Street Crash and the Great Depression

The 1928 presidential election matched Al Smith, who was handicapped by being Catholic and 'wet', as well as representing the still divided Democrats, against the greatly respected and enormously experienced Herbert Hoover for the Republicans. Hoover's overwhelming victory surprised no-one and most Americans looked forward to continued prosperity. These optimists were rudely disappointed in 1929, but through no particular fault of Hoover.

4.1 President Herbert Hoover.

Speculation in the 1920s

One of the less desirable products of the New Economic Era had been a series of 'speculative manias' in oil, land and shares in particular. A 'speculator' is someone who buys something with the sole aim of selling it, preferably quickly, at a profit. He has no interest at all in the enjoyment or benefit that might be obtained from actually owning this possession. Speculation can be a very dangerous business, but millions were so obsessed by the prospect of getting rich quickly with the minimum of effort, that they were prepared to take the risk. Many people made vast profits during the mid-1920s by speculating in land in Florida, then an underdeveloped, often inhospitable region, but with a climate attractive to holiday-makers. Disaster struck in 1926 when first, land values collapsed from their unrealistic levels, and then a hurricane devastated the area, destroying the dreams, as well as property, of thousands of people.

The Wall Street Crash

The speculation which attracted most attention was focused on the Wall Street Stock Exchange in New York. Throughout the 1920s share prices had risen slowly but steadily, mainly as a result of the general prosperity of American business. At this time those who bought shares in a company were mainly interested in obtaining a steady income from the dividends (share of the profits) paid out at regular intervals. The shares of a company which gave high dividends as a result of good profits could reasonably be expected to be bought and sold at high prices. During 1928 and 1929 share prices started to rise at a startling rate, not because of sudden rises in company profits, or even hopes of such rises in the future, but because speculation had started.

The *New York Times* average of twenty-five leading industrial shares which stood at $106 in May 1924, and $143 in March 1926, had reached $331 by December 1928 and peaked at $542 on 3 September 1929.

The Florida land boom

J. K. Galbraith is a prominent economist, author, former United States ambassador to India, and Democrat. In his study of the Wall Street Crash he examines other speculative disasters, and sees many common characteristics:

1 'The Florida boom contained all the elements of the classic speculative bubble. Florida had a better winter climate than New York, Chicago, or Minneapolis. Higher incomes and better transportation were making it increasingly accessible to the frost-
5 bound North. The time indeed was coming when the annual flight to the South would be as regular and impressive as the migrations of the Canada Goose.

On that indispensable element of fact men and women had proceeded to build a world of speculative make-believe. This was a
10 world inhabited not by people who have to be persuaded to believe but by people who want an excuse to believe. In the case of Florida, they wanted to believe that the whole peninsula would soon be populated by the holiday-makers and the sun-worshippers of a new and remarkably indolent era. So great would be the crush
15 that beaches, bogs, swamps, and common scrubland would all have value.

...In Florida land was divided into building lots and sold for a ten per cent down payment. Palpably, much of this unlovely terrain that thus changed hands was as repugnant to the people who bought it
20 as to the passer-by. The buyers did not expect to live on it; it was not easy to suppose that anyone ever would. But these were academic considerations. The reality was that this dubious asset was gaining in value by the day and could be sold at a handsome profit in a fortnight.
25 ...More land was subdivided each week. What was loosely called sea-shore became five, ten, or fifteen miles from the nearest brine. Suburbs became an astonishing distance from town.'

Source
Galbraith, J. K., *The Great Crash 1929*, Penguin Books, 1954, pp. 32–33

Questions
(1) Explain how the following extracts might, with only a little adaptation, be used to describe the speculation on Wall Street:
a 'This was a world inhabited ... by people who want an excuse to believe' (lines 9–11).

    b 'The buyers did not expect to live on it' (line 20).
    c 'This dubious asset was gaining in value by the day and could be sold at a handsome profit in a fortnight' (lines 22–24).
(2) What happened to most of those people who bought land in Florida?
(3) Why did the Wall Street speculation end in disaster?
(4) What were the effects of the Wall Street Crash on the American economy?

Individual shares often performed even better: in the eighteen months to September 1929 'Radio' rose from $94 to $505, despite never even paying a dividend. There are many reasons why this speculation occurred. The 1920s saw very low interest rates and so it was easy to borrow money, especially to 'play the market'. Most shares were bought, not with ready cash, but 'on the margin': that is to say, a buyer needed only to produce a small proportion of the actual price in order to obtain a share. He borrowed the rest. This meant that someone with a limited amount of money could actually buy a large number of shares, which encouraged prices to rise. The ease with which shares could be purchased by a wide variety of people is observed by F. L. Allen on this page. This was profitable for the speculator, and also for the lender of the money, so many businesses, including banks, were anxious to lend money and make gains much greater than those which could be made by investing in producing goods.

Wall Street fever sweeps America

It would be a mistake to exaggerate the number of people who 'played the market' in 1929, but there was certainly a 'Wall Street mentality' which was widespread, and accepted that speculation was desirable and foolproof:

'The rich man's chauffeur drove with his ears laid back to catch the news of an impending move in Bethlehem Steel; ... The window-cleaner at the broker's office paused to watch the ticker, for he was thinking of converting his laboriously accumulated savings into a few shares of Simmons. Edwin Lefevre (an articulate reporter on the market at this time who could claim considerable personal experience) told of a broker's valet who made nearly a quarter of a million in the market, of a trained nurse who cleaned up thirty thousand following the tips given her by grateful patients; and of a Wyoming cattleman, thirty miles from the nearest railroad, who bought or sold a thousand shares a day.'

Source
Allen, F. L., *Only Yesterday*, Harper, New York, 1931, p. 315

4.2 'Black Thursday', 24 October 1929: Panic in Wall Street as share prices collapse.

It appeared for a long time that it was impossible to lose because prices continued to soar, mainly because speculators wanted them to do so. The price of a share to a speculator is mainly decided by what he thinks it will be worth in the future. In September 1929 some people started to have doubts about whether share prices would continue to rise and started to sell shares without buying more. On 'Black Thursday', 24 October 1929 the uncertainty came to an end. Many people lost confidence (for reasons which were largely mysterious to them, to observers and to historians) in the possibility of future price rises, and started to sell all their shares for whatever price they could get. This became infectious and panic swept Wall Street. Nearly 13 million shares were sold and prices dropped sharply. Friday and Saturday saw some stabilisation in the market, but on Monday the real Crash occurred. Sales were over 9 million and the *New York Times* average fell $49. The next day sales were well over 16 million and average prices fell $43 to reach $275. The slide continued even after this panic until by June 1932 prices were down to $58. Some of the shares which had risen highest in the boom were the ones which collapsed furthest. Many companies disappeared totally.

The collapse in share prices

Between September 1929 and July 1932 the total value of shares on Wall Street fell from $89.6 billion to $15.6 billion. These statistics show what happened to some individual companies. (All prices are in dollars.)

	September 1929	*July 1932*
U. S. Steel	262	22
General Motors	73	8
Montgomery Ward	138	4
American Telephone and Telegraph Company	304	72
United Founders	70	0.50
American Founders	117	0.50

The collapse of the New Economic Era

About one million people were actively involved in speculating on Wall Street in 1929 and most of them lost nearly all their money. The sudden loss of wealth of so many people had a serious effect on those who relied on them for trade. This was bad enough, but of greater significance was the damage done to companies and banks who lost vast sums of money in unpaid debts. This was in large part made worse by the absence of suitable laws and rules to prevent much of the reckless and often dishonest practices which had been common. Many went bankrupt, causing widespread unemployment and poverty amongst millions who had no connection with any stock exchange. Very quickly America sank into a deep depression.

Some economists doubt whether the Crash was really responsible for the Depression. They point out that certain important industries, such as construction and automobiles, were starting to get into difficulties beforehand. Throughout the 1920s industrial production had grown considerably, partly because low interest rates had enabled companies to borrow money cheaply to build new factories. Unfortunately demand in America and the world had not been large enough to buy this increased supply of goods. Foreign trade was in the doldrums, agriculture was depressed (see pages 65–67): the economy was basically unsound. All this is undoubtedly true, but the Crash was of overwhelming importance in bringing about the collapse of this brittle structure. The orgy of speculation which preceded the Crash was known at the time to be dangerous, but those in authority preferred to leave well alone, often because they were making fortunes of their own in the process.

America without work

After the Crash there was a marked increase in the number of bankruptcies, and with this came massive unemployment – 5 million in 1930, 9 million in 1931, and 13 million in 1932. This was nearly a quarter of the workforce. The national picture was bad enough, but certain areas, industries and groups of workers were even more severely affected. Denora, Pennsylvania, had a population of 13 900 but only 277 had a job in March 1932. In the coal-mining communities of Williamson County, Illinois, there was no work at all. The hardship that was caused in California is examined on this page.

There were problems even for those who still had a job. Wages were often reduced by employers desperate to cut their costs and so remain in business. Women, children, negroes and Mexican immigrants suffered badly, and often had no choice but to work longer hours for reduced wages.

The already hard-pressed agricultural industry reached breaking point. Prices, at a low level throughout the 1920s, fell to levels which made it a pointless task to harvest, process and transport produce to market. In 1925 31% of all farms were mortgaged to banks due to debt. By 1932 this had risen to 40%. The problems were made worse because the earlier drift of the rural population to the towns in search of better jobs now halted due to the absence of jobs anywhere. In protest at this disastrous situation farmers in some areas organised

4.3 The Great Depression: a cheap food line in New York City, 1931.

The human cost of unemployment

In November 1932 the California Unemployment Commission reported to the Governor on the hardships suffered by the enemployed:

1 'Unemployment and loss of income have ravaged numerous homes. It has broken the spirits of their members, undermined their health, robbed them of self-respect, destroyed their efficiency and employability. Loss of income has created standards of living of
5 which the country cannot be proud. Many households have been dissolved; little children parcelled out to friends, relatives, or charitable homes; husbands and wives, parents and children separated, temporarily or permanently. Homes in which life savings were invested and hopes bound up have been lost never to be
10 recovered. Men, young and old, have taken to the road. They sleep each night in a new flophouse. Day after day the country over, they stand in breadlines for food which carries with it the suggestion "move-on", "We don't want you". In spite of the unpalatable stew

and the comfortless flophouses, the army of homeless grows
15 alarmingly. Existing accommodations fail to shelter the homeless;
jails must be opened to lodge honest job-hunters. Destitution
reaches the women and children. New itinerant types develop:
"women vagrants" and "juvenile transients". There are no
satisfactory methods of dealing with these thousands adrift.
20 Precarious ways of existing, questionable methods of "getting by"
rapidly develop. The law must step in and brand as criminals those
who have neither desire nor inclination to violate accepted
standards of society.
   Numerous houses remain physically intact, but morally shattered.
25 There is no security, no foothold, no future to sustain them. Savings
are depleted, and debts mount with no prospect of repayment.
Economic make-shifts are adopted. Woman and child labor further
undermine the stability of the home. The number of applicants for
charitable aid increases seriously. There is not enough money to do
30 the job well and adequately. Food rations are pared down, rents go
unpaid, families are evicted. They must uproot their households
frequently. Physical privations undermine body and heart. The peace
and harmony of the home vanish. The effect upon children differs,
but it is invariably detrimental.
35 Idleness destroys not only purchasing power, lowering the
standards of living, but also destroys efficiency and finally breaks
the spirit. The once industrious and resourceful worker becomes
pauperized, loses faith in himself and society.'

Source
California Unemployment Commission Report, quoted in Bernstein, I., *The
Lean Years,* Houghton Mifflin Company, Boston, 1960, pp. 321–322

Questions
(1) What caused the massive unemployment described here?
(2) a How did Hoover believe the poor should be helped? (See
        also page 44.)
    b Do the authors of this official report approve or disapprove
        of the government's economic policies? Use evidence from
        the document to support your case.
(3) a Explain what the authors mean by 'Numerous houses remain
        physically intact, but morally shattered' (line 24).
    b Why should 'woman and child labor' (line 27) be more of a
        problem during times of depression than in prosperity?

'farm holidays' in 1932, when supporters were told to 'stay at home – buy nothing – sell nothing'. This was not enough to save farmers from ruin.

The group which caught the nation's attention most dramatically were the veterans of the war who organised the Bonus Expeditionary Force in 1932 to march on Washington D.C. They had earlier been promised compensation for their war service and wanted the government to pay the money early because of their sudden poverty.

4.4 General Douglas MacArthur and his aide, Major Dwight D. Eisenhower, led the operation to clear the bonus marchers from Anacostia Field. Both men were important figures in the American Second World War effort. Eisenhower was President from 1953–61.

To pressurise Hoover and the Congress about 11 000 of them, including their families, made a shanty town on Anacostia Field in the centre of the city. Hoover ordered the army, led by General Douglas MacArthur, to clear the field, because he believed they were organised by revolutionaries and criminals, who posed a threat to the United States Government. The B.E.F.'s version of these events, on page 42, is rather different.

Attempts to end the Depression

In the early days of the Depression the official view of Hoover's administration and its many supporters in business was that there was no problem. There was a steady stream of public statements (presumably trying to rebuild the confidence shattered in October 1929) which claimed that these were only temporary difficulties, and that the American economy was basically still

The Battle of Anacostia Field

When Hoover ordered the army to clear the Bonus Expeditionary Force out of their shanty town on Anacostia Field in Washington D.C., he demonstrated how wide had become the gulf between his administration and the people of America by 1932. W. W. Waters, who was a leading figure in the B.E.F., gives his account:

'The troops reached Anacostia Field about eleven at night. Here Bedlam had broken loose, like a fire in a madhouse, when the news of the troops' coming was confirmed and few waited to meet them. The people had reason for being insane. Men and women were trying to gather what they could and flee. Some of them had had a whiff of gas over in the city and wanted no more of it. Men and women ran about wildly with packs and bundles on their shoulders. . . .

They came with their gas bombs and their bayonets. . . . The troops fired the shacks on the edge of the camp . . . .

Tanks and soldiers guarded the bridge back to the city so that no refugees could get into Washington. They could go where they wished but not back to their capital. They might disturb the sleep of a few of the Government officials.

The jeers and cries of the evicted men and women rose above the crackling of the flames. The clatter of the tanks was dulled by the sirens and horns of fire apparatus come to control the flames. . . .

The flames were mirrored in the drawn bayonets of the infantry as they advanced through the camp . . . . There is no way of knowing whether, in the debacle, a few homeless men perished or not.

On the evening after the crime against the B.E.F. had been done General MacArthur said: "That mob was animated by the essence of revolution . . . . In my opinion if the President had not acted . . . he would have been faced with a grave situation indeed." '

Source
Waters, W. W., as told to White, W. C. *B.E.F. The Whole Story of the Bonus Army,* John Day Company, New York, 1933, pp. 232–238.

Questions
(1) What was the aim of the Bonus Expeditionary Force?
(2) What was the official government opinion of this group?
(3) Waters is obviously sympathetic to the B.E.F. Quote from the document to show how his feelings are affecting his account of 'the Battle'.

healthy. Recovery was only just round the corner. On 25 October 1929, Hoover claimed: 'The fundamental business of the country ... is on a sound and prosperous basis.' In 1930, Secretary to the Treasury Mellon, who presumably could be expected to know, said: 'I see nothing ... in the present situation that is either menacing or warrants pessimism. ... I have every confidence that there will be a revival of activity in the spring and that during the coming year the country will make steady progress.' A book published in 1931 which collected these optimistic forecasts was aptly entitled *Oh, Yeah!*

Traditional Republican remedies

Ugly reality eventually started to impose itself on Hoover. His greatest worry to start with was that the government's budget was becoming unbalanced. As businesses failed and workers no longer earned wages, the amount raised in taxes fell dramatically, but spending remained at its former level, or even increased. Most economists believed that prosperity was impossible unless government finances were brought back into balance. Hoover tried to cut spending, but failed, which was probably merciful as this policy would probably have made matters even worse than they already were.

Another traditional, but in reality destructive, 'remedy' was to increase protection. The 1930 Hawley–Smoot Act raised tariffs to new record levels. Between 1925 and 1929 the average level of tariffs increased the price of imports by nearly 26%. In the years 1931–35 tariffs put up import prices by over 50%. The result was a further decline in world trade to the benefit of no-one.

Hoover began to shift the blame for America's problems onto other coutries. He argued that the world depression had dragged America down with it. The more convincing explanation is that it was America which had dragged the world down into depression. The example of Germany is particularly clear. Her recovery between 1924 and 1929 was based largely on American loans. After 1929 American money was withdrawn, with the result that by 1932 Germany had 6 million unemployed and political chaos, which contributed to the rise of Hitler. America's depression started earlier, was much more severe, and lasted longer than that of most other countries. Hoover's attempts to reduce international debts brought little improvement, but were moves in the right direction.

Charity begins at home

Hoover's government was soon forced to act at home as well. There was no system of government-financed social security or unemployment insurance to provide help for those in need. As Hoover explains on page 44, this was a deliberate choice. Most Americans believed it was wrong for government to take responsibility for the problems of individuals. In good times citizens should set aside money for sickness, old age or unemployment. Families should care for relatives in need. Should these means prove inadequate, then private charities, churches or public-spirited citizens would help. If government provided money it would merely encourage idleness and waste, which was damaging to morals and the economy.

This view was irrelevant to the condition of America in the 1930s. Families without a wage earner could not cope; private charities soon ran out of money; city and state governments raised funds to help out, but this too was not enough. No city was able to provide a family with more than $5 per week, and most gave much less. Chicago in May 1932 had 40% unemployment, 130 000 families on relief, and simply ran out of money. Wages of city employees were unpaid, and schools were forced to close. This was typical of many cities and states, so the Federal Government had little choice but to help.

Hoover, the government and charity

Hoover's views, expressed here, were shared by the vast majority of Americans during the years of prosperity. The Depression forced many to realise that these ideas no longer made practical sense:

Hoover's aim was to help 'the full mobilization of individual and local resources and responsibilities. ... Personal feeling and personal responsibility of men to their neighbor is the ... essential foundation of modern society. A cold and distant charity which puts out its sympathy only through the tax collector, yields a very meagre dole of unloving and perfunctory relief.'

Question
The unemployed, not surprisingly, generally thought Hoover did not care about their plight. Having taken into account all the evidence, write your own views about whether he was a heartless man.

Help for the unemployed

Hoover preferred to encourage rather than to spend. He urged employers and individuals to do their duty. In 1931 he started a 'Give-a-Job' scheme for householders to create jobs, but this achieved little. More important was his reluctant and delayed aid directly to business. He hoped that if business could recover then it could provide jobs for the unemployed. This has been described as 'the trickle down effect', or 'the theory of feeding the sparrows by feeding the horse'. The problem was that it did nothing immediately to help those who were actually starving. In 1931 about 100 died of starvation in New York hospitals alone. It is impossible to calculate the national death toll. This situation is all the more shocking when it is realised that America was producing too much food at this time.

Attempts to give federal aid to industry came in 1932 with the creation of the Reconstruction Finance Corporation led by Dawes. It was designed to give loans to industry, railways and banks to keep them going. It also financed a few public works, for example, constructing bridges and waterways, but this was on too small a scale to be really effective.

Farmers required urgent assistance, and the government realised what was required. Restriction of output was suggested, but only by voluntary agreement, not government control. Failure was inevitable. Some surpluses were bought up and given to the Red Cross, but the far more effective solution would have been to stop the surpluses being produced at all. Loans were provided for seed and fertiliser, and to help those in debt, but all to no avail.

These measures were hopelessly inadequate to deal with the social and economic disaster which had devasted the country. As America approached the 1932 presidential election there was an urgent need for new solutions, but it was by no means certain that these were available. Few politicians or economists ever suggested policies which differed much from those proposed by Hoover, or indeed the governments of most other countries. The outlook was bleak.

5 Roosevelt's New Deal 1932–36

1932 presidential election

To challenge Hoover in 1932 the Democrats, united for a change, chose Franklin D. Roosevelt as their candidate. Although he was a successful and likeable Governor of New York, he was by no means a commanding national figure who could hardly fail to win. Even though he promised Americans a 'New Deal' to end the Depression, his campaign did not really show him to be a crusader for radical changes in policy. Indeed his policies were often very traditional, confused and even self-contradictory, as extracts from some of his speeches show on page 47.

Roosevelt was described as 'a pleasant man who, without any important qualifications for the office, would very much like to be President'. He was, however, a politician of extraordinary skill who successfully capitalised on the unpopularity of Hoover, whose cause was damaged by the Depression, and who had none of his opponent's approachability and warmth. One wit said: 'If you put a rose in Hoover's hand it would wilt'. The result was a convincing victory for Roosevelt with 22 810 000 votes to

---

Lifeline

Franklin Delano Roosevelt (1882–1945)

Roosevelt was born into a very wealthy New York family, a factor which helped him rise up the political ladder of his home state at an early age. He served as assistant to Secretary of the Navy Daniels, under President Wilson, a man he greatly respected, and in 1920 he ran as Vice-Presidential candidate alongside Cox.

He seemed destined to hold high office, but tragedy struck in 1921 when he was attacked by poliomyelitis, a disease which prevented him from walking again without braces and a cane. His remarkable courage enabled him to remain in political life, and become Governor of New York State in 1928. During the Depression he gained a reputation as a humane and effective administrator. His most notable achievement was the creation of America's first state-run relief agency, a forerunner of later New Deal programmes.

His wife Eleanor, niece of Theodore Roosevelt and his distant cousin, was a great help to him, especially after his illness. She remained loyal to him after he had an affair with her social secretary, an 'indiscretion' which could have ruined his political career in an age when divorce was often treated with great disapproval. She became a very popular 'First Lady', and remained active in public life long after her husband's death.

5.1 President Franklin D. Roosevelt out meeting the public.

Hoover's 15 759 000. There were also heavy Democratic majorities in both Houses of Congress. This gave Roosevelt a strong position from which to work.

Roosevelt's approach to economics and politics

Roosevelt was above all a pragmatist, that is, a man who has no fixed ideas about the way the world works, and the solution to any problems facing it, but is prepared to experiment with a variety of different approaches. If a policy succeeds, fine; if it fails, find another one. He was guided by

some very generalised beliefs: he felt that private enterprise should be preserved; he accepted that the government had a duty to help the needy; he distrusted the concentration of too much power in any one place, be it the President, private businesses, labour unions, individual states or anyone else; he preferred to work by persuasion and co-operation rather than by the use of force. However, none of these beliefs would severely restrict his freedom to act in a flexible way.

Before taking power in March 1933, Roosevelt collected an impressive group of advisors, often from universities, to help him produce detailed policies to end the

Roosevelt's 'economic policies'

It is very difficult to say precisely what Roosevelt's economic policies were, either before or after the 1932 election:

1 'I accuse the present Administration of being the greatest spending Administration in peace times in all our history. It is an Administration that has piled bureau on bureau, commission on commission, and has failed to anticipate the dire needs and the
5 reduced earning power of the people.' (1932)

'If starvation and dire need on the part of any of our citizens make necessary the appropriation of additional funds which would keep the budget out of balance, I shall not hesitate to tell the American people the full truth and ask them to authorise the expenditure of
10 that additional amount.' (1932)

'Say that civilisation is a tree which, as it grows, continually produces rot and dead wood. The radical says: "Cut it down". The conservative says: "Don't touch it". The liberal compromises: "Let's prune so that we lose neither the old trunk nor the new branches".
15 This campaign is waged to teach the country to march upon its appointed course, the way of change, in an orderly march, avoiding alike the revolution of radicalism and the revolution of conservatism.' (1932)

'…we cannot review carefully the history of our industrial
20 advance without being struck with its haphazardness, the gigantic waste with which it has been accomplished, the superfluous duplication of productive facilities, … the thousands of dead-end trails into which enterprise has been lured, the profligate waste of natural resources. Much of this waste … could have been prevented
25 by greater foresight and by a large measure of social planning. Such controlling and directing forces as have been developed in recent years reside to a dangerous degree in groups having special interests in our economic order, interests which do not coincide with the interests of the Nation as a whole. … We cannot allow our
30 economic life to be controlled by that small group of men whose chief outlook upon the social welfare is tinctured by the fact that they can make huge profits.' (1933)

Questions
(1) What phrase from these speeches shows Roosevelt using the Republican's own ideas to attack Hoover?
(2) What is meant when a politician is described as (a) a radical, (b) a conservative and (c) a liberal?
(3) Give an example of Roosevelt apparently contradicting himself in different speeches.
(4) Which, in your opinion, is the most radical of the four passages? Give reasons for your choice.
(5) Give an example of 'a large measure of social planning' (line 25) carried out by Roosevelt after 1932.

(6) To whom is Roosevelt referring when he speaks about 'that small group of men whose chief outlook upon the social welfare is tinctured by the fact that they can make huge profits' (lines 30–32)? What events had made him describe them like this?

(7) After studying Roosevelt's policies when actually put into practice after 1933, which of these extracts do you think most accurately describes his true ideas? Explain your answer fully.

(8) How can you explain the fact that Roosevelt is so inconsistent in these speeches? Try to go beyond the possibility that he is either stupid or dishonest.

Depression. This 'Brains Trust', and also those whom he later appointed to government jobs, reflected his own lack of a fixed ideology. Some of them were very conservative and would have found much in common with Hoover. Others were radical left wingers who were very critical of the whole system of private enterprise. They believed Roosevelt should increase the power of government to plan the development of the economy; deliberately unbalance the budget to create jobs; produce a 'welfare state' to provide a decent standard of living for all Americans.

The Hundred Days

As soon as he took office, Roosevelt summoned Congress into emergency session to deal with a flood of bills which he wanted it to pass. This 'Hundred Days' of feverish activity laid the foundations for the New Deal, and set the tone for a Presidency eager to become involved in every aspect of economic activity. Roosevelt's ideas were all accepted and resulted in a bewildering variety of laws and organisations intended to end the Depression. These organisations, often known by their initials, are usually referred to as 'alphabet agencies'. Reflecting on this achievement, a journalist said: 'The oath of office seems suddenly to have transfigured him from a man of mere charm and buoyancy to one of dynamic aggressiveness'.

The banking crisis

The most urgent problem to solve in March 1933 was the potentially catastrophic wave of bank failures which was sweeping the country. Failures had been common even in the 1920s, but the Depression made life even more difficult for small, country banks as their customers were unable to repay their debts. In a desperate attempt to stop depositors from withdrawing their savings because they feared closure (an action which merely brought closure that much nearer) many states had declared 'bank holidays'. By 1933 the banking system neared collapse, and the whole American economy with it. Roosevelt quickly ordered a four-day national bank holiday, and obtained the Emergency Banking Act. This meant that any banks in danger of failing could be helped by grants of government money and the advice of experts in reorganising their affairs. Banks in a hopeless condition, about 5% in all, were closed down permanently. Roosevelt broadcast to the nation, in the first of his radio 'fireside chats', to explain what he had done, and to ask people to return money to the reopened banks. This vital appeal succeeded, and one of his aides claimed: 'capitalism was saved in eight days'.

Reforming Wall Street and business

Starting in 1933 there was a series of Acts to stop the bad practices which had led to the Crash of 1929. Companies who issued shares had to give full information about their activities. In 1935 banks were brought under central government control, and a Wealth Tax was introduced supposedly to redistribute wealth more evenly amongst the population, but this was not successful. Wall Street had to some extent learnt its lesson after the excesses of 1929, and these measures helped to prevent further problems. Roosevelt's relations with the business community had never been close: these and other New Deal policies distanced them still further.

Business was more impressed by his Economy Act which cut government spending by $500 million in 1933. This did nothing to cure the Depression, but was in line with some of his campaign promises. Most of his other policies concentrated on spending money.

The New Deal for agriculture

Agricultural recovery was vital to the future health of the economy, and it received great attention from the New Dealers. The main aim was to raise farm prices and incomes to enable them to buy goods from industry. The most important of many agencies established to help farmers was the Agricultural Adjustment Administration in 1933.

5.2 Bud Fields and his family, Alabama: a scene of rural poverty. The photographer was Walker Evans.

The first task of the AAA was to try to destroy surplus produce because it was too late to prevent sowing or breeding for that year, and pay compensation to farmers for loss of income. In later years the AAA preferred to offer loans to help store surpluses, and worked to obtain voluntary agreements, at a local level, to reduce production. It soon became necessary to use the force of law to prevent a small minority from breaking agreements welcomed by the majority.

In fact, the weather was far more important than the AAA when it came to reducing production. Drought brought a ten times greater decrease in wheat production than that achieved by the AAA. In 1934 and 1936 there were severe droughts in many regions, and the creation of a barren 'Dustbowl', as once fertile soil was destroyed by poor farming methods and lack of water. The increased prices could not benefit farmers in areas where it was impossible to grow anything at all. Nor could it help small tenant farmers who were evicted by landlords who had agreed to reduce the acreage of land in production. Countless families were forced to move to other areas in a generally useless search for a livelihood. The novelist John Steinbeck gives a moving account of the fate of one such family in his novel *The Grapes of Wrath*, an extract from which appears on page 51.

Soil conservation, and education of farmers into the use of better techniques, such as fertilisers, soil-enriching crops and contour ploughing, played a larger part in later AAA programmes. The resettlement of poor farming families also became a matter of great urgency. The government helped

5.3 A dust storm, Cimarron County, Oklahoma, 1936. The photographer was Arthur Rothstein.

The Grapes of Wrath

John Steinbeck's novel *The Grapes of Wrath*, first published in 1939, tells the story of the Joads, a family of poor farmers from Oklahoma, who are forced to leave their land. They migrated to California, where they believed work was to be found. This extract is from a discussion by the family, after having been told they have got to leave:

'What's the idear of kickin' the folks off?'

'Oh! They talked pretty about it. You know what kinda years we been havin'. Dust comin' up an spoiling ever'thing so a man didn't get enough crop to plug up an ant's ass. An' ever'body got bills at the grocery. You know how it is. Well the folks that owns the lan' says: "We can't afford to keep no tenants." An' they says: "The share a tenant gets is jus' the margin a profit we can't afford to lose." An' they says: "If we put all our lan' in one piece we can jus' hardly make her pay". So they tractored all the tenants off a the lan'. All 'cept me, an' by God I ain't goin'. Tommy, you know me. You knowed me all your life'.

'Damn right,' said Joad, 'all my life'.

'Well you know I ain't a fool. I know this land ain't much good. Never was much good 'cept for grazin'. Never should a broke her up. An' now she's cottoned damn near to death.'

Source
Steinbeck, J., *The Grapes of Wrath*, Pan, 1975, pp. 52–53

nearly $1\frac{1}{2}$ million families to move to better land, and equip small, self-sufficient farms.

In general, the fortunes of farmers did improve after 1933. By 1936 total farm incomes had risen by half, prices were up by two-thirds, and debts had fallen by $1 billion. By 1941 prices finally overtook 1929 levels, but this was due more to the Second World War than the New Deal.

Rebuilding industry

One of the most important, complex and controversial Acts of the Hundred Days was the National Industrial Recovery Act (NIRA). The first part of this Act set up the National Recovery Administration (NRA), and the second part, the Public Works Administration (PWA). The general aim was to reform the way industry ran its affairs, and then to help it expand, to the benefit of the whole community.

The National Recovery Administration

The main task of the NRA was to help private enterprise to survive and grow by obtaining the co-operation of management, labour unions, consumers and rival companies. Industries were encouraged to draw up codes of conduct dealing with matters such as wages, hours, conditions of work, and trade practices to rule out unfair competition between companies. The NRA's first director said that these codes would:

5.4 The National Recovery Administration's symbol which was displayed in shop windows and on advertisements.

'...eliminate eye-gouging and knee-groining and ear-chewing in business. Above the belt any man can be just as rugged and just as individual as he pleases.'

Progress on negotiating codes tended to be rather slow, so in July 1933 the President's Re-employment Agreement proposed a 'blanket code' to cover many industries. This established minimum wages, banned child labour, and led to better trade practices. Over $2\frac{1}{4}$ million employers of 16 million workers accepted this, and were thus entitled to display the NRA's Blue Eagle emblem, and the motto, 'We Do Our Part'.

The usefulness of all this was limited however: large firms dominated the formation of codes, and small firms and consumers were generally ignored; codes were often used as a way of simply pushing up prices; enforcing them was almost impossible. There were temporary increases in the numbers employed, but recovery had to wait a long time.

A New Deal for labour

Section 7a of the NIRA, and the Wagner Act, which replaced it in 1935, were great steps forward for organised labour unions. Workers were given the legal right to form unions, and to bargain collectively with their employers, through representatives of their own choosing. Employers were not allowed to insist that workers should join a 'union' run by the company, and 'yellow dog' contracts were banned.

It is probably easier to make a law than to enforce it. When workers tried to take advantage of their legal rights and form independent unions, many employers resisted fiercely. Throughout the 1930s there was a series of bitter strikes, with violence a common occurrence. Many companies bought arms to fight strikers. The evidence on page 53 shows how determined many employers were to stand up for what they believed to be their right to hire whomever they chose. Perhaps the most brutal fights took place in the steel industry, where the 1937 'Memorial Day Massacre' in Chicago, resulting in seven deaths, was only one of several bloody encounters. The year 1937 saw the invention of a perhaps less provocative tactic, the 'sit-down strike', used with great effect against General Motors and Chrysler.

In all of this, Roosevelt's administration tried to stay neutral, in contrast with the Republican Presidents who preceded him. By the end of the decade unions were stronger, increasing their membership from under 3 million in 1933 to over 10 million in 1941.

Relief for the unemployed

Although Roosevelt recognised that the only real cure for the problem of unemployment was economic recovery, he had to help those already living in poverty. The Federal Emergency Relief Administration (FERA), set up in 1933, gave grants totalling $500 million to the individual states to help with relief. He then moved towards providing the

'Industrial relations' in the 1930s

Many companies acquired impressive arsenals of weapons to 'protect their property' and break strikes. In 1937, half of all tear gas and the equipment needed to use it was bought by industrial companies. In the same year Youngstown Sheet and Tube Co. possessed the following munitions:

machine guns	8
rifles	369
shotguns	190
revolvers	454
gas guns	109
rounds of gas ammunition	3000
rounds of ball ammunition	6000
rounds of shot ammunition	3950

It was very common in the 1930s for companies to go to great lengths to prevent unions from organising their workers. The Ford Company was particularly hostile:

'There are about eight hundred underworld characters in the Ford Service organization. They are the Storm Troops. They make no pretense of working, but are merely "keeping order" in the plant community through terror. Around this nucleus of eight hundred yeggs there are, however, between 8000 and 9000 authentic workers in the organization, a great many of them spies and stool-pigeons and a great many others who have been browbeaten into joining this industrial mafia. ... Because of this highly organized terror and spy system the fear in the plant is something indescribable. ... Workers seen talking together are taken off the assembly line and fired. Every man suspected of union sympathies is immediately discharged, usually under the framed-up charge of "starting a fight", in which he often gets terribly beaten up.'

Sources
Stolberg, B., *The Story of the CIO,* Viking, New York, 1938, p. 116. Quoted in Major, J., *The New Deal,* Longmans, 1968, pp. 136–137.

unemployed with work rather than a 'dole'. He explains his reasons on page 54.

The Public Works Administration

This was established by the NIRA to launch a programme of public works to benefit those who would be given jobs, as well as the nation as a whole. Led by the rather conservative Harold Ickes, the PWA built an impressive array of schools, courthouses, hospitals, railways, bridges, tunnels and ports. Ickes wanted value for money ($6 billion was spent in the years 1933–39) and did not see his major task as being to relieve poverty and provide jobs, but rather to provide America with high quality public facilities.

Roosevelt's opinion of relief

Roosevelt was forced to start a programme for the relief of poverty, but he was not happy about the long-term effects of 'hand outs' or 'the dole', as he explained in 1935:

The dole is 'a narcotic, a subtle destroyer of the human spirit ... I am not willing that the vitality of our people be further sapped by the giving of cash, of market baskets, of a few hours of weekly work cutting grass, raking leaves or picking up papers in the public parks. The Federal Government must and shall quit this business of relief.'

Questions
(1) What sort of scheme started by Roosevelt provided the sort of relief described here?
(2) Which speech by Hoover, quoted earlier in this book, expresses similar ideas?

Civil Works Administration

The more impatient, ambitious and radical Harry Hopkins believed that the PWA's approach was too limited, and that immediate operations should be started by the government to employ as many people as possible. Later in 1933 the Civil Works Administration (CWA) was launched to provide emergency, short-term jobs. By January 1934, $4\frac{1}{4}$ million were employed in building roads, schools and airports, as well as on conservation projects. The cost was nearly $1 billion. The CWA attracted criticism from those who believed many of the jobs were useless (so-called 'boondoggling') and that the money could have been better spent. It was only meant to be a temporary organisation, so the CWA ended its work in July 1934, when FERA was forced to take up the burden of relief again.

Works Progress Administration

The Works Progress Administration (WPA) was started in 1935 and performed much of the work done by the CWA. Again led by Hopkins, the WPA employed 8 million people and in the years 1935–41 spent over $11 billion. Most of the work was in construction, but there was also a variety of 'community service' programmes in fields such as education, theatre and music. The Federal Writers Project run by the WPA gave employment to writers. Part of the result can be seen in the extract on page 55, which gives a valuable insight into many aspects of working life in the 1930s.

One section of society which suffered particularly badly from unemployment was young people. Many left home in search of work and drifted around the country. Henry Ford said: 'Why it's the best education in the world for those boys, that travelling around. They get more experience in a few months than they would in years at school.' Others were less sure.

Civilian Conservation Corps

Established in 1933, the Civilian Conservation Corps (CCC) aimed to give work to young men by helping to look after the countryside. Conservation was a cause very dear to Roosevelt's heart. They were paid $30 per month, $22 of which went to their families. Work included fire prevention, building tracks, flood control and forestry. About $2\frac{1}{4}$ million were enrolled in seven years. The average stay in the CCC was over nine months.

Housing

During the Depression, there sprang up around many cities squalid shanty towns, bitterly referred to as 'Hoovervilles', inhabited by those who were forced to leave their homes because they could not afford to pay for shelter. A thousand families per day were forced to leave their homes in early 1933 as they were unable to repay loans for house purchases. The Home Owners Loan Corporation (HOLC) helped with the repayment of such loans to the benefit of both the lender and the borrower. There was also an urgent need to build more new houses, especially for the poor, but in this direction, despite efforts by the PWA and other bodies, the results were unimpressive.

Organising a union in the 1930s

The Federal Writers Project was started by the WPA to give work to writers without a job. These reminiscences were related to a member of the Project by a labour union activist:

'In the meantime I'd joined a labor union. It was the United Textile Workers of America. ... I was very active in the union work. ...

Somehow the management found out about it – I hadn't been keepin' it any secret – and the superintendent called me in the office one day and began tellin' me how much they thought about me, and he said if I'd give up the union why they'd find me a better job. And they did. ... But I didn't promise nothin', see?

Well I held the job all right; I could do the work, but I didn't give up my union activities. So they demoted me back to a "learner-weaver". It was just about that time a union organizer asked me if I'd take a trip with him for two weeks ... so I went to the boss and asked him to let me off. ... I didn't tell 'em for what purpose. ...

Well they let me off and I went with the organizer. ... We organized several towns and then we came back to Pheonix.

As soon as I reported at the mill the overseer fired me. They'd heard about what I'd done and he said I didn't need the job because they understood I had another one. Bein' sarcastic, y'know. ... Losin' that job didn't matter so much, but they blackballed me from all the other mills. ...

Well there was nothing to do but apply for relief. I did, and finally got a job on the WPA. Worked on a labor project; dug ditches, rolled wheelbarrows, and things like that. I did all sorts of temporary jobs between the WPA work. ... And I kept up my union activities.

...Then I heard about the Adult Education Program. ... Well I told the WPA office I was interested in that kind of work ... My job was to teach, just that and nothin' more. If the workers wanted me to tell 'em about unions then it was all right, but I wasn't supposed to encourage 'em or discourage 'em about the unions.'

Source
Federal Writers Project, *These Are Our Lives,* W. W. Norton and Company,
Inc., University of North Carolina Press 1939 and 1967, pp. 403–406.

Questions
(1) What does this document suggest was the attitude of
    Roosevelt's administration to labour unions?
(2) Which New Deal laws were supposed to protect workers from
    the type of treatment suffered by this man?
(3) In times of high unemployment unions are often not able to
    stand up to employers. When there is a shortage of workers
    unions become much more powerful. Explain why this should
    be so. (Think about the practical alternatives open to workers
    and employers at different times.)
(4) How strong were unions at the end of the 1930s?

The Social Security Act

Unlike many other industrialised countries,
America had no system of social security to
help those who were in no position to help
themselves. The reasons for this apparent
neglect of the elderly, sick or unemployed
are examined in Chapter 3. The 1935 Social
Security Act started a system of insurance
(with costs to be shared by employers,
employees and the government) to provide
money for some, but not all, of those in
need. Farm labourers and domestic servants
were not covered, which meant that negroes
and women fared badly. Nor was there an
insurance scheme for the sick, because most
doctors feared that this would threaten their
incomes and independence. Although the
Act had severe weaknesses, it was a
considerable breakthrough, and was the basis
for many improvements in later years.

The Tennessee Valley Authority

Probably the most depressed region of
America was the Tennessee Valley, an area
of 40 000 square miles in seven states. The
farm land of the valley had been gradually
eroded by years of deforestation, damaging
farming methods and heavy rainfall. In 1933

only 2% of farms had electricity, and over
half the population of $2\frac{1}{2}$ million were on
relief. Annual flood damage was valued at
about $1\frac{3}{4}$ million.

The Tennessee Valley Authority (TVA)
was created in 1933 with the intention of
planning the economic development of the
region. The creation of the TVA was bitterly
opposed by those who objected to federal
interference in the affairs of the seven states.
This experiment in planning was considered
by critics to be a dangerous step in the
direction of the destruction of free enterprise
and the creation of a socialist system.
Roosevelt intended to do neither, but wanted
merely to help this poverty-stricken region.
The TVA was able to build dams to
generate electricity, and to sell it to
consumers. These dams would help with the
creation of a programme of flood control,
improvements in agricultural methods,
reforestation and industrialisation. The TVA
was, and continues to be, an outstanding
success, transforming the valley by the end
of the decade into a show-piece for
progressive agriculture.

Within ten years a fifth of farms in the
valley were electrified. This progress was
repeated across the nation. In 1935 one out
of ten farms had electric power: by 1941 four
out of ten were electrified.

5.5 An unemployed man selling apples outside his Hooverville shanty town home.

End of Term Report

During Roosevelt's first term as President there had been government activity on a scale never before considered in America. New Dealers justified all this 'interference' by saying that desperate circumstances required desperate remedies. At first glance the results were less than impressive: unemployment remained high; industrial production was low; farmers were still poor. No end to the Depression appeared to be in sight. Perhaps the best that can be said is that the Depression was getting no worse, slow improvement was taking place in some areas, and Roosevelt's boundless optimism had given many millions of Americans hope where previously there had been only despair.

'Hooverville'

'Hooverville' became a common sight in towns all over America during the Depression. In this extract from Steinbeck's *The Grapes of Wrath,* a family is looking for somewhere to camp for the night, on its journey to California:

'He drove his old car into a town. He scoured the farms for work. Where can we sleep the night?

Well, there's Hooverville on the edge of the river. There's a whole raft of Okies there.

He drove his old car to Hooverville. He never asked again, for there was a Hooverville on the edge of every town.

The rag town lay close to water; and the houses were tents, and weed-thatched enclosures, paper houses, a great junk pile. The man drove his family in and became a citizen of Hooverville – always they were called Hooverville. The man put up his own tent as near to water as he could get; or if he had no tent, he went to the city dump and brought back cartons and built a house of corrugated paper. And when the rains came the house melted and washed away. He settled in Hooverville and he scoured the countryside for work, and the little money he had went for petrol to look for work.'

Source
Steinbeck, J., *The Grapes of Wrath,* Pan, 1975, p. 249.

6 The politics of the New Deal

The 1936 presidential election

The New Deal had made Roosevelt extremely popular with the majority of Americans after 1933, but by 1935 some powerful opposition was developing, not from the Republicans, but from various radical personalities and their supporters. Senator Huey P. Long of Louisiana was a skilful politician who ran his state with an iron hand. In return for complete control, obtained by more or less legal (if not moral) methods, he proposed policies which were much more radical than Roosevelt would have wished. His Share-Our-Wealth Scheme, apparently supported by 7½ million people in 1935, involved confiscation of large fortunes, pension schemes, minimum wages,

6.2 Senator Huey Long of Louisiana was a dangerous opponent of Roosevelt. He was shot dead in 1935 by an Austrian immigrant whom Long was persecuting.

6.1 Father Charles Coughlin was once an ally of Roosevelt, but turned into a fanatical opponent of the New Deal. After 1941 his reputation suffered badly because of his alleged sympathy for Fascism.

veterans' bonuses and much more. Had he not been assassinated in 1935, Long may well have been able to split the non-Republican vote, and bring about Roosevelt's defeat.

Another formidable opponent was the Catholic priest, Charles Coughlin, whose radio broadcasts reached audiences of up to 45 million in 1932. He believed at first that 'the New Deal is God's Deal', but by 1934 he had broken with Roosevelt. He argued for state ownership of banks and natural resources, large scale government spending to create jobs, and a system of government which seemed very similar to Mussolini's

Coughlin on Roosevelt

'The Radio Priest', Fr Charles Coughlin, was one of the most popular and influential men in America. His support for Roosevelt up to 1934 was very valuable; his later attacks could have posed a real threat in the 1936 election:

1   'Any jackass can spend money. Any crackpot with money at his disposal can build for himself a dictatorial crown. It takes no brains to be liberal with other people's money.

It is time for the American public to perform a sit-down strike –
5   not on industry, not on men of commerce, but on politicans. They are sitting down on you, waiting for the government executioner, waiting for the last chapter of the Bill of Rights to be burned at the stake like a witch, waiting for the Supreme Court to put its head on the chopping block.'

(Coughlin 1937)

Source
Quoted in Tull, C. J., *Father Coughlin and the New Deal*, Syracuse University Press, 1965

Questions
(1) What evidence could be produced to back the criticisms of Coughlin and others that Roosevelt wasted money and achieved very little?

(2) Why was the 'sit-down strike' (line 4) a topical issue in 1937? (It may help you to refer to Chapter 5).

(3) To what episode is Coughlin referring in lines 8–9?

(4) Coughlin and many others feared Roosevelt was trying to become a dictator in the style of Hitler, Mussolini or Stalin. Apart from the answer to question 3 what other evidence might they produce from the period 1933–45 to prove their case? It will be necessary to do some research into these other topics before you answer this question.

Fascist Italy. Coughlin's Union Party was not able to take advantage of his popularity and the challenge never came to anything. His speeches on this page show that Coughlin had become increasingly violent in his language, and his audiences fell sharply by 1941.

The Republican candidate, Alfred Landon, who actually agreed with much of the New Deal, was unable to make a real challenge. The result was no surprise: Roosevelt, with 27 753 000 votes, crushed Landon with 16 675 000, and the Democrats increased their majorities in Congress. This was the high point of Roosevelt's success. Within weeks he was under severe attack, and had managed to turn many former supporters into opponents.

The Supreme Court 'packing plan'

Since 1933 Roosevelt had controlled the Presidency and Congress, but had been unable to dominate the Supreme Court. The court has the power and duty to examine laws to decide whether they are 'constitutional'. For example, has Congress acted in the way the Constitution said it could? Has the President been given powers which should belong to someone else? Has the Federal Government taken over powers

Study this cartoon and answer the questions which follow:

Source
Punch, 1937, in Bullock, A., *History of the 20th Century,* Octopus, 1976, p. 170

Questions
(1) In what year would this cartoon have appeared?

(2) a   Who is the man riding the horse 'New Deal'?
     b   Why is he appearing to torment the 'Supreme Court'?
     c   Why is the 'Supreme Court' shown as an old man?

(3) What happened as a result of this episode?

(4) The incident described here brought problems for the New
     Deal. For what other reasons over the following two years did
     the New Deal run into difficulties?

---

reserved for the individual states? If a law is declared 'unconstitutional' it ceases to have any effect.

By tradition, there are nine justices, who hold their posts for life. The President makes new appointments, with the approval of the Senate, only when vacancies occur through death or retirement. At any time, the chances are that the President will have a court mainly appointed by previous Presidents. In 1937, only three justices were 'New Dealers', four were definitely conservative opponents, and two were 'neutral'.

During 1935 and 1936 the court had declared unconstitutional several New Deal measures, including the NRA and AAA, and it was very likely that others would go the same way. This forced Roosevelt to introduce new laws which tried to do what the old ones had done, but still satisfied the critics on the court. Roosevelt, believing that the 1936 elections had given him the nation's support, proposed that the President should have the power to appoint up to six new justices to balance those who had served over ten years, or had reached the age of seventy. Opponents called this 'packing the court'.

Although many people agreed the court needed to be reformed, they disliked Roosevelt's apparently heartless attack on elderly justices, and believed he was doing this, not for reasons of justice or good government, but to get rid of opposition. One critic said: 'Our President evidently has noted the apparent success of Hitler and is aiming at the same dominance.' It is by no means certain that the court was biased against the New Deal: it had approved many other laws, and had only rejected these because they were poorly designed or obviously unconstitutional. Even the New Dealers had voted against the NRA, because it illegally interfered in the affairs of individual states.

Roosevelt's usually loyal supporters in Congress were very divided over packing the court, and he was eventually forced to abandon the idea. Very soon the problem was solved in the usual way: some of his opponents retired and he was able to appoint his own supporters to replace them.

The end of the New Deal

This whole episode damaged Roosevelt's reputation, and it helped to strengthen the anti-New Deal group in Congress, which would have sympathised with most of what the Liberty League has to say on page 63. His popularity was further reduced by his decision to cut government spending in 1937 in an attempt to balance the budget, apparently a long-forgotten ambition. This caused industrial output to fall sharply, and 2 million people to lose their jobs. It showed that the slow recovery, which had taken place since 1933, needed continued government spending if it were to carry on. He started to spend heavily again in 1938, and the numbers out of work fell, but by 1939 there were still 9 million without a job.

The 1938 mid-term elections saw important gains for Republicans and conservative Democrats, who were unenthusiastic about extending the New Deal. A stalemate developed after this, as neither reformers nor conservatives were able to dominate Congress. The New Deal was to make few new advances, but neither was it to be dismantled.

The American Liberty League attacks the New Deal

In 1934 some businessmen formed the American Liberty League to defend themselves against the New Deal's alleged interference. These are extracts from some of its pamphlets:

1   'The New Deal is nothing more or less than an effort by inexperienced sentimentalists and demagogues to take away from the thrifty what the thrifty and their ancestors have accumulated, or may accumulate, and give it to others who have not earned it, or

5   whose ancestors haven't earned it for them, and who never would have earned it and never will earn it, and thus indirectly to destroy the incentive for all future accumulation. Such a purpose is in defiance of all the tenets upon which our civilisation has been founded.'

Source
Shaw, R., *The New Deal: Its Unsound Theories and Irreconcilable Policies* (1935) p. 13

10   'Nothing could threaten the race as seriously as this. It is begging the unfit to be more unfit. Even such a measure as old-age insurance, which I am sure must touch the sympathies of every one, especially if he has the intelligence to think things through, removes one of the points of pressure which has kept many persons up to

15   the strife and struggle of life'.

Source
Cutten, G. B., *Professors and the New Deal* (1936), p. 15

'(The New Dealers) contend that there is a tremendous disparity in the distribution of the "good things of life" due to greed, corruption, and crookedness in the economic system; I contend that ... the distribution of wealth under our system is infinitely more

20   widespread than ever attained by any other; that what maladjustment there is, is due largely to the difference in human capacity and human capability; that the amassing of wealth honestly made is but a badge of service performed to the community, and that the remedy of the defects of the present system lies not in the

25   destruction but in the improvement of the character of the race, through Christian education'.

Source
Utley, S. W., *The Duty of the Church to the Social Order* (1936), pp. 2–3

All are attributed to Wolfskill, G., *The Revolt of the Conservatives,*
Houghton Mifflin, Boston, 1962, p. 124 in Major, J., *The New Deal,*
Longmans, 1968, pp. 80–81

Questions

(1) Which New Deal schemes would most provoke the phrases
'take away from the thrifty ... and give it to others who have
not earned it' (lines 2–4), and 'begging the unfit to be more
unfit' (lines 10–11)?

(2) What sort of 'tenets upon which our civilisation has been
founded' (line 8) do you think the writer believes have been
most threatened?

(3) When was 'old-age insurance' (line 11) introduced? Explain in
your own words why Cutten is critical of this scheme.

(4) Which two labels could be most appropriately attached to all
the writers of these passages?

a	Radical	f	Conservative
b	Communist	g	Anarchist
c	Fascist	h	Atheist
d	Capitalist	j	Monetarist
e	Socialist	k	Christian

1940 presidential election

The campaign in 1940 was dominated by the
crisis in Europe, which brought jobs to
American workers, but threatened to drag
America into war. Roosevelt decided to try
for a third term of office, which had never
been done before. The Republicans chose
the relatively unknown, but talented,
Wendell Wilkie, who was sometimes
distrusted because he was an ex-Democrat.
One leading Republican said: 'I don't mind
the church converting a whore, but I don't
like her to lead the choir the first night.'
Roosevelt won comfortably, but the
27 308 000 to 22 321 000 margin was the
smallest since 1916.

The achievements of the New Deal

The economic statistics on page 65 show that
when America entered the Second World
War in 1941, she was only just starting
genuinely to recover from high
unemployment, low farm prices and
stagnation in business. Important advances
had been made in working conditions, relief
of poverty and the running of business, but
there had been no economic miracle. To
have achieved such a miracle would have
required policies of government spending
and planning on a scale beyond Roosevelt's
dreams or nightmares. Instead his policies
were often hesitant or contradictory, perhaps
due to his lack of interest in, or

understanding of, economics.

More effective than the New Deal in building prosperity was war, in Europe from 1939, and throughout the world from 1941. This increased the demand for American manufactured goods and food, and forced Roosevelt to spend vast sums of money, which helped America to break economic records. Some commentators, perhaps cynically, compare Roosevelt's reluctance to spend enough on peaceful, humanitarian reconstruction, with his eagerness to commit all the nation's resources to producing weapons of destruction. Nonetheless, it was the war which was to consume all of Roosevelt's enormous energy for the rest of his life, as economic problems faded into the background.

The American economy before 1945

The Gross National Product (GNP) is a measure of how much a country produces in a year. All the figures are in billions of dollars:

1919	78.9	1933	56.0
1920	88.9	1934	65.0
1921	74.0	1935	72.5
1922	74.0	1936	82.7
1923	86.1	1937	90.8
1924	87.6	1938	85.2
1925	91.3	1939	91.1
1926	97.7	1940	100.6
1927	96.3	1941	125.8
1928	98.2	1942	159.1
1929	104.4	1943	192.5
1930	91.1	1944	211.4
1931	76.3	1945	213.6
1932	58.5		

Unemployment (% of workforce)

1929	3.14	1938	18.91
1930	8.67	1939	17.05
1931	15.82	1940	14.45
1932	23.53	1941	9.66
1933	24.75	1942	4.41
1934	21.60	1943	1.66
1935	19.97	1944	1.01
1936	16.80	1945	1.59
1937	14.18		

Questions

(1) a Account for the fact that the GNP falls sharply after 1920.
   b Name the Presidents of the United States and give the dates they were in power in the years 1921–33. To which political party did each of them belong?

c What were the economic policies followed by the United States in the years 1921–33?

d What sort of industries were responsible for the steady rise in the GNP 1922–29?

(2) a Why did unemployment rise and the GNP fall in the years 1929–33?

b Name the President and his political party for the years 1933–45.

c What slogan was applied to his economic policy in these years? How did it differ from that of his predecessors before 1933?

d Using these statistics outline the successes and failures of government economic policies 1933–39. Give the reasons for the fluctuations which take place.

(3) a What happens to GNP and unemployment figures in the years 1939–45?

b Why did this occur?

American farm prices

	Head of cattle ($)	Cotton per lb. (c.)	Wheat per bushel ($)
1917	43.34	27.09	2.05
1918	50.01	28.88	2.05
1919	54.65	35.34	2.16
1920	52.64	15.89	1.83
1921	39.07	17.00	1.03
1922	30.39	22.88	0.97
1923	31.66	28.69	0.93
1924	32.11	22.91	1.25
1925	31.72	19.61	1.44
1926	36.80	12.47	1.22
1927	39.98	20.19	1.19
1928	50.63	17.98	1.00
1929	58.47	16.78	1.04
1930	56.36	9.46	0.67
1931	38.99	5.66	0.39
1932	26.39	6.52	0.38
1933	19.74	10.17	0.74
1934	17.78	12.36	0.85
1935	20.20	11.09	0.83
1936	34.06	12.36	1.03
1937	34.06	8.41	0.96
1938	36.58	8.60	0.56
1939	38.44	9.09	0.69

1940	40.60	9.89	0.68
1941	43.20	17.03	0.94
1942	55.00	19.05	1.10
1943	69.30	19.90	1.36
1944	68.40	20.73	1.41
1945	66.90	22.52	1.50

Questions

(1) a Describe the trends taken by these prices in the years 1917–29.

b Give the reasons for the changes in direction.

c How do cattle prices compare with cotton and wheat in these years? How do you account for this?

(2) a Why did prices fall dramatically after 1929?

b Let us assume inflation was non-existent. If you were a farmer totally dependent on (a) cotton (b) wheat, what percentage of your 1919 income would you receive in the following years: (i) 1922 (ii) 1929 (iii) 1932 (iv) 1936 (v) 1938 (vi) 1945? Why might the 1919 figures not be the fairest ones to choose for comparison with later years?

c What was the AAA and when was it formed? Describe its activities after this date.

d Use these statistics to assess how successful the AAA was.

(3) When did prices start to show a consistent improvement after this date? Explain why this was so.

7 United States foreign policy 1933–41

In 1933, most Americans had problems enough at home, without worrying about what the United States' policy towards the rest of the world should be. Roosevelt, in his early career, had been an enthusiastic supporter of Wilson and internationalism, but his inaugural speech made only brief mention of foreign policy: 'I would dedicate this nation to the policy of the good neighbor – the neighbor who resolutely respects himself and, because he does so, respects the rights of others.' This hope was mainly taken to concern the United States' relations with her southern neighbours in Latin America.

America's 'back yard'

The United States' relations with Latin America had been governed since 1823 by the 'Monroe Doctrine'. This was a warning to all European countries not to interfere in the affairs of the New World, and so endanger American security. It also meant that the United States believed she had the right and duty to maintain peace and order in her 'back yard'. This could result in some involvement in the internal affairs of these countries.

By the early twentieth century, Americans were less worried by threats to their security than by threats to their important economic interests in Latin America. American industry found it easy to sell goods there, and obtained many vital raw materials at a low cost. Large sums of money were invested in factories, mines and plantations, or in loans to governments. So great was the involvement in some of these countries that when a company was a great landowner, a major employer and creator of 'wealth', then it actually dominated the government. Wars or left-wing revolutions could mean that this position was put at risk.

Business expected the United States government to make sure that their interests were properly protected. Successive Presidents did their best, often providing aid for pro-American governments or sending troops to countries where there appeared to be the danger of anti-American disturbances. By the time of the First World War, the United States had ensured that most Latin American governments were friendly to American interests. The people of the region were often less happy about what they called 'Yanqui imperialism'.

In the 1920s attitudes slowly started to change. Military intervention probably poisoned relations with many countries, so the United States tried to act more tactfully. When there were threats to American oil companies, and attacks on the Catholic Church in Mexico, there loud demands in America that vigorous action should be taken. Coolidge preferred a softer line, and tried, with some success, to negotiate with that country's left-wing government. In 1925, when the handful of United States troops based in Nicaragua were withdrawn, there was anarchy. Five thousand troops were immediately sent back, not only to restore order, but also to produce a peaceful, long-term solution to the troubles. Elections were held, and the troops left in 1933.

'The good neighbor'?

Latin America greeted Roosevelt with optimism. 'Yanqui imperialism' was still distrusted, with good reason, but there appeared to be now the prospect that there could be the creation of a relationship between genuine equals.

Roosevelt continued in the direction already started by the Republicans. The United States withdrew her troops from Haiti and the Dominican Republic, and in

---

A new approach to Latin America

Charles Evans Hughes, Secretary of State in the 1920s, tried to improve relations with Latin American countries:

1   'We covet no territory, we seek no conquest; the liberty we cherish for ourselves we desire for others; and we accept no rights for ourselves that we do not accord to others.'

'Our interest does not lie in controlling foreign peoples; that
5   would be a policy of mischief and disaster. Our interest is in having prosperous, peaceful and law abiding neighbors with whom we can co-operate to mutual advantage.'

Source
Quoted in Hicks, J. D., *Republican Ascendancy,* Harper and Row, Publishers; Chapter 11

Questions
(1) How successful were attempts in the 1920s and 1930s to improve relations with Latin America?
(2) What does Hughes mean by 'prosperous, peaceful and law abiding neighbors' (line 6)? Why might this actually be a reason for dissatisfaction towards America's policies by many Latin Americans?

1936 abandoned her right to intervene in Panama. Relations with Mexico were still strained, but there was no attempt to prevent her government from nationalising American property, so long as compensation was paid. Intervention in the region was more likely when American lives, rather than property, were at risk. Bi-lateral (two sided) trade agreements were made with several countries. These made it easier to sell goods, as each side reduced tariffs. Not only trade was increased: so was goodwill.

Despite all this, the overall position did not really improve. It is impossible to have an equal relationship between a small country, which does nearly all of its trade with one large customer, America. The small country inevitably becomes a dependent. This was the reality for many Latin American countries between the wars, and remains so today. Being a 'good neighbor' was never a realistic idea.

Relations with Russia

The 'February Revolution' in 1917 brought the Provisional Government to power in Russia, and was widely welcomed in America. The United States recognised the new government, which appeared to offer the hope of introducing democratic reforms. When the 'October Revolution' brought the Bolsheviks to power later that year, Wilson refused to recognise the new regime as the legal Russian government. He believed the Bolsheviks were undemocratic, did not represent the wishes of the Russian people, and probably would be unable to stay in control. Perhaps more important was the new regime's determination to take Russia out of the war with Germany. This would make America's fight more difficult.

In 1918, Wilson followed the example of his allies, and sent about 14 000 troops to Russia to help the anti-Communist 'White' armies in the Civil War. The intervention was a failure, and they returned home in 1920. This episode did nothing to improve relations with Russia in the years to come.

The United States did not recognise the Communists throughout the 1920s because they had confiscated American property, refused to repay a loan made before the Revolution, and spread their propaganda inside America. The 'Red Scare' in the years after 1918 made recognition of the Communists even more unlikely. Roosevelt decided in 1933 to normalise relations between the two countries, and recognised Stalin's government. Few Americans now felt threatened by Communism. As one newspaperman put it: 'I think the menace of Bolshevism in the United States is about as great as the menace of sunstroke in Greenland or chilblains in the Sahara.' Some hoped that trade would be increased by this, but, in fact, there were very few benefits. A prominent historian described it as 'an event of monumental unimportance'.

Isolationism in Congress

So long as Roosevelt's attention was turned towards the Depression at home, Congress took the initiative in deciding foreign policy. Isolationists were in a large majority. These were of two basic types in the 1930s. The 'positive' isolationists were passionately concerned with the welfare of other nations, and believed America should, and could, help to prevent war. This could best be done by moral persuasion, not military methods. The 'negative' isolationists were not much interested in world affairs, and felt that other countries could do as they pleased. America was far enough away from danger, and economically self-sufficient, so she could safely concern herself only with events in the Western Hemisphere. It was the 'negative' isolationists who were most influential in the 1930s.

Isolationists of all sorts were encouraged by the findings of the Nye Committee which investigated the arms industry. In 1934 it reported that American involvement in the First World War had been caused largely by the greed of arms manufacturers and bankers eager to make profits. Congress was determined to prevent a repetition of this by passing a series of Neutrality Acts after 1935.

The Neutrality Acts

There seemed to be an increasing likelihood of war in the 1930s as Germany, Italy and Japan built up their armed forces, and made aggressive gestures towards their neighbours. Isolationists were determined to keep America neutral.

Roosevelt's intentions were not very clear. He appointed as Secretary of State the suspiciously internationalist Cordell Hull, who seemed to welcome closer contacts with other countries. No matter what Roosevelt wanted, though, Congress was anxious to make policy, and he had no choice but to accept it. He did so with little protest.

The Neutrality Acts were intended to decide precisely how America should behave in the event of a war elsewhere in the world. Isolationists believed that if contact with those involved was removed altogether, then there was no risk of being dragged in by accident, or by the trickery of profiteers. The 1935 Act gave the President the power to prohibit American ships from carrying American-made munitions to belligerents (countries at war). The 1936 Act extended this ban to loans. Food and raw materials were not affected by either Act. The intention was purely 'negative', only to keep America out of wars, not to help prevent them happening at all.

In 1937 a new formula, known as 'Cash and Carry', was established. Congress had no wish to hurt American manufacturers in the pursuit of neutrality. It now decided the only danger came from the 'shipment' of goods, not from their 'sale'. The new Act allowed nations involved in a war to buy goods other than munitions from America, provided that they paid cash and used their own ships. It was hoped that America could then have 'peace *and* prosperity'. 'Cash and

Timeline 3

The drift to war 1931–41

	United States	Europe	Asia
1931			Japan invades Manchuria.
1935	Neutrality Act (August)	Italy invades Abyssinia (October).	
1936	Neutrality Act.	Spanish Civil War starts (July).	
1937	Cash and Carry Act (April).		Japan attacks rest of China (July).
1938		Germany unites with Austria (March). Munich Agreement gives Germany Czechoslovakia's Sudetenland (September).	
1939	Americans allowed to sell arms to belligerents under 1937 Act (November).	Germany takes over rest of Czechoslovakia (March). Germany attacks Poland (September).	
1940	Rearmament starts (April). Economic sanctions imposed on Japan (July). 'Destroyers for Bases' deal (September).	Germany conquers most of European continent (June). Submarine warfare starts.	Japan moves troops into French Indo-china (September).
1941	Active aid to Britain starts. 'Lend-Lease' (March). Aid to Russia (July). 'Atlantic Charter' (August). Ban on trade with Japan (September). Declarations of war on Japan and Germany (December).	Germany attacks Russia (June). Britain allies with Russia (June). Germany declares war on United States (December).	Attacks on Pearl Harbour, Philippines, Malaya, etc. (December).

Roosevelt's views on neutrality

(1) The 'platform' (manifesto, or statement of policies) on which Roosevelt and the Democrats fought the 1936 election, contained the following 'plank' on foreign affairs:

1   'We shall continue to observe a true neutrality in the disputes of others; to work for peace and to take the profits out of war; to guard against being drawn, by political commitments, international banking, or private trading, into any war which
5   may develop anywhere.'

(2) In Roosevelt's 'Quarantine' speech in 1937 he described war in these terms:

'War is a contagion, whether it be declared or undeclared. It can engulf states and peoples remote from the original scene of hostilities. We are determined to keep out of war, yet we cannot insure ourselves against the disastrous effects of war
10   and the dangers of involvement. We are adopting such measures as will minimize our risk of involvement, but we cannot have complete protection in a world of disorder in which confidence and security have broken down.'

(3) In a 'fireside chat' in September 1940, Roosevelt explained why he believed the European crisis made Lend-Lease necessary:

'... the Axis not merely admits but *proclaims* that there can be
15   no ultimate peace between their philosophy of government and our philosophy of government. ...

Some of our people like to believe that wars in Europe and in Asia are of no concern to us. But it is a matter of most vital concern to us that European and Asiatic war-makers should not
20   gain control of the oceans which lead to this hemisphere....

If Great Britain goes down, the Axis powers will control the continents of Europe, Asia, Africa, Australasia, and the high seas.... It is no exaggeration to say that all of us, in all the Americas, would be living at the point of a gun – a gun loaded
25   with explosive bullets, economic as well as military.'

Source
The source of 2 and 3 is Zevin, T. D., *'Nothing to Fear', The Selected Addresses of Franklin Delano Roosevelt 1932–1945*, Hodder and Stoughton, 1947, pp. 115 and 249–250

Questions
(1) a   How does the 1936 Democratic platform compare with the findings of the Nye Committee?
    b   In what ways did Congress try to put these principles into practice in the 1930s?
(2) a   What events probably urged Roosevelt to make his 'Quarantine' speech?
    b   In what ways do you think Roosevelt believed 'the disastrous effects of war' (line 9) might reach America?
(3) a   What was the 'Axis'?

b   Roosevelt tried to appeal to matters of principle as well as self-interest in his 1940 speech. Quote from the passage to show how he did both of these.

c   Why would the defeat of Britain be particularly damaging to America? (Think about Britain's political, economic and military position in the world in 1940).

Carry' favoured those countries which were rich, and also had large navies, notably Britain, France and Japan.

The decline of isolationism

Whether they liked it or not, many Americans were forced to pay more attention to world affairs in the late 1930s. Italy invaded Abyssinia in 1935. The Spanish Civil War, which started in 1936, concerned many who had Spanish or Latin American origins, or who were Catholic. In 1937 Japan attacked China, and broke America's 'Open Door' policy there. This was supposed to mean that all countries should have equal opportunities to trade in China. Japan was determined to take China for herself. An American gunboat on the Yangtze River was sunk, and two sailors were killed, but no action was taken after Japan apologised. In

7.1 Hand grenades being used by Fascist troops during Spanish Civil War 1936–39.

7.2 Sino-Japanese War. Japanese troops enter Manchuria.

the same year, the Rome-Berlin-Tokyo Axis was signed. Many believed that America was now less secure.

In October 1937 Roosevelt made a speech which appeared to argue for a more positive policy to prevent war (see page 72). 'When an epidemic of physical disease starts to spread, the community approves and joins in a quarantine of the patients in order to protect the health of the community against the spread of the disease.' To isolationists this sounded very much like 'collective security'. He was severely criticised, and forced to drop the issue.

In 1938 and 1939, events in Europe disturbed many Americans. The Nazis' anti-Semitism forced many Jews to seek refuge across the Atlantic. Germany, having taken

America's role in the Far East

The United States ambassador to Japan outlines in 1934 his view that America's interests in the Far East should be protected vigorously in the face of increasing Japanese pressure.

1   'The firm stand of our Government and delegation to maintain the present naval ratios intact in the face of Japanese intransigence, as well as their decision that the action of the Japanese Government in denouncing the Washington Naval Treaty, automatically created a
5   new situation in which the conversations must be suspended *sine die,* leaving the Japanese to return home empty handed. ...

The thought which is uppermost in my mind is that the United States is faced, and will be faced in future, with two main alternatives. One is to be prepared to withdraw from the Far East,
10   gracefully and gradually perhaps, but not the less effectively in the long run, permitting our treaty rights to be nullified, the Open Door to be closed, our vested economic interests to be dissolved and our commerce to operate unprotected. There are those who advocate this course and who have advocated it to me personally, on the
15   ground that any other policy will entail the risk of eventual war with Japan. In their opinion, "the game is not worth the candle" because the United States can continue to subsist comfortably even after relinquishing its varied interests in the Far East, thereby eliminating the risk of future war.

20   The other main alternative is to insist, and to continue to insist, not aggressively yet not the less firmly, on the maintenance of our legitimate rights and interests in this part of the world and, so far as practicable, to support the normal development of those interests constructively and progressively. ...

25   In following this second and logical course, there should be and need be nothing inconsistent, so far as our own attitude is concerned, with the policy of the good neighbor. The determination to support and protect our legitimate interests in the Far East can and should be carried out in a way which, while sacrificing no point
30   of principle, will aim to restrict to a minimum the friction between the United States and Japan inevitably arising from time to time as a result of that determination.'

Source
Grew, J. C., *Peace and War: United States Foreign Policy, 1931–1941,* Washington, D.C., 1943

Questions
(1) a   When was the Washington Naval Treaty signed? What were its conditions?
    b   Who was the President of the United States at the time of the treaty? To which party did he belong?
    c   What label is frequently used to describe his foreign policy?
(2) a   What does Grew mean by 'the Open Door' (line 11)?

b Why is the United States interested in events in the Far East?

c Grew outlines two alternative courses of action (lines 9–24). Describe each course and say which one Grew prefers.

d Grew uses the phrase 'good neighbor' (line 27). This was commonly used to refer to the United States policy towards another part of the world. Which part of the world was this?

(3) a Name the President of the United States at this time. To which party did he belong?

b Briefly describe his general approach to world affairs.

(4) a Was Grew's advice to the Secretary of State followed in the next few years?

b How did relations between the United States and Japan develop until 1941?

---

over Austria and Czechoslovakia, by more or less peaceful means, attacked Poland in September 1939. This provoked a declaration of war by Britain and France. An opinion poll showed that 84% of Americans wanted an Allied victory, but only 2% wanted the Germans to win. The decline of isolationism and neutralism is indicated by small number who had no opinion.

The United States and the European War

In response to this change of attitude, the United States became steadily more involved in the struggle against Germany. Genuine neutrality was a thing of the past. Americans began to accept that their main priority should be to safeguard their security, not merely to avoid war.

It was now widely believed that if Germany dominated Europe she would close the continent to any outside economic contacts. The United States would be severely damaged by this loss of trade.

Congress revised the Neutrality Acts again in 1939. Belligerents were now allowed to buy arms and munitions on a 'Cash and Carry' basis. Congress was consciously favouring the Allies and running a risk. Senator Vandenberg said: 'In the long run, I do not believe that we can become an arsenal for one belligerent without becoming a target for another.'

America became even more concerned when Germany swept through Scandinavia, the Low Countries and France in the spring and summer of 1940, leaving Britain alone in the war. Churchill said Britain would fight 'until in God's good time, the New World, with all its power and might, steps forth to the rescue and liberation of the old.' Roosevelt did not offer direct aid, but he did obtain sharply increased defence spending from Congress. In January 1940 he had asked for $2 billion, but had had to settle for less. In September 1940 $10.5 billion was granted. The United States armed forces were in a sorry state, poorly equipped and undermanned. 'The draft' (conscription) was started in September 1940, and rearming proceeded hastily.

Aid to Britain

From the autumn of 1940, the United States provided steadily increasing help to Britain. In September Roosevelt agreed to let Britain have up to fifty over-age destroyers to replace those which had been sunk. In return America was given eight former British bases on the American continent.

7.3 German soldiers race through a French town during the drive towards Dunkirk, 1940.

After an appeal by Churchill, the United States agreed in March 1941 to help Britain further with the 'Lend-Lease' agreement. This allowed Britain to obtain armaments immediately, but delay payment until later. Roosevelt explained his reasons in a 'fireside chat', part of which appears on page 72. He hoped that the United States would be 'the great arsenal of democracy'.

Active military co-operation started in the spring of 1941. Submarine attacks on Britain's supply lines were threatening to bring defeat in 1941. Although to start with, she did not attack submarines herself, American patrols reported their whereabouts in the western Atlantic to the British. When an American ship was attacked in September, Roosevelt ordered a 'shoot on sight' policy against these 'rattlesnakes of the Atlantic'. To prevent a German takeover, the United States also established bases in Greenland and Iceland, both strategically important in the 'Battle of the Atlantic'.

In August Roosevelt and Churchill met secretly in a ship off Newfoundland, and issued the 'Atlantic Charter' of war aims (see page 81). Many of its details were reminiscent of Wilson's 'Fourteen Points', and confirmed that it was only a matter of time before the United States declared war herself.

Relations with Japan

Germany's successes gave Japan the encouragement and opportunity to extend her ambitions beyond China. Germany's victims had extensive colonial possessions in East Asia and the Pacific, most of which were rich in vital raw materials.

In 1940 Japanese policy took a more aggressive direction. From September, Japan forced the defenceless 'Vichy' French authorities (a puppet government dominated by Germany) in Indochina to allow her troops to be based there. The United States had ordered her fleet to stay at Pearl Harbor as a warning, but to no effect. Aid was given to China in her continuing war with Japan. During 1940 and 1941, the United States imposed increasingly severe economic sanctions on Japan, which finally led to a ban on all trade in September 1941. Japanese industry was damaged, suffering shortages of vital raw materials, especially oil.

The two countries were now on a collision course. One or other had to step down to avoid war, but both sides felt that their vital interests were at stake. Japan was basically asking the United States to give her a free hand in Asia and the Pacific. This was totally unacceptable to the Americans who were not prepared to be shut out from this region. In November 1941, Roosevelt sent 'war warnings' to his commanders in the Pacific, after the failure of half-hearted attempts, by both sides, to seek a peaceful solution.

The United States enters a global war

On 7 December, 1941 Japan launched a surprise attack on the United States' Pacific fleet at Pearl Harbor in Hawaii. The losses included 18 ships, sunk or seriously damaged, 188 planes destroyed and 2403 killed (half of whom were on one ship, the *Arizona*). Roosevelt described this as 'a date that will live in infamy'. In fact, Japan failed

7.4 The USS *Virginia* and the USS *Tennessee* blazing in Pearl Harbor after the Japanese attack in December, 1941.

to destroy her major objectives, the aircraft carriers, which were at sea, and most of the damaged ships were able to be repaired quite quickly. At the same time, Japan attacked colonies all over Asia and the Pacific. These included the Philippines (an American colony), Hong Kong, Malaya and the Netherlands East Indies (N.E.I.). She soon controlled a vast area (see the map on page 83).

The next day Roosevelt obtained from Congress an overwhelming vote in favour of declaring war on Japan. In theory, nothing had changed to make the United States declare war on Germany as well, but Hitler solved this problem by making the declaration himself on 11 December. This move has never been satisfactorily explained, as now Germany found herself in the unenviable position of having to face Russia and the United States at the same time, potentially the two most powerful nations in the world.

The isolationists and Roosevelt in 1941

Many isolationists were very bitter about the way Roosevelt led the United States into war. Some of their views are expressed on this page. They accused him of deliberately lying to the country: speaking about peace, but consistently planning for war. It has even been claimed that Roosevelt knew of the possibility of an attack on Pearl Harbor, but did nothing, so that he could have a good excuse to declare war. There is no evidence to prove this accusation.

It is clear, however, that Roosevelt was in advance of opinion in Congress, and the nation as a whole. He felt he had carefully to

Isolationism in 1941

'America First' was an organisation founded by isolationists to resist what appeared to be the drift to war. This statement was issued by them on 23 June 1941 in response to the attack by Germany on Russia. The United States started to give aid to Russia in July:

1   'The entry of Communist Russia into the war certainly should settle once and for all the intervention issue here at home. The war party can hardly ask the people of America to take up arms behind the red flag of Stalin. With the ruthless forces of dictatorship and
5   aggression now clearly aligned on both sides the proper course for the United States becomes even clearer. We must continue to build our defences and take no part in this incongruous European conflict.'

Philip La Follette, the prominent Progressive Republican from Wisconsin, was a vigorous opponent of Roosevelt's apparent warmongering:

'Two years ago the President and the War Party launched us on a
10   course of action labelled "steps short of war" to "keep us out of war". That was the most cunning of the many deceitful phrases employed in the propaganda campaign to get us into the war .... The sin of the War Party is not that they advocate war. The sin is that their only answer to the menace of Hitlerism in Europe is step
15   by step to create Hitlerism in the United States. Every step taken in the past two years has been put over on us by the same fraudulent methods practised by the European dictators.'

Source
Both quoted in Cole, W. S., *America First, the Battle Against Intervention 1940–1941,* Octagon Books, New York, 1971

Charles A. Lindbergh, who became a hero to millions when he flew across the Atlantic, lent his support to the isolationist cause:
   'I would a hundred times rather see my country ally herself with England, or even Germany with all her faults, than with the cruelty, the Godlessness, and the barbarism that exists in the Soviet Union.'

Source
Quoted in Divine, R. A., *The Reluctant Belligerent*

Questions
(1) What had been America's policy towards Russia in the decade before 1941?
(2) Roosevelt tried to convince Americans that matters of principle were at stake in the European war. Why does America First disagree and describe it as an 'incongruous' conflict (line 7)?

Churchill welcomes the Americans as Allies

Churchill made no secret of his delight when the United States joined Britain in the war against the Axis powers. Many isolationists believed the United States was the victim of a deceitful campaign to lure her into a war fought mainly to preserve the undemocratic British Empire, not on behalf of freedom:
   'To have the United States at our side was to me the greatest joy.... Now at this very moment I knew the United States was in the war, up to the neck and in to the death. So we had won after all!... Hitler's fate was sealed. Mussolini's fate was sealed. As for the Japanese, they would be ground to powder.... No doubt it would take a long time.... But there was no more doubt about the end.... Being saturated and satiated with emotion and sensation, I went to bed and slept the sleep of the saved and the thankful.'

Source
Churchill, W. S., *The Grand Alliance* pp. 510–12. Quoted in Dallek, R., *Franklin D. Roosevelt and American Foreign Policy 1932–1945,* OUP, 1979, p. 312

mould American opinion until it accepted that there was no satisfactory alternative to war. In the process he was not absolutely straightforward about his actions and intentions for the future. One of the major functions of a President is to lead the nation: it is his failure to do this throughout the 1930s that is perhaps the greatest criticism that can be levelled at him. He allowed foreign policy to drift, and to be planned by those whose ideas he believed to be short-sighted. If he had been bolder, the United States might have been able to help keep the peace.

8 Global war 1941–45

The Grand Alliance

In December 1941 the United States found herself a member of an extraordinary 'Grand Alliance', composed of countries which had very little to keep them together apart from their hatred of Germany. The three leading members of this Alliance (also known as the United Nations) faced totally different problems, and had war aims which were often contradictory. In theory they all supported the 'Atlantic Charter' on this page, but this document was, in reality, meaningless.

Stalin, the ruthless dictator of Communist Russia, had very little in common with Churchill, who had been a strong supporter of intervention in the Russian Civil War on the side of the 'Whites'. Britain was determined to protect her vast empire, but the Soviet Union and the United States felt that all empires should be broken up. Britain and the United States supported the idea of multi-party democracies; the Soviet Union had only one legal political party.

Differences such as these caused constant difficulties during the war, but Roosevelt was always confident that his charm and diplomacy could keep the Alliance together. This was often true, but as the war drew to

---

The Atlantic Charter

When Roosevelt and Churchill met aboard HMS *Prince of Wales* off the coast of Newfoundland, they produced this declaration of ideals. It was also supported by China, the Soviet Union and twenty-two other nations fighting against the Axis powers:

(The President and the Prime Minister) 'deem it right to make known certain common principles. . . .

First, their countries seek no aggrandisement, territorial or other;

Second, they desire to see no territorial changes that do not accord with the freely expressed wishes of the peoples concerned;

Third, they respect the rights of all peoples to choose the form of government under which they will live; . . .

Fourth, they will endeavor . . . to further the enjoyment by all States . . . of access . . . to the trade and to the raw materials of the world. . . .

Fifth, they desire to bring about the fullest collaboration between all nations in the economic field with the object of securing, for all, improved labor standards, economic advancement and social security;

Sixth, . . . they hope to see established a peace which will afford to all nations the means of dwelling in safety within their own boundaries. . . .

Seventh, such a peace should enable all men to traverse the high seas and oceans without hindrance;

Eighth, they believe that all of the nations of the world ... must come to the abandonment of the use of force....'

Source

Zevin, B. D. (ed.), *Nothing to Fear: The Selected Addresses of Franklin Delano Roosevelt 1932–1945,* Hodder and Stoughton, 1947, pp. 285–286

Questions

(1) In what ways do the details of the Atlantic Charter match Wilson's Fourteen Points on page 11?

(2) Which sections were most likely to produce disagreement between the United States and the Soviet Union? Explain your reasons in each case.

(3) Give three of these principles which were not put into practice at the end of the war. Outline what happened in each case. You will be better able to do this after studying the next two chapters.

---

an end, and it became necessary to make important decisions about the way the world was to be organised in peacetime, disagreements became more serious. It was for this reason that Roosevelt concentrated purely on military victory, and hoped that these decisions could be made later. This had dangerous consequences as can be seen in Chapter 9.

The task facing the Alliance

In 1941 and early 1942 the Axis powers made enormous and rapid advances on nearly all fronts. The map on page 83 shows that Japan's empire had extended far enough to menace India and Australia. The Allied forces were ill-equipped, often poorly led, and were forced to retreat.

In the Atlantic, German submarines were sinking ships faster than they could be replaced, and were strangling Britain. In North Africa, Rommel's forces were threatening to take the Suez Canal, and cut off Britain's oil supplies. German armies,

having driven deep into Soviet territory, appeared likely to take Leningrad, Moscow and Stalingrad.

Although most Americans probably felt more emotionally involved in the war against Japan, the United States decided to concentrate its main efforts on the defeat of Germany and her European allies. Germany would continue to fight regardless of the fate of Japan, but Japan's cause was made much easier by the fact that Germany was successfully destroying her own European opponents. The Pacific War, involving the extra problems of vast distances and inhospitable terrain, was also more difficult to win.

The peripheral strategy

The United States gave high priority to helping the Soviet Union. Lend-Lease facilities were offered, and arms were sent mainly by way of Vladivostok, Iran and Murmansk. In 1942 only half the promised amount was sent, to the annoyance of Stalin,

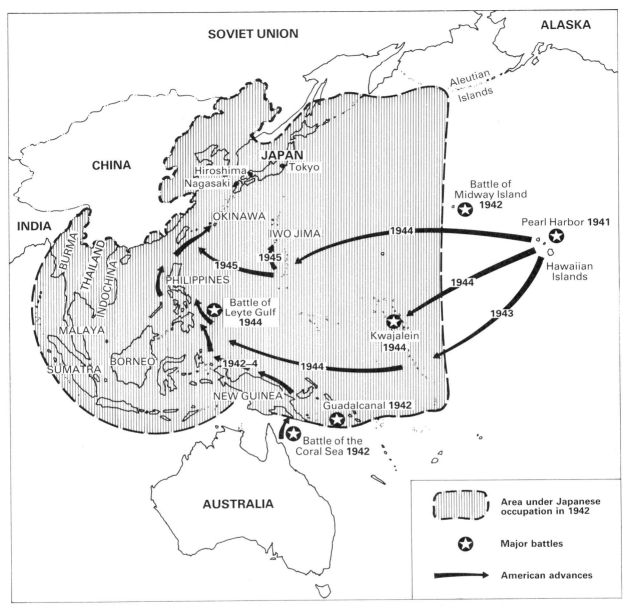

8.1 The Pacific War.

but the supply improved in later years. This aid proved very important to Russia's survival.

Both the United States and the Soviet Union were anxious that a second front should be opened in Western Europe in 1942. This would be very hazardous move, but it would make the Germans divide their forces and so relieve the pressure on the Red Army. Britain was determined to avoid conflict on the continent until it was certain that victory could be obtained quickly, and with the minimum of losses. Churchill overcame Roosevelt's objections, and they agreed to follow a 'peripheral strategy' to draw a net round the Axis powers and starve them of vital supplies. He was also anxious to protect Britain's position in the

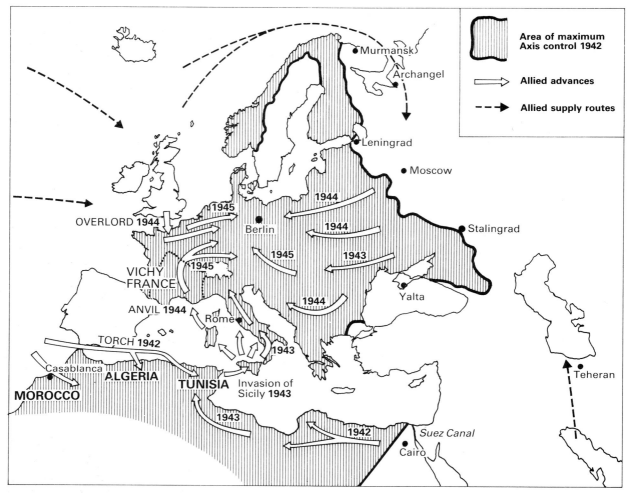

8.2 The defeat of Fascism in Europe and North Africa.

Mediterranean and the routes to her colonies in the East. He wanted landings in North Africa, then held by the Vichy French government. There was no real awareness of the problems that this would create for the Russians, who had already lost 5 million men, and in September 1942 were starting the bloody defence of Stalingrad. In this one battle they lost more men than the United States did during the whole war. This lack of consideration for the Russian position strained relations between Stalin and his Allies, and encouraged him in future to act purely in the Soviet Union's self-interest, as he believed his partners were behaving in a similar way.

TORCH November 1942

General Eisenhower led a force of 110 000 British and American troops against the French colonies in North Africa in an operation codenamed TORCH. (See the map on this page.) They overcame fierce resistance and were then able to turn their attention to Rommel's forces towards the east. He was also faced by Montgomery's army from Egypt and was forced to surrender in May 1943.

The Italian campaign

Roosevelt and Churchill met at Casablanca in January 1943, and decided to continue the 'peripheral strategy' by attacking Italy. In July 1943 a joint force landed on Sicily. (See the map on page 84.) Within two weeks Mussolini was deposed by Marshall Badoglio, an enthusiastic Fascist. When Allied troops landed on mainland Italy in September, Badoglio surrendered, and then declared war on his former partners, the Germans. The Allies found themselves co-operating with a man whose views they claimed to detest. The 'war against evil' had taken on an even stranger appearance.

The Germans managed to regain control of most of the Italian peninsula and made the Allied advance very slow. Churchill had described Italy as 'the soft underbelly of the crocodile', but it turned out instead to be a 'tough old gut'. The whole of Italy was not captured until the spring of 1945. The campaign only tied down a small proportion of the enemy forces, and so was of very little value to the overall task of defeating Germany.

The offensive against Germany

From 1942 a bombing campaign of mounting intensity was started. The United States Air Force played a major role in this. The objectives were not just confined to industrial and military sites, but also included civilian targets. The intention was to destroy morale as well as military capability, but the results were less impressive in both respects than had been hoped. Industrial production remained

8.3 Hamburg after Allied bombing.

remarkably high, and attacks, such as those on Hamburg and Dresden, probably increased German bitterness towards the Allies. The cost of the raids for the Germans was high. They lost 305 000 dead, 780 000 wounded, and had 5.5 million houses damaged or destroyed.

In Teheran at the end of 1943, Roosevelt met Stalin and Churchill for the first time. They decided that the second front would finally be opened in 1944. The operation was to be code-named OVERLORD, and would be led by Eisenhower. This invasion dominated all American strategy during 1944, and meant that Churchill's constant desire for further operations in the Mediterranean, Greece and the Balkans, was now opposed.

OVERLORD June 1944

D-Day was 6 June 1944. In twenty-four hours the Allies landed 156 000 men on the beaches of Normandy. They met with fierce opposition, but the beach-head was held. By 26 July a million men were in France, and by early September there were 2 million. (See the map on page 84.)

On 15 August ANVIL was launched, when seven Free French and three American divisions landed in the South of France to divert the German forces. This operation, too, was a success.

Paris was liberated on 26 August, and the Allies advanced cautiously on a broad front towards the Low Countries and Germany. The only major set-back to their progress

8.4 American troops aboard a landing craft bound for Normandy.

8.5 Army troops on 'Omaha' Beach during the initial landings there, 6 June 1944.

8.6 A German sniper is searched in Normandy, June 1944.

occurred at the 'Battle of the Bulge' in December. The Germans made a desperate, last counter-attack which forced a fifty mile bulge in the Allied lines in the Ardennes, Belgium. The Allies were able to continue their advance in January 1945, and crossed the Rhine into Germany in March.

From the east the Red Army had been steadily pushing the Germans back since 1943: by mid-1944 they had cleared Russian territory; by early 1945 most of Eastern Europe was under Soviet control. On 25 April the Americans met the Russians on the River Elbe. Hitler committed suicide on 30 April, and his successor Doenitz surrendered unconditionally to Eisenhower on 7 May.

Study this cartoon and answer the questions below:

Source
Bullock, A., *History of the 20th Century*, Octopus, 1976, p. 330

Questions
This poster was produced by the Nazis in the Netherlands. What is its message to the Dutch about the United States? Explain as many aspects of this poster as you can.

The Pacific War

The United States had to take the major role in the war against Japan. The most important factors in this conflict were naval and air power. Aircraft carriers were obviously vital in both sides' calculations. Relatively few troops were involved in land battles. American troops were never committed to fight on the mainland of Asia.

Throughout 1942 her forces were mainly on the defensive, but some notable victories were won. In May the Battle of the Coral Sea stopped the Japanese from invading New Guinea. The Battle of Midway Island in June was a significant turning point, when heavy losses were inflicted on the Japanese navy and air force. The ferocious struggle for Guadalcanal lasted six months. The Japanese were forced to retreat after suffering 20 000 casualties.

During 1943 the United States started to advance as they gained the all-important control of the sea and air. In October 1944 the United States won the Battle of Leyte Gulf, the largest sea battle in history, after which the Japanese navy was never again able to challenge the United States' supremacy. Japanese supply routes were also heavily attacked by American submarines, which sank 4 million tons of merchant shipping. Japanese industry was never able to match the Americans when it came to replacing lost ships and planes. This was of great significance in the United States' victory.

Rather than drive the Japanese out of all their occupied territories, the Americans adopted the tactic of 'island hopping'. Major enemy strongholds were avoided as they made rapid advances, often by way of relatively unimportant islands. Control of the sea and air meant that the Americans could starve these bases of supplies. Bloody encounters were frequent as the Japanese put up heroic and fanatical resistance. The example of Kwajalein, where the Japanese lost twenty-two men for every American

8.7 American troops landing on Eniwetok Atoll, a Japanese-held island, in February 1944. Marines wait for a tank crew to prepare the way ahead for them to advance.

casualty, was not unique. In desperation, 'kamikaze' attacks were started. There appeared to be no shortage of volunteers prepared to commit suicide by steering a plane or boat, packed with explosives, towards its target. These accounted for 21 ships sunk, 66 damaged and 45 000 casualties.

By early 1945 the capture of Iwo Jima and Okinawa put Japan itself within reach of American bombers. The raids on Japanese cities, with her air defences overwhelmed, were the worst of the war. On 9 March

Tokyo alone had 267 000 buildings destroyed, 84 000 killed, and about half that number wounded. When Japan surrendered, there were no more worthwhile military or industrial targets left.

Atomic warfare

In 1939 Roosevelt had been warned by the eminent physicist and Jewish refugee, Albert Einstein, that Hitler was planning to develop an atomic bomb. Although this was a false

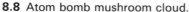
8.8 Atom bomb mushroom cloud.

alarm, he responded by secretly ordering the 'Manhattan Project' to beat the Germans in the race. On 16 July, 1945 the first atomic bomb was tested in New Mexico, with results which exceeded the scientists' expectations. J. Robert Oppenheimer, leader of the Project, as he watched the test, quoted Hindu scriptures: 'Now I am become death, destroyer of worlds.'

The new President, Harry S. Truman, who had succeeded Roosevelt when he died on 12 April 1945, decided to use this awesome weapon against the Japanese unless they surrendered unconditionally. They refused to do so. On 6 August an atomic bomb was dropped on Hiroshima. It killed 70 000 people, and wounded as many again. On 8 August, as they had promised in February at the Yalta Conference (see Chapter 9), the Soviet Union declared war on Japan, and swept into Manchuria. The stunned Japanese still failed to submit, and so a second bomb was dropped on Nagasaki, killing 40 000. The Japanese remained unwilling to give in unless the position of the Emperor was safeguarded. More conventional air raids were mounted until Hirohito himself announced the unconditional surrender by radio on 15 August. The Second World War was over.

Although there appeared to be very little doubt in the minds of those who had to decide at the time, in recent years there has been considerable discussion about whether the bomb should have been used. Many would argue that it is an immoral act to use such an indiscriminate weapon under any circumstances. The long-term effects of radiation, which were not fully realised before the bombs were dropped, put this type of warfare into a different category from even the most devastating of conventional attacks, which, it should be noted, often caused more death and destruction than these bombs. It has also been suggested that it would have been possible to show the Japanese what the bomb could do by demonstrating its power at sea.

8.9 U.S. Navy photo of the destruction in Hiroshima, taken in October 1945.

An eye-witness remembers the destruction of Hiroshima

Futaba Kitayama, then a thirty-three year old housewife, was 1.7 kilometres from the centre of the blast when the atomic bomb exploded over Hiroshima. This is her account of the experience:

'I don't remember which came first – the flash of light or the sound of an explosion that roared down to my belly. Anyhow, the next moment I was knocked down flat on the ground. Immediately, things started falling down around my head and shoulders. I couldn't see anything; it seemed pitch dark. I managed to crawl out of the debris.

Soon I noticed that the air smelled terrible. Then I was shocked by the feeling that the skin of my face had come off....

What happened to the sky that had been such a clear blue one only a moment ago? It was now dark, like dusk. I ran like mad toward the bridge, jumping over the piles of debris.

What I saw under the bridge was shocking: Hundreds of people were squirming in the stream, I couldn't tell if they were men or women. They looked all alike....

As far as I could see with my declining eyesight was all in flames....

... I saw on the street many victims being carried away by stretcher. Carts and trucks, heavily loaded with corpses and wounded who looked like beasts, came and passed me. On both sides of the street, many people were wandering about like sleepwalkers.'

Source
New Scientist, 25 August 1977, pp. 472–475, in Jolly, R. (ed.), *Disarmament and World Development,* Pergamon Press, 1978, pp. 32–33.

The defenders of Truman's action stress the horrific alternatives. The Japanese army was still intact. Two million soldiers were in Manchuria alone. Their record of zealous defence in 1945 suggested that any American invasion of Japan would result in terrifying casualties. A demonstration at sea was by no means certain to have convinced them that their position was hopeless. The debate continues.

Superpower

The United States emerged from the war in an unrivalled position of wealth and power. She controlled or strongly influenced four of the five major industrial regions of the world: Western Europe, Japan, Britain and America. Only the Soviet Union was beyond her control. Her own economy was extraordinarily prosperous. Her armies were spread all over the globe, and she was the only atomic power. She was in a unique situation to influence world affairs, because all other powers, including the Soviet Union, had been devastated by the most destructive war in history, and were in great need of American aid. All this is somewhat ironic, as America had probably made, in relative

The relationship between war-time military policy and post-war foreign policy

The strategy which the United States adopted in the Pacific War had consequences which extended far beyond the defeat of Japan, as American historian Stephen E. Ambrose explains:

'American military policy in the Pacific was geared only in a negative way to the nation's foreign-policy aims. The military effort was dedicated to the destruction of Japan. That was a goal of the first magnitude, to be sure, but just stopping the Japanese was not enough. It became increasingly clear as the war went on that it would be difficult, perhaps impossible, to restore the old order in Asia. Nor did Roosevelt want to return to business as usual, for he was a sincere opponent of old-style colonialism and wanted the British out of India, the Dutch out of the N.E.I., the Americans out of the Philippines, and the French out of Indochina.

For the Americans the question was what form independence would take, and here, as in Europe, power would reside with the man on the spot with a gun in his hand. Except in Japan, the Philippines, and the N.E.I., that man would not be an American. This fact opened the possibility that Communists would replace the old colonial rulers and that they might shut the Americans out of their Asia just as thoroughly as did the Japanese. The challenge for American policy-makers was how to simultaneously drive out the Japanese, prevent the resurgence of European colonialism, and foster the growth of democratic, capitalist local governments, all without actually making the effort necessary to put the man with a gun on the spot. In China, Indochina, and North Korea it turned out to be impossible'.

Source
Ambrose, S. E., *Rise to Globalism,* Penguin, 1980, pp. 76–77

terms, the smallest sacrifices in the conflict. She had not been invaded or bombed. Her industries and cities were still intact. Over 11 million Americans had gone overseas to fight, and 300 000 had been killed, but this pales into 'insignificance' alongside Russia's total losses of 20 million. Her main contribution had often been to provide her Allies with the supplies with which to fight.

As Stephen E. Ambrose points out on this page, there were weaknesses in America's position, which were to cause enormous problems in the years to come. In 1945, however, problems were far from most American minds as they surveyed their status as a superpower. Most were optimistic that they could help to rebuild a world in America's own image. Disillusionment and dissent rapidly set in.

9 The start of the Cold War

As long as the Axis powers remained undefeated, Roosevelt did his best to put off the evil moment when it would be necessary to make decisions about the organisation of the post-war world. It was clear from an early stage that Stalin, Churchill and Roosevelt had totally different ideas on the subject, but Roosevelt remained optimistic to the end of his life that all differences could be resolved.

Spheres of Influence or Open World?

The Soviet Union's major concern was about her security. Throughout her history she had suffered from invasions from Europe, and was determined to create a 'buffer zone' of friendly countries in Eastern Europe to help protect her from future attacks. Her greatest fear was that a revived Germany would strike at her again, and so Stalin wanted to ensure that Germany was either friendly or severely weakened. A buffer zone could also serve the additional purpose of helping the devastated Russian economy to recover by supplying raw materials or reparations.

This policy was totally contrary to the United States' hopes. Roosevelt believed that peace and security were more likely to be obtained in an 'Open World', in which all nations would be able to trade and invest without any restrictions. No state could have a 'sphere of influence' where its interests dominated.

Churchill was very concerned about post-war reconstruction long before the war ended. He feared that the Soviet Union would extend its power deep into Europe, including the Balkans and the Mediterranean. In 1944 he concluded the Moscow Agreements with Stalin. These gave the Soviet Union influence over Bulgaria and Rumania, while Britain was to have authority over Greece. Yugoslavia and Hungary were to be shared. Roosevelt refused to have anything to do with this deal, which went contrary to his 'Open World' ideals.

Timeline

Foreign policy 1945–60

1945   Yalta Conference (February).
        Truman replaces Roosevelt (April).
        End of Lend-Lease to Russia in retaliation for her Polish policies (May).
        Potsdam Conference (July).
        Demobilisation starts.

1946   United States dispute with Russia over Iran and Turkey (March and August).
        Bizonia formed (December).

1947   Truman Doctrine approved (May).

1948   Marshall Plan announced (June).
        Blockade of Berlin by Russia. Airlift started (June).
        OAS formed (September).

1949   NATO established (April).
        Russia ends blockade of Berlin (May).
        Russia explodes atomic bomb (September).
        Separate states established in West and East Germany
        (September and October).
        Victory by Communists in China. Nationalists flee to
        Taiwan (October).

1950   United States aid to France in Vietnam (May).
        Korean War starts. United States and UNO send troops
        (June).
        Communist China intervenes in Korea (November).

1951   Peace treaty with Japan (September). American
        occupation ends the following year.

1953   Eisenhower becomes President (January).
        Stalin dies (March).
        Armistice in Korea (July).

1954   Geneva Agreements (June). America sends aid to South
        Vietnam.
        SEATO formed (September).
        Communist Chinese pressure on Taiwan over Quemoy and
        Matsu.
        United States–Taiwan Mutual Defense Treaty (December).

1955   End of four power occupation of Austria (May).
        Geneva Summit (July).
        Baghdad Pact formed.

1956   Suez Crisis (October).

1957   Start of violent opposition to Diem's regime in South
        Vietnam.
        More American support to Taiwan in dispute with
        Communists.

1958   American troops to Lebanon (July).

1959   Castro takes power in Cuba (January).

1960   NLF formed in Vietnam.
        U-2 spy plane shot down by Russians (May).

The Yalta Conference, February 1945

The 'Big Three' met at Yalta to plan the final defeat of the Axis, and to make decisions about the future world order. The United States was anxious for the Soviet Union to attack Japan as she then believed that the Pacific War could last a long time. In return for this help, Stalin obtained several territorial concessions at the expense of China.

The United Nations Organisation

Roosevelt was also pleased by the compromise agreement on the creation of the United Nations Organisation (UNO) whose main purpose was to help keep world peace. Progress had been made during 1943–44, with the formation of several bodies designed to help with reconstruction, including the Food and Agriculture Organisation, the United Nations Relief and Rehabilitation Administration and the International Monetary Fund. Roosevelt would have preferred a UNO composed of members with equal power acting under the principle of 'collective security'. Stalin, believing that the United States and her friends would always be able to dominate if this were the case, insisted that the Soviet Union should have votes for its sixteen constituent republics (it eventually settled for three votes) and that any great power should be able to veto a decision.

The Declaration on Liberated Europe

The three powers produced a formula which appeared to set rules for their behaviour in occupied territories. Each power was to

9.1 Roosevelt, Churchill and Stalin at Yalta, 1945.

establish governments representing the wishes of the people and to hold free elections. All actions in these areas required three-power agreement. This made the declaration meaningless as one power could always obstruct the others. It had no influence on future developments.

The occupation of Germany

It was decided to divide Germany into four zones, to be run by the 'Big Three' and France. An Allied Control Council would co-ordinate these zones, which at some future date, presumably, were to be reunited. (See the map on this page.) The precise fate of Germany, and the equally sensitive subject of Poland, were left ominously vague.

Later critics were to accuse Roosevelt of a 'betrayal of democracy', by failing adequately to prevent Communist domination of Eastern Europe. The fact is that he had little choice but to accept the unarguable reality of Soviet power in 1945, and that a 'sphere of influence' in Eastern Europe was going to be created with or without American consent.

Truman's attitude towards the Soviet Union

When Truman succeeded Roosevelt in April, the United States' attitude towards the Soviet Union became less tolerant. He was inexperienced, ill-informed about foreign affairs, and could not understand many of Stalin's concerns. He soon confronted the

9.2 Occupied Germany 1945–49.

9.3 President Harry S. Truman. President of U.S.A., 1945–53.

Soviet Union over Poland.

Stalin had installed the Communist 'Lublin Poles' in power, in preference to the 'government in exile' in London. Without consulting his Allies, he made a treaty with the Poles which gave them German territory in compensation for land to be taken by the Soviet Union. (See the map on page 97.) Truman responded by putting economic pressure on the Russians to encourage a more acceptable policy. He ended Lend-Lease in May, and delayed an agreed loan of $1 billion. The Soviet Foreign Minister, Molotov, was given a very clear and sharp lecture on what the United States expected in future.

Stalin could not understand this attitude. He had always made policy in his own country's self-interest, and fully expected his Allies to do the same. For the United States to develop a concern for Poland, a country of great importance to the Russians, was in Stalin's view clearly mischievous.

The Potsdam Conference, July 1945

This conference, attended by Stalin, Truman and Britain's new Labour Prime Minister,

---

Stalin accuses the Western powers of double standards

In April 1945 Stalin responded to Truman's attacks on his policies towards Poland:

'Poland borders on the Soviet Union, which cannot be said about Great Britain or the U.S.A.... I do not know whether a genuinely representative Government has been established in Greece, or whether the Belgian Government is a genuinely democratic one. The Soviet Union was not consulted when those Governments were being formed, nor did it claim the right to interfere in those matters, because it realises how important Belgium and Greece are to the security of Great Britain. I cannot understand why in discussing Poland no attempt is made to consider the interests of the Soviet Union in terms of security as well.'

Questions

(1) a Name the conference which was supposed to decide the fate of countries liberated from the Axis powers.
    b What agreements were reached?

(2) a What had Stalin done to Poland which angered Truman?
    b How did Truman retaliate?
    c Which superpower won this dispute?

(3) a What arrangements had been made in 1944 concerning the government of Greece after her liberation?
    b Explain the American attitude towards this deal.
    c What events in Greece made relations between the United States and Soviet Union even worse by 1947?
    d What did Truman do about this situation?

Attlee, saw a worsening of the already strained relations within the Alliance. Further details were agreed over the zones of occupation in Germany (and Austria), but serious differences emerged over reparations. The Soviet Union believed it had been promised a substantial sum at Yalta, but now had to settle for less. It was accepted that she could take anything she wanted from her own zone. In addition, the Western Powers would give considerable amounts from their zones in exchange for food and raw materials. These arrangements proved unsatisfactory, and caused many disputes, so that in May 1946 the United States ceased to send its share of goods eastwards.

It is probable that at this stage Stalin had not decided to turn the whole of Eastern Europe, including its zone in Germany, into a bloc of Stalinist Communist states. What he considered to be an increasingly hostile Western attitude persuaded him that this would be the safest course for the Soviet Union to pursue. Furthermore, Stalin noted that the United States was determined to maintain her own domination of the American continent for economic and strategic reasons. He could not see why the Soviet Union should not have similar privileges in Eastern Europe when the dangers she faced were in fact far greater.

The United States' military strategy after 1945

The Republicans in Congress were determined that government spending should be reduced from its abnormal wartime levels. The defence budget was cut from $45 billion in 1945 to $13 billion in 1949. By 1947 the armed forces were down to $1\frac{1}{2}$ million men.

Strategists believed that the United States no longer needed large conventional forces, and that the bomb would be able to deter any aggressors. It was assumed that this weapon would be able to 'persuade' the Soviet Union into changing her policies. On the eve of the Potsdam Conference, just before the bomb was tested, Truman said: 'If it explodes, and I think it will, I'll certainly have a hammer on these boys.' Many observers suspected that its use in 1945 had been just as much a warning to the Soviet Union as a blow against the Japanese.

It was not expected that there would be a Communist bomb for at least another five years. In the meantime, the language of Western leaders became increasingly hostile towards the Soviet Union. Truman claimed to be upholding 'righteousness and justice', and referred to the Communists as 'barbarians'. He was reluctant to give ground: 'Negotiation would involve compromise with principle and complicity with evil.' Churchill's 'Fulton Speech' in March 1946 described what he saw as 'an iron curtain' dividing Western Europe from the East, where the Soviet Union was imposing Communism on unwilling peoples. Comparisons started to be made between the behaviour of Stalin and Hitler.

Iran, Turkey and Greece

The United States' policy was forced to take a different direction by events, not in Europe, but in the Eastern Mediterranean and Middle East, a region of vital concern to the economies of Europe.

In 1942 Britain and the Soviet Union had agreed to divide Iran between them to stop the oil fields falling into Nazi hands. The Soviet Union failed to leave after the war, as had been planned, and instead started to encourage revolts against the government. In early 1946 she appeared ready to invade, so the United States put strong diplomatic pressure on her to stay out. Although she backed down, it seemed to the Western Powers that the Soviet Union was eager to expand her territories.

It had been a centuries-old ambition for the Russians to dominate the Dardanelles which connected the Black Sea to the Mediterranean. The Soviet Union claimed some Turkish provinces in 1946, which provoked the United States into sending part of the navy as a warning to leave Turkey alone. Truman was firm: 'We might as well find out whether the Russians were bent on world conquest now as in five or ten years'. The Soviet Union again backed down in the autumn of 1946.

The Moscow Agreements gave Britain influence over Greece. She installed a right-wing royalist government and based a 40 000 strong army there. The government was soon under attack from largely Communist guerrilla forces. Britain, whose economy was in a state of near collapse, was unable to provide the necessary military and financial aid to the Greeks, and in February 1947 appealed to the United States to help. It was assumed that the guerrillas were being supplied and directed from Moscow, but this was not true. Stalin was content to let Yugoslavia and Hungary provide the aid instead.

Peace, freedom and world trade

Truman claimed that 'peace, freedom and world trade' were the main aims of the United States' foreign policy, and that it was impossible to have one without the others. After 1947 he became much more active in the pursuit of these goals. In so doing, he appeared to consciously divide the world into 'Us' and 'Them', in much the same way as Stalin did. The wartime Alliance seemed far away.

The Truman Doctrine: containment

Truman asked Congress for $400 million aid to Greece and Turkey for the purpose of 'containing' Communist aggression. He made it clear that any other governments which faced similar threats should also receive help. Freedom and peace, he claimed, were being menaced by Communists throughout the world. It was essential that the Soviet Union, which it was assumed directed all Communist parties, should be contained in a 'ring of freedom' financed by the United States.

Congress, which was still trying to cut government spending, was convinced by this warning and accepted the Truman Doctrine. The United States foreign policy has been dominated by the idea of containment ever since.

The Marshall Plan

The Truman Doctrine largely concerned itself with military aid in the defence of 'freedom', but Communists could gain power by means other than outright aggression. European economies were in a shambles after 1945, suffering from severe shortages, disrupted communications, low production and much else besides. Many believed that these were the ideal conditions to encourage support for Communism. The success of the French and Italian Communist parties appeared to be proof of this. This economic crisis could also create problems nearer home. There were fears that unless trade in Europe recovered, America would soon return to economic depression. A large proportion of American exports went to Europe, but this could only continue if there was prosperity there.

This situation persuaded the Secretary of State, General George C. Marshall, to propose that the United States should help to rebuild European economies by giving them massive sums of money. Congress approved this 'Marshall Plan' in 1948. The Soviet Union was invited to take part in the scheme; few expected (or hoped) that she would, and they were not disappointed. Nor did any other countries under her control participate. The Communists dismissed the plan as 'Dollar Imperialism', a United States attempt to control those countries which received aid. If it was aid 'with no strings attached', why did she not take up the offer

Communism and economic depression

George Kennan was one of the most influential State Department officials, with great experience in the United States Embassy in Moscow. In this telegram he shows his concern about the European economic crisis after 1945:

1   'Much depends on health and vigor of our own society. World communism is like malignant parasite which feeds only on diseased tissue. This is point at which domestic and foreign policies meet.'

Another State Department official wrote on the same subject:

'Hungry people are not reasonable people. Their thoughts are
5   concerned with their own misery and particularly with the tortured cries of their hungry children. They are easy victims of mass hysteria. When people become frightened elements of a mob, democratic precepts mean nothing.'

Source
Both quoted in Paterson, T. G., *The Quest for Peace and Prosperity* in Bernstein, B. J. (ed.), *Politics and Policies of the Truman Administration*, Quadrangle, Chicago 1970

Questions
(1) For what reasons are both of these writers so concerned about the economic crisis in Europe?

(2) Give two examples of countries where Communism was feeding on 'diseased tissue' (line 2) in 1945. Do not include anywhere under the control of the Soviet Union.

(3) What did the United States eventually do to help solve this problem? How successful was this policy?

by the UNO to distribute the money?

The sixteen nations who took part formed the Organisation for European Economic Co-operation (OEEC) to administer the aid. They were expected to reduce tariffs, and encourage free competition – all part of the ideal 'Open World'. In the years 1948–52 $13 billion were spent under the plan, and the results were impressive. By 1950 production had risen 25% higher than pre-war levels: by 1952 this had reached 200%. Trade with America increased substantially.

The threat of economic and political collapse in Europe receded, and these countries were in a stronger position to deal with a more direct, military threat.

The creation of a Soviet bloc in Eastern Europe

During 1945–46 elections in Soviet occupied countries had usually produced coalition governments which included Communists.

Study this Czechoslovakian cartoon of 1952 and answer the following questions:

Source
Dikobraz 1952 in Bullock, A., *History of the 20th Century,* Octopus, 1976, p. 369

Questions

(1) Who is the man holding the ace of diamonds?

(2) Identify the figures seated at the table.

(3) Which policies are represented here by (a) the pile of money, and (b) the gun?

(4) Explain the relationship alleged by this cartoon between the seated and the standing figures.

(5) What alternative opinion about this relationship could be put forward by an opponent of the Czechoslovakian government?

By 1948 the Communists had taken sole power by a variety of methods – underhand, skilful or violent. The unity of this bloc was strengthened in 1947 by the creation of Cominform to dictate policy. In response to the Marshall Plan, Comecon was established in 1949 to tie the East European economies firmly to the Soviet Union. The last thing Stalin wanted was an 'Open World'. By this time he wanted, and obtained, a bloc of Communist 'satellites' obedient to the will of Moscow, and immune to either threats or temptations from the United States. Any opposition within this bloc was to be ruthlessly eliminated.

Who caused the Cold War?

After 1945 relations between the Soviet Union and her former Allies had deteriorated to such an extent that a 'Cold War' was said to exist. This term is generally taken to mean a position of armed hostility but where no fighting actually takes place between the major rivals. When fighting occurs it is between the superpowers' smaller friends.

The question of who caused this Cold War is a matter of active historical and political debate.

Both East and West were responsible for acts of deception designed to secure an advantage over the other. The Soviet Union's meddling in Turkey, Iran and elsewhere convinced those who were already suspicious, that her intentions were to expand. The United States' language, and her unwillingness to share her atomic secrets, 'obviously' proved that she was bent on destroying the Soviet Union. When negotiations took place there was no meeting of minds, no agreement on the basic principles to be put into practice. The United States' 'Open World' was in direct conflict with the Soviet Union's need for security. Compromise was almost impossible, and communication broke down.

Whoever was to blame, there was no doubt that in 1948 Europe, at least, was divided firmly into two antagonistic camps. The major concern was whether this hostility would actually result in open warfare.

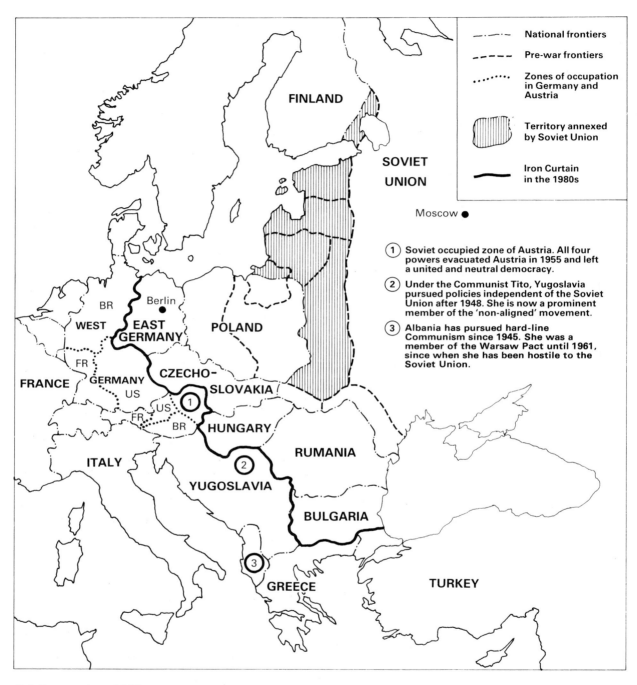

9.4 Europe since 1945.

10   The testing of containment 1948–53

The Berlin Crisis 1948–49

The future of Germany had been the major issue which produced the tension between the Western powers and the Soviet Union. When it became clear to the United States that it was impossible to reach agreement on the country's long-term future, it was decided that the Western powers' zones should be made economically self-sufficient, so that they would cease to be a financial burden to their occupiers. Moves were made in this direction when the British and American zones united in 1946 to form Bizonia, an arrangement later joined by the French. The Soviet Union was deeply suspicious towards this policy. She believed that an economically powerful Germany would eventually become a military threat. Attempts to build up the German economy were therefore interpreted as an attack on her security.

In June 1948 a new currency, the Deutschmark, was introduced into Western Germany. This showed a readiness to create two separate German states if necessary. Stalin retaliated by cutting all land communication between the Western powers' sectors in Berlin and their zones in the rest of Germany. West Berlin was left as a helpless island surrounded by Soviet controlled territory. The $2\frac{1}{2}$ million inhabitants of West Berlin could only survive if the Western powers were able to fly in vast quantities of supplies.

Truman immediately announced the United States' determination to stay in Berlin, and thus prevent Communist expansion. The policy of containment was being put to the test. A massive airlift was organised, mainly by the United States, but with some contributions from Britain and France. A minimum of 4000 tons per day were required for survival, but after early shortages, the incredible level of 13 000 tons was reached. This was made possible by a constant stream of planes flying at three minute intervals along the three air corridors to the city. They had to face the hazard of Soviet fighters 'buzzing' them, but no actual attacks were made, and outright war was avoided.

After 324 days Stalin surprisingly lifted the blockade in May 1949. Although he had failed in his aim of forcing the Western powers out of Berlin, he had caused them considerable difficulty and expense at relatively little cost to the Soviet Union. By giving in he accepted that Germany and Berlin would remain divided.

In September 1949 the Western zones united to form the Federal Republic of Germany (West Germany), and in October the Soviet Union turned her zone into the German Democratic Republic (East Germany) with East Berlin as its capital. West Berlin continued to have an insecure life-line to West Germany along the previously agreed routes. Each rival German state loyally followed its superpower sponsor in the years to come.

The North Atlantic Treaty Organisation (NATO)

The policy of containment made it necessary for the United States to keep her armed forces stationed in Europe. This was a reversal of her original intentions. To do this it was necessary to reintroduce the draft in 1948 after it had been ended by Congress the previous year.

The United States also felt it was important that her European friends should contribute to their own protection. Their efforts were to be co-ordinated by the North Atlantic Treaty Organisation (NATO) formed in 1949. This was a defensive alliance of the United States and, originally, eleven other countries. They all promised to treat an attack on one of them as an attack on all. This was the first occasion when the United States had ever entered into a peacetime alliance, and clearly shows how far her foreign policies had changed since the Neutrality Acts.

In the short term NATO's military importance was limited, as the United States was the only member with enough wealth and power to oppose the Red Army. In later years, when European countries had recovered from the war, they were able to make a more effective contribution to containment.

Attempts were later made to imitate NATO elsewhere in the world. The South East Asia Treaty Organisation (SEATO) in 1954, and the Baghdad Pact in 1955, later renamed the Central Treaty Organisation (CENTO) in 1959, were intended to help contain the Communist world. These alliances never worked as effectively as NATO, however.

The American public was given a rude shock when it was announced in September 1949 that the Soviet Union had tested her first atomic bomb. This convinced the United States that much greater defence spending was needed urgently. Not only were conventional forces enlarged, but it was also decided to produce the hydrogen bomb, whose destructive power would dwarf any existing nuclear weapon.

American strategists believed it was necessary to allow West Germany to rearm. This would inevitably annoy the Soviet Union, but France too was concerned that a revived Germany would one day threaten her. French fears were reduced by the creation of the European Coal and Steel Community. This forerunner of the European Economic Community was designed to ensure that control over these vital raw materials would be shared. Germany would not be able to use her natural resources for unchecked military expansion. By 1955 West Germany was largely accepted as an equal member of the Western community of nations and was admitted to NATO.

The Cold War in Asia

From 1945 to 1949 Truman was mainly concerned by events in Europe. Policy in Asia had received less attention, but it was in this region that the United States started to suffer the most severe blows. Many of Truman's opponents had long argued for an 'Asia First' policy, and events in China and Korea appeared to confirm the truth of their views.

The occupation of Japan

Following her unconditional surrender, Japan was occupied by United States forces under the very personal control of General Douglas MacArthur. Although he had the title of Supreme Commander for the Allied Powers (SCAP), he only took orders from his President, and he often was reluctant to take orders even from him.

The United States wanted to make Japan into a friendly power able to take a leading political and economic role in East Asia. Originally it was intended that she should be totally disarmed, but as the Cold War became more bitter, Japan was allowed some military power. Japan could play a very significant role as a valuable trading partner for America, and also for other Asian countries. This would help the region to prosper and resist Communism.

MacArthur's first priority was to establish a democratic system of government to replace the old military and imperial order. In 1946 elections to a Diet (Parliament) were held, and power was gradually handed over to the Japanese. The economy was able to recover quickly, and was given an unexpected boost by the Korean War in 1950 when Japanese industry supplied the UNO's forces with a wide range of goods. Japan's strategic value became quite clear in this conflict as much of the United States' effort was based there.

In 1951 a peace treaty was signed at San Francisco. Japan's status as an ally of the United States was obvious when the Soviet Union refused to sign the treaty. The American occupation formally ended the next year.

The United States and China

Throughout the war Roosevelt had tried to encourage his allies to recognise Chiang Kaishek's China as a 'great power'. This was a hopeless attempt as Chiang's government was notoriously corrupt and inefficient, and his country was incredibly backward. Until 1945 he was more concerned about fighting a civil war against Mao Tsetung's Communists than about defeating Japan. The United States provided Chiang with substantial aid in full knowledge of this.

After the fall of Japan a Communist victory appeared most unlikely. Mao controlled only a small part of the country, and on paper his poorly equipped army would be crushed by Chiang's Nationalist forces, most of whose materials had been supplied by the United States. Neither superpower had much confidence in 'its' man. Mao was not obedient to Stalin's orders. Chiang was reluctant to make long overdue reforms, and consistently disgraced the cause of freedom and democracy. His regime was an embarrassment to well informed Americans.

The course of the civil war was an unpleasant suprise to many Americans. Mao profited from Chiang's unpopularity. He obtained the support of most peasants, and many Nationalist troops defected to the Communists and took their arms with them. The United States decided to end aid as the

10.1 Mao Tsetung at a Communist victory parade in Peking, 1949.

Nationalists disintegrated in 1948–49. Mao announced the establishment of the People's Republic of China in October 1949. The Nationalists ignominiously fled to Taiwan where they continued to defy the Communists. Few people expected them to survive for very long.

The victory for Communism was all the more shocking to Americans because it was sudden. Most assumed (falsely) that it could only have happened because of direct aid and planning from Moscow, and that this was further evidence of the Soviet Union's expansionist policies. The 1950 Treaty of Friendship between the two countries simply confirmed the theory.

Chiang's supporters in America, mostly Republicans, attacked Truman bitterly. He was accused of 'selling out China to the Reds'. Anti-Communist campaigners in America were given considerable fresh ammunition. (See Chapter 11.) On this page the statements of those who were actually involved give a more realistic account of the causes of Chiang's defeat.

The United States refused to recognise the People's Republic and blocked her admission to the UNO. This prompted the Soviet Union to boycott its proceedings in January 1950. Only lukewarm support was given to

---

The loss of China

General Barr, head of the United States' military mission in China, gave his explanation for the Nationalists' defeat:

1   'No battle has been lost since my arrival due to lack of ammunition or equipment. Their military debacle, in my opinion, can all be attributed to the world's worst leadership and many other morale-destroying factors that led to a complete loss of the will to
5   fight.'

Dean Acheson, Secretary of State from 1949, responded to the fierce attacks levelled at the Truman administration:

'Nothing that this country did or could have done within the reasonable limits of its capabilities could have changed that result; nothing that was left undone by this country has contributed to it. It was the product of internal Chinese forces, forces which this
10   country tried to influence but could not. A decision was arrived at within China, if only a decision by default.'

The Republican Senator Hugh Butler of Nebraska directed his onslaught at Acheson personally:

'I watch his smart aleck manner and his British clothes and that New Dealism, everlasting New Dealism in everything he says and does, and I want to shout, "Get out! Get out! You stand for
15   everything that has been wrong with the United States for years."'

Questions
(1) What was the United States' policy towards China in the years 1945–49?
(2) What were the 'internal Chinese forces' (line 9) which brought about the Nationalists' defeat?
(3) How did the 'loss of China' affect America's own politics? It might be helpful to consult Chapter 11.

Taiwan at this stage, although Chiang's regime was still recognised as the legal government of the whole of China. Relations between the People's Republic and the United States rapidly went from bad to worse because of events in Korea.

The Korean War

It was agreed in 1945 that the former Japanese colony of Korea should be temporarily divided along the line of latitude 38°N. Until order could be restored the Soviet Union would occupy the North, and the United States, the South.

As relations between the occupying countries deteriorated it became imposssible to reach agreement on the reunification of the country. Neither power had any wish to remain in Korea, so they both set up a rival state, each claiming the right to rule the whole country. In the North Kim Il-sung led a Communist regime. In the South Syngman Rhee ran an apparently democratic government. In reality, Rhee acted as a virtual dictator, showing scant respect for political freedom. The United States regarded him with little affection, and even tried to have him assassinated. The North had an efficient Soviet-trained army of 135 000 men. Although its chief American

10.2 Korean War 1950–53.

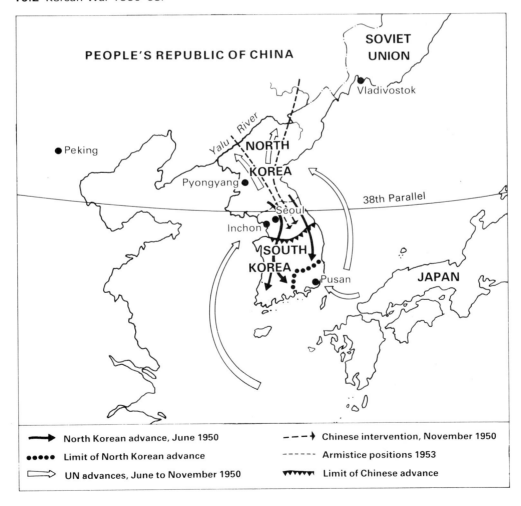

10.3 An American G.I. interrogates a captured North Korean nurse.

adviser described the South's force as 'the best doggoned shooting army outside the United States', its 98 000 troops were poorly equipped and ill-disciplined.

In early 1950 the United States had declared that her major line of defence in the region was not on mainland Asia, but in the offshore islands stretching from the Aleutians, to Japan and the Philippines. This could have been treated as an invitation to the North to try to reunite Korea.

After a period of tension along the 38th Parallel, the North attacked the South on 24 June, 1950. (See the map on page 109.) The Communists advanced rapidly and managed to capture most of the peninsula. Rhee's government was helpless and appealed for United States aid. In order to show her determination to help her friends against Communists, the United States decided to change her earlier lack of enthusiasm for South Korea and sent immediate aid.

Since the Soviet Union was boycotting it, the United States managed to get the UNO to condemn North Korea's aggression. More significantly, for the first time ever, the UNO also agreed to send an international force to help the United States to defend the South. The contribution of countries other than the United States was relatively small, however, and all anti-Communist forces were clearly under the American commander, MacArthur. The United States was thus using the UNO largely for her own purposes.

United States and UNO forces started to arrive just in time to prevent a North Korean victory. After the Communists were halted at Pusan, a bold counter-attack was launched at Inchon. This cut the over-extended enemy lines, and turned near triumph into a rout.

Until that time the United States' war aims had been to repel the aggressors and to restore the South Korean border to the 38th Parallel. As the North's forces fled in disarray, Truman now declared the aim was to create a 'free, independent and united' Korea. He wanted to liberate the North from, as he saw it, an unpopular Communist tyranny. MacArthur enthusiastically advanced north of the 38th Parallel in October, and moved rapidly towards the borders with China and the Soviet Union.

Chinese intervention

The Soviet Union took no active role in the fighting, but her aid was vital to the North Korean campaign. China had been only an onlooker up to this time. As United States troops came nearer, China's attitude changed. She warned the Americans not to come close to her border. Truman ordered MacArthur not to provoke Korea's formidable neighbours, but this had little effect on his independent-minded general. He believed it was necessary to strike at China across the Yalu River.

After a warning attack followed by a withdrawal, the Chinese secretly infiltrated 300 000 troops across the border to hide in

Face to face with the Chinese Red Army

Anthony Farrar-Hockley was a British officer fighting in Korea as part of the UNO's force. He describes here the Chinese forces which intervened in the Korean War:

1   'The attackers enter; hundreds of Chinese soldiers clad in khaki suits; plain, cheap cotton caps; rubber soled, canvas shoes upon their feet; their shoulders, chests and back criss crossed with cotton bandoliers of ammunition: upon their hips, grenades.... Those in
5   the forefront of the battle wear steel helmets that are reminiscent of the Japanese. Their weapons – rifles, carbines, 'burp' guns, and Tommy guns that we supplied to Chiang-Kai-shek – are ready in their hands. Behind on mule or pony limbers are their guns and ammunition. Between the two lines, on sweating backs, or slung
10 between two men upon stout bamboo poles, their mortars and machine-guns travel forward. No Oxford carriers, no jeeps or trailers, no gun prime-movers here; but if they lack these aids to war, they do not lack what we do most: men. The hundreds grow to thousands on the river bank, as, padding through the night, they
15 close with us: eight hundred Gloucesters astride the road to Seoul – the road the Chinese mean to clear at any cost.'

Source
Rees, David, *Korea – The Limited War,* St Martins Press, New York, 1964

Questions
(1) What were the events which led to the intervention of Communist China in the Korean War?
(2) Describe and explain the likely course of events which resulted in the Red Army using weapons sent by Britain and the United States to Chiang Kaishek (line 7).
(3) What was the military result of the Chinese attack?
(4) When did this war come to an end and what was the outcome?

the rugged mountains. On 26 November a sudden onslaught by these troops put MacArthur's army into a headlong retreat, which was only halted below the 38th Parallel. The United States' forces gradually recovered and a stalemate developed around the old border in early 1951.

This set-back meant that no more talk was heard of liberating the North from Communism. The aim was again to repel the aggressors. MacArthur disliked this 'weakness', and stated openly that the United States should concentrate on the Communist threat not in Europe, where Truman believed there was the greatest danger, but in Asia where China was presenting the new challenge. Truman dismissed MacArthur for interfering in policy-making. On his return home, the first time in fourteen years, he was given a 'ticker-tape' reception in New York, and treated as a national hero, especially by Republicans who wanted to attack Truman by supporting the 'Asia First' policy. This

Truman, Korea and the world

1   'The Communists in the Kremlin are engaged in a monstrous
conspiracy to stamp out freedom all over the world. If they were to
succeed, the United States would be numbered among their
principal victims. It must be clear to everyone that the United States
5   cannot – and will not – sit idly by and await foreign conquest. The
only question is: When is the best time to meet the threat and how?

The best time to meet the threat is in the beginning. It is easier to
put out a fire in the beginning when it is small than after it has
become a roaring blaze.

10   And the best way to meet the threat of aggression is for the
peace-loving nations to act together. If they don't act together, they
are likely to be picked off, one by one . . . .

This is the basic reason why we joined in creating the United
Nations. And since the end of World War II we have been putting
15   that lesson into practice – we have been working with other free
nations to check the aggressive designs of the Soviet Union before
they can result in a third world war.

That is what we did in Greece, when that nation was threatened
by the aggression of international Communism.

20   . . . With our help, the determination and efforts of the Greek
people defeated the attack on the spot.

Another big Communist threat to peace was the Berlin blockade.
That too could have led to war. But again it was settled because
free men would not back down in an emergency . . . .

25   Our resolute stand in Korea is helping the forces of freedom now
fighting in Indochina and other countries in that part of the world. It
has already slowed down the timetable of conquest . . . .

We do not want to see the conflict in Korea extended. We are
trying to prevent a world war – not to start one. The best way to do
30   this is to make plain that we and the other free countries will
continue to resist the attack.

But you may ask: Why can't we take other steps to punish the
aggressor? Why don't we bomb Manchuria and China itself? Why
don't we assist Chinese Nationalist troops to land on the mainland
35   of China? . . . .

I believe that we must try to limit war to Korea for these vital
reasons: to make sure that the precious lives of our fighting men are
not wasted; to see that the security of our country and the free
world is not needlessly jeopardized; and to prevent a third world
40   war.

A number of events have made it evident that General MacArthur
did not agree with that policy. I have therefore considered it
essential to relieve General MacArthur so that there would be no
doubt or confusion as to the real purpose and aim of our policy.

45   It was with deepest personal regret that I found myself compelled
to take this action. General MacArthur is one of our greatest military
commanders. But the cause of world peace is more important than
any individual. . . .'

Source
Department of State Bulletin, April 16, 1951. Quoted in Commager, H. S.,
Documents of American History, Meredith Corporation 1973, pp. 567–568

Questions
(1) Outline the course of events in the Korean War which led to this speech by Truman.
(2) a When and why did the United States send aid to Greece (line 18)?
    b Truman believed that the threat to Greece came from 'the aggression of international Communism' (line 19). Is this an accurate interpretation of the situation?
    c What is meant by 'the Berlin blockade' (line 22)? How did the United States react?
    d What name is usually given to the United States' policy towards the Soviet Union in the years after this aid to Greece? How was it put into practice in the period before this speech?
(3) a Consult Chapter 16. Who were 'the forces of freedom now fighting in Indochina' (line 25)?
    b Why and when did the United States start to help these forces?
    c Why, in Truman's opinion, is it so important for 'other free countries' (line 30) that the United States is fighting in Korea?
(4) a Why might some people have argued that the United States should 'bomb Manchuria and China' (line 33)?
    b Who were the 'Chinese Nationalist troops' (line 34)? Why might they wish 'to land on the mainland of China' (line 34)?
(5) a How did American public opinion react to MacArthur when he returned home? Which political party gave him strongest support?
    b Study pages 120–3. Explain how these events in Korea gave the 'anti-Communist witch hunters' in America more 'evidence' with which to attack Truman's administration?

---

was an astonishing reception for a man who had just been sacked, and showed how unpopular Truman had become.

The end of the war

The high optimism with which the United States had crossed the 38th Parallel had turned into deep disillusionment by mid-1951. It had been a bloody conflict, with atrocities on both sides, and fought in a severe climate over inhospitable terrain. There appeared to be little likelihood of an early victory for either side, and so negotiations started at Panmunjom in July 1951.

These talks were frustrating as neither side was prepared to make any real concessions to end the continued fighting. No progress was made throughout 1952 which was election year in America.

Eisenhower promised in his election campaign to visit Korea to try to end the war. He kept his word, but achieved little. As President, in May 1953 he threatened to use nuclear weapons; the Communists were unimpressed. More influential was the change in mood between East and West. Eisenhower was determined to avoid being bogged down in costly warfare, and after Stalin's death in March 1953, the Soviet Union was more prepared to reduce tension.

An armistice was finally signed in July 1953. The new border was to be almost identical to the 38th Parallel. The United States continued to strengthen the South with substantial military and economic aid, and to support its far from democratic regimes in their resistance to Communism.

The impact of the Korean War on United States foreign policy

The war had a far-reaching effect on United States foreign policy. The defence budget rose sharply and remained at a high level. Owing to their involvement in Korea, relations between Communist China and the United States appeared to be irreparably damaged. The American government's attitude could best be described as merely 'unfriendly' in 1949. By the end of 1950 it was hostile. No improvement took place until the 1970s. Taiwan immediately benefited by receiving aid which had earlier been refused. The French also started to obtain United States aid in their war in Indochina. (See Chapter 16.)

In Europe NATO was extended to include Greece and Turkey. Spain, ruled by Franco, one-time associate of Hitler and Mussolini, was given aid in 1951, and in 1953 she agreed to have American air force bases on her territory. At the UNO the United States took advantage of the Soviet Union's absence in 1950 to obtain the Uniting for Peace resolution. This would make it possible for the General Assembly of all members (where the United States had clear support) to overcome a great power's veto. The Soviet Union was the obvious target.

In 1952 most voters felt that Truman's foreign policies had failed. The 1945 ideal of an Open World had long been abandoned and replaced by containment. Korea had shown that this was enormously costly, not only in dollars, but also in American lives. The United States appeared to have wasted the considerable advantages over the Soviet Union which she had held at the end of the Second World War. Truman was held responsible. His difficulties abroad had a damaging effect on his policies at home, and made him one of the most unpopular Presidents of all time.

11 America at home 1941–52

From 1941 Roosevelt's administration was totally dominated by the war. Not only was attention given to events overseas, but it was also vital to organise the American economy so that it could efficiently provide the vast quantities of war materials for Allied armed forces across the globe. This brought many long-term changes to America's society, economy and government.

The task was supervised by the Office of Economic Stabilisation in 1942, and by its successor the Office of War Mobilisation from 1943. They ensured that war production came first in the allocation of raw materials. Industries were converted from the production of consumer goods to the manufacturing of munitions. These defence plants recruited large numbers of workers, often from previously depressed agricultural areas. Many women worked for the first time, attracted by high wages and propaganda about the patriotic achievements of 'Rosie the Riveter'. Women accounted for 36% of the labour force by 1945, and two-thirds stayed at work after then. Many cities expanded rapidly as their industries boomed.

In 1940 unemployment was 14.6%. By 1944 it had fallen to 1.2%. Wages rose considerably more than prices, and many people were afraid that high inflation might develop. The Office of Price Administration (OPA) was successful in its attempts to prevent this. Many newly prosperous workers were frustrated when they tried to spend their money, because there were widespread shortages of consumer goods.

Timeline

America at home 1941–60

1942   Republicans make gains in mid-term elections (November).

1944   Roosevelt elected for fourth term of office (November).

1945   Roosevelt replaced by Truman (April).

1946   Republicans win control of Congress for first time since 1928 (November).

1947   Taft–Hartley Act.

1948   Truman elected for second term in office (November).

1950   McCarthy starts campaign against Communism (February).

1950	McCarran Internal Security Act.
1951	Twenty-Second Amendment ratified.
1953	Eisenhower becomes President (November).
1954	*Brown* v. *Board of Education* decision.
1955	Start of Montgomery Bus Boycott (December).
1957	Little Rock disturbances (September).
1960	'Sit Ins' by SNCC (April). Civil Rights Act.

Food too was often in short supply, so many restaurants were forced to serve up delicacies like 'beaverburgers'. Farm prices rose as worldwide demand swallowed up the pre-war surpluses. Agricultural production

11.1 Unknown Norma Jean, who later became famous as Marilyn Monroe, promoting the war effort.

expanded by 15% to cope with this.

The war forced the Federal Government to increase its spending by 1945 to levels ten times higher than those during peacetime. To pay for this taxes were sharply increased on incomes and business profits, which were very high because of the war boom. Heavy borrowing also played its part because Congress was reluctant to allow the raising of money by excessive taxation. High spending and taxation by the Federal Government remained a permanent feature of the American scene after 1945.

The emergency conditions made it necessary for the government to start to censor the news media, and to engage in a certain amount of propaganda. By and large civil liberties were well protected, but with one major exception. It was decided to evacuate 110 000 Japanese-Americans from their West Coast homes as they were accused of being a security risk. They were put in miserable 'relocation camps' until 1945. No evidence was ever produced to show that they would have helped the enemy. Much of the agitation against them came from racist farmers who wanted to take their land. German-Americans were not treated in this way.

Communists, who had been persecuted in the past, met with approval from unexpected

'Wilson'

The film *Wilson*, made during the Second World War, was, according to its producer Darryl F. Zanuck, intended 'to show the mistakes of the past so they could be avoided in the future'. The scene shows President Wilson talking to Count von Bernstorff:

'WILSON. Count von Bernstorff, for more than two years this Government has exercised every restraint in its efforts to remain neutral in this conflict. But you and your military masters apparently are determined to deny us that right.

VON BERNSTORFF. But I assure you, sir –

WILSON (*ignoring the interruption*). Every way we turn we run into a blank wall of German cruelty and stupidity. Every time we think we've escaped, you blindly – and *deliberately* – block us with some new outrage!

VON BERNSTORFF (*rising – full of German indignation*). Mr. President! . . .

WILSON. Sit down. Won't you Germans ever be civilised? Won't you ever learn to keep your word? . . . We are not exactly fools. We know about the spies and conspirators you've sent amongst us in an effort to corrupt our opinions through lies and rumors. . . . Unfortunately some of our own people have fallen in with your plans, and day after day I see them going up and down this country doing your work, crying out in their innocence that this is "just another European war" which can't touch America – . . . Is your Kaiser . . . so drunk with power that he can't understand that . . . this, is, in truth, a fight for freedom and decency against the most evil and autocratic power the world has ever seen? . . . Good night, sir!

. . . (*Wilson looks after von Bernstorff as he leaves.*) *Slowly he turns and crosses and stands in front of the great, dimly-lit portrait of Washington, the scene moving with him, as we hear faintly the strains of "Yankee Doodle".*'

Source
Gassner, J. and Nichols, D., (eds) *Best Film Plays of 1943–1944,* Crown Publishers, Inc., New York, 1945, in Polenberg, R., (ed.) *America at War: The Home Front, 1941–1945,* Prentice-Hall, Inc., 1968, pp. 12–15

Questions
(1) This film is probably intended to say as much about the Second World War as the First. In what ways does the script suggest the two wars had similar causes and were fought for the same principles?

(2) a How does this extract try to convince people that the Germans are not just a threat to Europe but also to America?
   b What other reasons could be added to this argument?

(3) Choose five phrases from the script to show that this film is biased.

sources. The Daughters of the American Revolution had a remarkable change of heart: 'Stalin is a university graduate and a man of great studies. He is a man, who, when he sees a great mistake, admits and corrects it. Today in Russia, Communism is practically non-existent'. *Life* described the Soviet secret police, the N.K.V.D., as 'a national police force similar to the F.B.I.'.

Wartime politics

Unlike Britain, normal political activity continued during the war. The issues remained familiar as Republicans tried to dismantle the New Deal. They made big gains in the 1942 mid-term elections, and approached the 1944 presidential contest with optimism. Their candidate was Thomas Dewey, a moderate conservative.

Roosevelt's health was obviously poor, but his doctor still gave him permission to stand for a fourth term. The Democrats rejected the existing Vice-President, the liberal Henry A. Wallace, and replaced him with the more conservative, though less talented, Harry S. Truman. Roosevelt accepted this to keep his party united.

The result was a comfortable victory for Roosevelt with 24 607 000 against Dewey's 22 015 000. The Democrats also strengthened their position in Congress.

Truman takes over

On 12 April 1945 Roosevelt died after suffering from a cerebral haemorrhage. His successor, Truman, was something of an unknown quantity. He was noted for hard work and honesty, but had never been an enthusiastic New Dealer so many liberals feared that their influence would decline.

The Fair Deal

Liberals were encouraged when Truman sent a message to Congress requesting passage of a series of reforms which later came to be known as the 'Fair Deal'. These included programmes to create full employment, improve the social security system, increase the minimum wage, build more houses and provide equal employment opportunities for all races. Many of these ideas would certainly have been proposed by Roosevelt had he lived.

Congress was more interested in abolishing the extensive wartime controls over the economy, and either ignored or totally rejected the Fair Deal. Most controls were successfully abandoned, but Truman had a long dispute with Congress over the OPA.

Inflation remained a major worry as high wartime wages still tried to buy the few consumer goods available. Unions fought for increased wages and reduced hours, but Truman urged the country to 'hold the line'. This did not halt the large number of strikes. Truman believed the OPA was necessary to avoid inflation, but employers and workers alike were opposed to it. When it lapsed in 1946 inflation reached 38% for several months. Compromise was reached when a weaker OPA was reintroduced.

Truman was losing the support of many groups in society, and this was reflected in the 1946 mid-term elections. For the first time since 1928 the Republicans won control of both Houses and were now in a position to dictate policy. Their most notable victory was the 1947 Taft–Hartley Act which undid much of the work of the NRA and the Wagner Act, by placing considerable restrictions on the power of unions. Truman's veto was decisively overridden.

The 1948 presidential election

As the 1948 election drew near, Truman's popularity in the country was very low. Even his party was disenchanted with him. Henry Wallace, the leading liberal, was deeply opposed to Truman's policy towards the Soviet Union. He formed a 'third party', the Progressive Citizens of America, and decided to run for the Presidency. His was a serious challenge, and many believed he could

Wallace v. Truman

Wallace was the most influential liberal critic of Truman's foreign policies and ran for President in 1948:

'We must not let British balance-of-power manipulations determine whether and when the United States gets into a war ... "getting tough" never bought anything real or lasting – whether for schoolyard bullies or world powers. The tougher we get, the tougher the Russians will get.'

Truman responded to his criticism in 1948:

'We must not fall victim to the insidious propaganda that peace can be obtained solely by wanting peace. I do not want and I will not accept the political support of Henry Wallace and his Communists.'

Questions

(1) On what occasions before 1948 did Truman 'get tough' with the Russians? How did the Russians respond in each case?

(2) To what political party had Wallace previously belonged?

(3) What was the result of the 1948 Election?

(4) What action had Truman taken against Communists inside America at the time of this election? (Consult pages 120–1.)

attract up to ten million votes, mainly from the Democrats.

In a desperate attempt to win back liberal support Truman attacked the Republican controlled 'Do Nothing' Congress, and called it into emergency session to pass his Fair Deal. As he expected, no legislation resulted, but he did regain much of the support on which Roosevelt had relied. Wallace's campaign withered away, while another Democratic revolt developed. The conservative, racist Democrats from the South were angered by Truman's support for laws which would give equal rights to blacks and other racial minorities. These 'Dixiecrats' nominated Strom Thurmond from South Carolina, but his campaign was never more than a protest. However, Wallace and Thurmond together could certainly stop an already unpopular Truman from winning.

The Republican candidate, Dewey, was understandably confident. Dr Gallup's new 'opinion poll' gave him a clear lead. His campaign was that of a man who expected, rather than hoped, to be President. Truman responded with an exhausting 'whistlestop tour' of the country, hitting out in all directions. The result was the biggest upset in any election this century. Truman proved all the pundits wrong with a 24 106 000 to 21 907 000 victory. He also had the bonus of Democratic majorities in both Houses of Congress.

Truman's second term

The 1948 result was not a victory for reform: it was more a defeat for reaction. The voters appeared not to want an attack on the New Deal, but they were no more enthusiastic about the Fair Deal. Congress was still dominated by a conservative coalition of Republicans and right-wing Democrats. Truman's programme for reform met with little more success. He did manage to obtain an improvement of the social security system, and a Housing Act to provide for the building of 810 000 dwellings for low income families. His major achievement, however, is probably less easy to appreciate. It was simply to prevent the New Deal from being dismantled despite constant sniping by an unsympathetic Congress.

Korea, Communism and corruption

Whatever hopes Truman had of getting the Fair Deal through were totally destroyed by the Korean War and the resulting criticism of his foreign policies. The Republicans made gains in the mid-term elections of that year, and were able to mount increasingly effective attacks. The situation was not helped by revelations of corruption by his subordinates. Nine officials ended up in prison. Truman himself was totally innocent, but the episode weakened his administration.

Anti-Communist witch-hunts

The most damaging issue Truman had to deal with in his last years as President was 'Communism'. A bizarre 'witch-hunt' against alleged Communists in positions of influence swept the country, and did untold damage to the United States' image throughout the world.

In order to get Congress to approve the policy of containment and Marshall Aid, Truman had highlighted the Communist menace to shock America out of her inactivity. He described a situation where, in many countries, small minorities of Communist traitors conspired to weaken and overthrow their governments. The United States needed to be constantly alert and protect her friends against this continual danger.

11.2 Truman displaying the newspaper headline: 'Dewey Defeats Truman', the morning after his election victory in November 1948.

Truman's Loyalty Program

Many believed that if other countries were at risk, so too was the United States. Truman's own Attorney-General McGrath agreed in 1949: 'They are everywhere – in factories, offices, butcher stores, on street corners, in private businesses. And each carries in himself the germ of death for society.' Many Americans became far more worried about the Communist menace inside America rather than the more obvious threat from outside the country. This hysterical campaign is all the more remarkable when it is realised how insignificant the American Communist Party always has been.

In 1947 Truman approved the Federal Employee Loyalty Program designed to get rid of security risks in government. In five years it checked on 4 million people and dismissed a mere 379 employees, but as the head of this program pointed out, 'not one single case or evidence directing towards a case of espionage has been disclosed'. This 'dismal' record merely convinced committed anti-Communists that the program was not doing its job properly.

The truth of this view seemed to be confirmed by a series of sensational trials of alleged spies and Communists. Congress was frightened into passing the McCarran Internal Security Act in 1950. This clumsy and unworkable law placed many restrictions on Communists. Truman vetoed it, but Congress overrode it with massive majorities.

The House Un-American Activities Committee

The House of Representatives' Un-American Activities Committee was also worried. It produced a booklet of questions and answers entitled *100 Things You should Know About Communism*. One extract read: 'What is the difference in fact between a Communist and a Fascist? Answer: None worth noticing.' From 1947 it investigated Hollywood. A stream of star witnesses testified about Communist infiltration of the highly influential film industry. Very few 'Reds'

were unearthed and only three 'Communist films' were identified, all made during the war. This did not stop the studios drawing up black lists of artists who were suspected of Communist sympathies. Those who appeared on the list could never obtain work. Several careers were destroyed, and Charlie Chaplin even decided to leave the country in disgust. By 1960 witch-hunts in Hollywood were fortunately a thing of the past.

McCarthyism

The outstanding Red-baiter was the Republican Senator Joe McCarthy of Wisconsin. His political career up to 1950 had been at times either disreputable or entirely uneventful. He went totally unnoticed, until in February 1950 he almost casually took up 'Communism' as an issue. He made allegations of large numbers of Reds in the State Department. His story was confused, and his numbers varied over the next few days from one traitor to as many as 205. The Tydings Committee of the Senate investigated his accusations and found them to be a 'fraud and a hoax'. Neither he nor his supporters were discouraged.

The setbacks to the United States in China and Korea gave the McCarthyites the opportunity to make charges of treachery in high places. Marshall, now Secretary of Defense, he accused of deliberately allowing Communist victories. He was apparently a member of 'a conspiracy so immense and an infamy so black as to dwarf any previous such venture in the history of man'. Marshall was forced to resign in 1951. Acheson was dubbed the 'Red Dean'. The whole period of Democratic rule he believed to be 'twenty years of treason'.

His tactics were extraordinary. He manipulated the press with great skill, providing scoops and headlines with regularity. A typical speech would last for many hours, and contain a bewildering stream of supposedly incriminating facts, all backed up by a briefcase full of documents which no-one could inspect. One biographer described his main weapon as the 'multiple untruth'. As the speech on this page indicates, he made so many 'revelations' that no-one could actually keep track of what he was saying. This did not stop millions from believing him.

Truman's attempts to stand up to him failed hopelessly. No other national leader dared attack him either, because McCarthyite votes could mean defeat at the next election.

McCarthy campaigning for Eisenhower

This extract from a speech McCarthy gave on television in 1952 is an example of the 'multiple untruth' in action:

'Tonight I shall give you the history of the Democrat candidate ... who endorses and would continue the suicidal Kremlin-shaped policies of this nation.... Keep in mind that each item which I give you taken alone is a small part of (the) jigsaw puzzle.... Stevenson's biography ... states that (Archibald) MacLeish was the man who brought him into the State Department. MacLeish has been affiliated with ... Communist fronts.... The Democrat candidate says: Judge me by my friends.... Alger Hiss and Frank Coe recommended Adlai Stevenson as delegate to a conference which was to determine our post-war policy in Asia.... I hold in my hand the official record of the series of lectures.... I hold in my hand a photostat of the *Daily Worker* of October 19, 1952.... While you may think there could be no connection between the debonair Democrat candidate and a dilapidated Massachusetts barn, I want to show you a picture of the barn.... In Detroit the other day the Democrat candidate made a statement that I had not convicted a single Communist.... While his statement is technically correct, its implication is viciously untrue.... Of course I have not convicted a single Communist. I am neither a judge nor a jury nor a prosecutor.... We must have a Republican administration ... and Congress.... (Then) we will have the power to help Dwight Eisenhower scrub and flush and wash clean the foul mess of corruption and Communism in Washington.'

Source
Rovere, R., *Senator Joe McCarthy*, Harper and Row, 1973, pp. 146-147

The fall of McCarthy

At the Republican convention in 1952 McCarthy was the star of the show. The Republican candidate, Eisenhower, although he found McCarthy distasteful, had no choice but to go along with him.

In 1953 McCarthy became Chairman of the Senate Committee on Government Operations, and used this position to mount investigations into matters such as embassies and the propaganda radio station 'Voice of America'.

McCarthy's power surprisingly dis-

11.3 Senator McCarthy exhibiting 'evidence' during a house of representatives Un-American Activities' committee.

integrated in 1954 when the Army-McCarthy Hearings were broadcast on television to audiences of over 20 million. He tried to prove that the Army was playing into Communist hands, but in so doing, showed himself to be a coarse bully with little respect for the freedom he claimed to be defending. His popular support declined sharply from the position at the beginning of the year when 50% positively favoured him and only 29% were opposed to him. In December the Senate at last plucked up the courage to condemn his behaviour by 67 votes to 22.

He disappeared from public view as rapidly as he had appeared, and died of drink-related diseases in 1957. In his heyday he had dominated two Presidents and terrified or delighted politicians of all parties. Between 1950 and 1954 no foreign policy could safely be made without reference to him. The London *Times* believed he was the 'essential factor in policy making for the West'. Despite all this, he probably unearthed not a single 'genuine card-carrying Communist'.

12 Eisenhower's America

The 1952 presidential election

When Truman decided not to run again the Democrats nominated Adlai Stevenson as their candidate. He was an inspiring figure, great orator and considerable intellectual, but all the odds were stacked against him. The Republicans selected Dwight D. Eisenhower, a man of international reputation who was admired by all sections of society. He successfully used 'Korea, Communism and Corruption' to attack the Democrats and was clear favourite to win. His running mate was Richard M. Nixon, the darling of right wing, Red-baiting Republicans. The result was decisively in Eisenhower's favour, 33 848 000 to 27 307 000.

Lifeline

Dwight D. Eisenhower (*1890–1969*)

'Ike', as he was popularly known, was brought up as a sincere Christian and pacifist, and so his decision to join the army was a great shock to his family. After steady but unspectacular progress, he was promoted to high rank during the Second World War, and directed the invasion of Europe in 1944. It was his skill in resolving the many disputes between the rival forces, powerful personalities and nations which made OVERLORD such a success. This diplomatic ability made him well qualified to take command of NATO's forces in 1951.

Despite his lack of interest in, or experience of, domestic politics, members of both parties hoped he would run for President. Many leading Democrats would have liked him to have been their candidate in 1948, but he was more at home as a Republican. Once he had decided to run for President in 1952 one of his main strengths was his all-party appeal. He rarely took a strong stand on any issue and was always a moderate.

As President, Ike was never known for overworking, partly because he suffered from several heart attacks while he was in the White House. It was noted that he took a remarkable number of holidays and was particularly fond of golf. This did not stop him being regarded with great affection as a somewhat 'grandfatherly' figure who represented what was best in 'Americanism'.

Domestic policies

In later decades, when America appeared to be almost overwhelmed by troubles at home and abroad, the Eisenhower years seemed to be a golden age. The United States was undoubtedly the most powerful nation in the world, and most of her citizens enjoyed the benefits of an orderly and prosperous society. Unlike most other Presidents, Eisenhower remained popular throughout his eight years in the White House. The journalist James Reston described him as 'a national phenomenon, like baseball. The thing is no longer just a remarkable political fact, but a kind of national love affair.' In 1956 he was again able to defeat Stevenson, this time by the increased margin of 35 559 000 to 26 017 000.

He felt no mission to change America as he was basically content with most features of her way of life. Perhaps his major concern was to restore the cherished Republican principle of the balanced budget which had

been overtaken by twenty years of paying for the New Deal, World War, Cold War and Korea. Spending was reduced in the early years, although not enough to satisfy the right wing and bring the desired tax cuts. By the end of his second term, though, he was being forced to increase spending to help the economy out of a sharp recession. The 1959 deficit was a record for any peacetime year. Eisenhower was quite prepared to spend money where he believed it was necessary. He further extended the social security system, tripled the federal education budget and expanded road building.

At first sight it would appear that there was no need for more adventurous policies. Most Americans had an improving standard of living. The visible signs of this were sprawling suburbs, an unrivalled education system, and a bewildering variety of consumer goods. Families now appeared to expect to own a television and more than one car. By 1960 America was the first society to have more people employed in 'white collar'

12.1 President Eisenhower whispering an aside to Vice-President Nixon during a Republican rally at the Coliseum.

All things to all men

Study this cartoon and answer the questions which follow:

AFTER GENERAL EISENHOWER HANGS UP HIS UNIFORM, WILL HE DON —

AN 'ABE LINCOLN' — A 'TEDDY ROOSEVELT' — A 'WOODROW WILSON' — A 'HERBERT HOOVER' — AN 'F.D.R' — OR A 'HARRY TRUMAN'?

Source
Vicky in *News Chronicle* (Associated Newspapers Group, Ltd, London)

In 1948 and 1952 Eisenhower was approached by sections of both parties to be their Presidential candidate. The British cartoonist Vicky satirises this uncertainty about Eisenhower's political opinions.

Questions
(1) To which party did each of the Presidents shown here belong?

(2) Which party did Eisenhower eventually represent?

jobs (professional, managerial, technical and clerical) than in 'blue collar' jobs (craftsmen, operatives and miners). This was proof of a sophisticated, technically advanced and prosperous nation.

What was less obvious to those who did not want to see, was the severe poverty which still existed in this affluent society. The plight of American blacks in particular was starting to force itself on a rather self-satisfied nation and President. Eisenhower only reluctantly became involved with this issue, as can be seen in Chapter 14. He was perhaps fortunate that this and several other problems abroad were only starting to emerge in the 1950s. Later Presidents were compelled to cope with these neglected matters.

Eisenhower and Dulles

As an outstanding general, Eisenhower's major interest and expertise were in foreign affairs. He developed a close working relationship with his Secretary of State, John Foster Dulles, who was given considerable freedom in making policy until his retirement in April 1959 and subsequent death from cancer.

The New Look

Eisenhower had strongly attacked containment in 1952, and argued instead for a policy of 'Liberation' of the peoples under Communist rule. (See this page.) This inspiring call to arms was combined with the attractive idea of reducing expenditure on defence. As he said in 1953: 'Every gun that is made, every warship launched, every rocket fired signifies, in the final sense, a theft from those who hunger and are not fed, those who are cold and are not clothed'. This meant that the United States should

---

Eisenhower and Dulles' foreign policies

In 1952 Eisenhower and his foreign policy adviser Dulles were very critical of containment. The Republican platform had this to say on the subject:

1   'Containment is defensive, negative, futile and immoral (in abandoning) countless human beings to a despotism and Godless terrorism.'

Eisenhower believed the policy was like a treadmill 'which at best might perhaps keep us in the same place until we drop exhausted'.

Dulles argued for a different approach:

(The United States) 'should make it publicly known that it wants
5   and expects liberation to occur. The mere statement of that wish and expectation would change, in an electrifying way, the mood of the captive peoples. It would probably put heavy new burdens on the jailers and create new opportunities for liberation.'

Later, as Secretary of State, Dulles described his approach to diplomacy as 'brinkmanship':

'You have to take chances for peace, just as you must take
10 chances in war. Some say that we were brought to the verge of war. Of course we were brought to the verge of war. The ability to get to the verge without getting into the war is the necessary art.... If you try to run away from it, if you are scared to go to the brink you are lost. We've had to look it square in the face.... We walked
15 to the brink and we looked it in the face. We took strong action.'

Questions

(1) a   What is meant by the policy of 'containment' (line 1)? When did it start and how was it put into practice?

b   Explain why the Republicans described containment as 'defensive, negative, futile and immoral' (line 1).

(2) a   What did Dulles mean by his alternative policy of liberation?

b   How successfully was this enforced in the 1950s? Explain why this was the case. (See following pages.)

(3)   On what occasions did the United States 'go to the brink' (line 13 of war under Eisenhower? (See following pages.)

adopt a 'New Look' military strategy and rely, not on large conventional ground forces, but on the relatively cheaper, but more devastating nuclear deterrent. Curtis LeMay, chief of the Strategic Air Command, believed that 'Communism could best be handled from a height of 50 000 feet'. Allies would be supplied with arms, not men, and so the risk to the United States should be minimal.

The reality was that, although the size of the United States' armed forces was slightly reduced, the military strategy remained much the same. The nuclear deterrent was not appropriate in all conflicts, and so it was still necessary to maintain a military presence throughout the world.

Relations with the Soviet Union

After the death of Stalin in 1953 the Soviet Union, under first Malenkov and then Khrushchev, was more inclined to co-exist peacefully with the United States. This did not mean an end to rivalry, as was proved when the Soviet Union tested a hydrogen bomb in 1953, and the Warsaw Pact was created in 1955 to counter NATO. Competition now, however, was less likely to lead to direct confrontation and the risk of war.

It soon became clear that Liberation was an unrealistic policy. When the Red Army crushed a workers' revolt in East Germany in 1953, the United States limited her help to encouragement by her radio station in West Germany. In 1956 nothing was done to assist the opposition in Poland, and even though 30 000 died fighting the Russians in Hungary, the United States stood helplessly aside, more concerned by the simultaneous 'Suez Crisis'.

There were areas of progress. In 1954 the Geneva Agreements were designed to end a war which could have brought the United States into direct conflict with Communist China. (This is dealt with in more detail in Chapter 16.) In 1955 the Austrian State Treaty was signed. This ended the four power occupation, and left a united, independent and neutral country. Relations had improved far enough for a summit meeting to be held, although nothing but a 'Spirit of Geneva' was achieved at the conference.

The missile gap

The Soviet Union scored a considerable propaganda victory in 1957 when she launched Sputnik, the world's first man-made space satellite. Defense Secretary Charles Wilson dismissed this as 'a nice technical trick', but many Americans feared the military potential of the new rockets. This danger became more real when the Soviet Union tested the first intercontinental ballistic missile (ICBM) which threatened to bring immediate destruction to American cities.

There were loud demands for the United States to make good this 'missile gap'. In 1958 the modest Explorer satellite was launched in reply, and the National Aeronautics and Space Administration

12.2 Hungarian anti-Soviet fighters in 1956.

(NASA) was created. This was not enough for critics who believed America was falling behind in important ways, notably education in science and technology. Books appeared with titles like *What Ivan Knows and Johnny Doesn't*.

Eisenhower was less concerned. The United States had long been secretly sending U-2 spy-planes over the Soviet Union to photograph activity on the ground. It was revealed that the 'gap' was a myth, and that there were severe technical problems preventing progress towards a 'first strike capability'. This was not public knowledge, and so critics such as John F. Kennedy continued to warn Americans of the dangers facing them.

It was in this atmosphere that Khrushchev renewed pressure on Berlin in 1958. Although the Soviet Union had recognised West Germany in 1955, she remained unhappy about the position of West Berlin. A flood of East Germans, usually well skilled and intelligent, were leaving for the West despite elaborate precautions to prevent them. The East German economy could not afford to lose these people. Eisenhower refused to give way. No agreement was reached when Khrushchev visited America in 1959, so a summit was arranged for 1960.

The day before the Paris Summit was due to open the Soviet Union announced it had shot down a U-2 spy-plane, and accused the United States of aggressive intentions. The pilot, Gary Powers, was exhibited after Eisenhower claimed it was only a 'weather plane'. He ended all further flights over Russia, but the summit was ruined with great embarrassment on one side and glee on the other.

Taiwan and Communist China

Ties between the United States and Taiwan were strengthened when the Communists threatened to invade the tiny off-shore islands Quemoy and Matsu in 1954–55. A mutual defence treaty was signed because these Nationalist controlled islands were declared to be strategically vital. The United

States seriously considered the use of atomic weapons to defend them. The Soviet Union helped to avoid war on this occasion, but the issue was reopened in 1958. This time Taiwan was given sophisticated weapons, and the Seventh Fleet helped to supply Quemoy. Tension was again reduced, and the uneasy 'truce' continued, but with regular artillery displays from both sides as symbols of the constant state of war.

The Soviet Union was not prepared to back China in 1958 because Mao had become increasingly hostile to Khrushchev's policies. By 1960 her aid to China had ceased, and there was a real possibility of an armed conflict within the Communist world.

Competition in the Third World

There was a growing interest from all the major powers in gaining support in the poorer 'Third World' countries, many of them newly independent ex-colonies. These nations were usually in desperate need of aid for economic development and security. The United States joined in a competition with the Soviet Union and Communist China to provide aid, but usually with the strings of military and political co-operation attached. However, many of these countries did not want to attach themselves to any great power, preferring to be 'non-aligned'.

The United States was usually more inclined to give aid to governments which were unlikely to make great changes in their economic and social systems. She was determined to prevent revolutions which might make life difficult for American businessmen and politicians. This often meant that the United States became opposed to reforms of any sort. The unfortunate result was described in 1958 by Senator Fulbright of the influential Senate Foreign Relations Committee. He believed the United States had 'dealt with princes, potentates, big business, and the entrenched, frequently corrupt, representatives of the past'. As many of these governments were overthrown the United States frequently became linked with them, and lost influence because of it. The amount of aid given was constantly attacked by a cost-conscious Congress against Eisenhower's wishes, and was in fact reduced by 19% in the years 1953–61.

The Middle East

In the post-war period the Middle East, a region vital to Western economies, became increasingly unstable. Two major factors in the turmoil were the rise of Arab nationalism and the controversy over the existence of the state of Israel. The latter issue was, and continues to be, of special interest to the sizeable and influential Jewish community in America. No politician interested in winning an election could affort to ignore this fact.

Israel and the Arabs

In 1948 both superpowers supported the UNO's decision to divide the formerly British-controlled Palestine into two sectors, one for Arabs, and the other for Jews. This new state, Israel, was immediately attacked by neighbouring Arab countries who believed she had no right to exist. After a desperate struggle, Israel survived and managed to capture more territory from the Palestinian Arabs. A cease-fire was eventually agreed in 1949 with the help of the American, Dr Ralph Bunche, but most Arab nations remained committed to the destruction of the state of Israel.

Nasser and Egyptian nationalism

In 1952 the playboy King Farouq of Egypt was overthrown in a military coup. By 1954 the strongly nationalist Colonel Nasser had come to power, committed to make Egypt a truly independent, powerful nation able to lead the Arab world.

Egyptians had long resented the presence of British troops in the zone surrounding the Suez Canal. This economically vital

12.3 Gamal Abdul Nasser, President of Egypt.

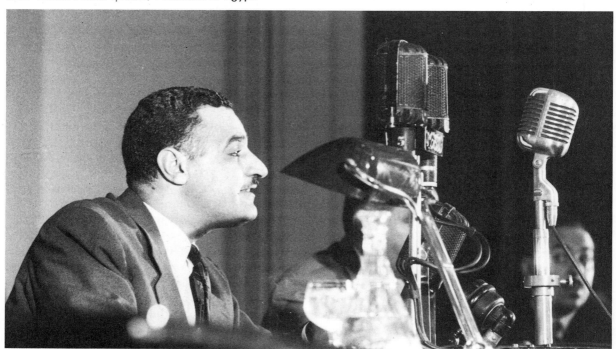

waterway was jointly owned by Britain and France. Nasser negotiated the evacuation of these forces in 1955, but the Canal Company remained under European ownership. He also started a programme of modernisation of the armed forces and economy. Arms were obtained from Czechoslovakia, and the construction of the ambitious Aswan Dam was planned.

American policy in the Middle East was to encourage stability and exclude any influence from the Soviet Union. With this in mind the Baghdad Pact was signed in 1955 by Iraq, Turkey, Iran, Pakistan and Britain. (When Iraq withdrew in 1958 it was reorganised as CENTO in 1959.) The United States was interested in friendly relations with the Arab world, but Nasser believed this pact was merely a device to maintain outside control of the region.

The United States, along with Britain and the World Bank, had offered to help pay for the Aswan Dam, but at the last minute tried to put pressure on Nasser to change some of his policies by threatening to withdraw this money. Dulles thought Egypt was becoming pro-Communist and aggressively anti-Israel. The latter was true, but Nasser most certainly was not a Communist. Dulles' tactics backfired. Nasser resented what he saw as American interference in Egypt's affairs, so to finance the dam he obtained Soviet aid instead and nationalised (with compensation) the Suez Canal Company.

The Suez Crisis 1956

Britain and France were outraged and feared that a pro-Soviet nation could now threaten their oil supplies. In October 1956 Israel, who was afraid of an Arab attack, made a secret treaty with Britain and France to strike at Egypt. Later that month, without consulting the United States, first Israel and then Britain and France attacked Egypt.

Eisenhower was furious, especially as this came in the middle of the Hungarian uprising and his election campaign. He was determined to prevent the Soviet Union helping Egypt (Khrushchev had threatened to use atomic weapons against Britain and France) but also wanted to maintain good relations with Arab nations. He put heavy pressure on Britain and France to leave the captured canal and allow a UNO force to replace them. Israel followed suit in early 1957 and evacuated the Sinai Peninsula.

Eisenhower failed in his ambition to remain on good terms with the Arabs. Khrushchev's aggressive words achieved more than his own practical deeds. In the next decade Egypt in particular became heavily dependent on the Soviet Union, and the United States committed herself to Israel.

The Eisenhower Doctrine

Eisenhower's concern about the Middle East was shown when Congress approved his scheme to give any economic or military aid to the region if it were threatened by Communism. This 'Eisenhower Doctrine' was first put into practice in Jordan, where King Hussein was embattled with pro-Nasser forces. In 1958, 14 000 marines were sent to Lebanon when she was in dispute with Syria. They left without any major incident later that year.

When Eisenhower stood down from office in 1961 it seemed that he had largely failed in his foreign policy goals set forth in 1952. Liberation had never been a realistic idea, and if anything, Communism was stronger than it had been when he took over from Truman. He had helped to stabilise for a while the conflict between the superpowers, but this uneasy calm was soon disturbed by events in the United States' own back yard.

13　John F. Kennedy and the New Frontier

13.1 President John F. Kennedy.

An end to stagnation

Eisenhower was the first President to be compelled not to stand for a third term of office by the Twenty-Second Amendment to the Constitution. This amendment, ratified in 1951, forbad any President to serve more than two terms in office. Richard M. Nixon was his successor as Republican candidate in 1960, and was challenged by the handsome, intelligent, but inexperienced, John F. Kennedy. The contest was the most closely

fought of the century with Kennedy just winning by 34 227 000 to 34 109 000. In Congress there was no real majority to support his promises of liberal reforms, as a coalition of conservative Southern Democrats and Republicans could dominate the voting.

In 1960–61 Kennedy claimed that America had stagnated under Eisenhower: the Soviet Union had strengthened her military power; the United States' economy was growing much more slowly than her superpower

Lifeline

John F. Kennedy (1917–63)

John Kennedy came from a very wealthy, Catholic family. His father was ambassador to Britain 1937–41, but was unable to reach higher office because of the large number of enemies he had accumulated. John was expected to pursue a political career from an early age and entered Congress in 1946. His record was by no means outstanding, but in 1958 he was re-elected as Senator for Massachusetts by a record majority.

He won the 1960 Democratic nomination despite tough competition and the fact that no Catholic had ever been President. To balance this was his family's wealth (an indispensable qualification for a Presidential campaign) and his 'star quality': he was one of the few politicians who can genuinely be described as a 'sex symbol'; he possessed great personal charm; he had a reputation as an intellectual and author, winning the much valued Pulitzer Prize; his war record revealed considerable bravery. The image that he deliberately cultivated was one of youth, vitality and high ideals in what was often felt to be a very drab age.

rival; American leaders were ageing and following outdated ideas; the Third World was slipping out of the United States' sphere of influence. He hoped to inspire the Americans to act boldly in a wide range of fields at home and abroad, and to create a 'New Frontier' to challenge the nation's pioneering spirit. In his inaugural speech in January 1961 he said: 'And so, my fellow Americans, ask not what your country can do for you, ask what you can do for your country'. He also had a message for the world: 'Let every nation know, whether it wishes us well or ill, that we shall pay any price, bear any burden, meet any hardship, support any friend, oppose any foes, in order to assure the survival and success of liberty.'

Military superiority or sufficiency?

Kennedy had attacked the Republicans for allowing the Soviet Union to create a 'missile gap' so that she could soon have the ability to make a successful 'first strike' at America. When he actually took office he discovered that this 'gap' was a myth, but he still wanted the United States to strengthen her armed forces and aim for a position of clear superiority over the Soviet Union. Eisenhower had been satisfied with forces which were merely 'sufficient' to defend the United States' interests. Kennedy preferred a more dynamic approach and hoped to spread American influence and virtues throughout the world: 'Without having a nuclear war, we want to permit what Thomas Jefferson called "the disease of liberty" to be caught in areas which are now held by the Communists.' This sounded very much like Dulles in 1952.

Defense Secretary Robert McNamara planned substantially increased military expenditure so that the United States would have the ability to make a 'flexible response' to a variety of situations. Nuclear weapons were becoming more numerous and powerful to deal with the Soviet Union, while

Timeline

Foreign policy since 1961

1961   Kennedy becomes President (January).
        Alliance for Progress (March).
        Cuban exiles attempt to invade Cuba at Bay of Pigs
        (April).
        Berlin Wall built (August).

1962   Neutral government established in Laos (June).
        Cuban missile crisis (October).

1963   Buddhist uprising in Vietnam (May).
        Test Ban Treaty (September).
        Military coup overthrows Diem (November).
        Johnson replaces Kennedy (November).

1964   Gulf of Tonkin Resolution (August).

1965   Rolling Thunder (February).
        American troop build-up in Vietnam.
        American intervention in the Dominican Republic (April).

1967   Arab–Israeli War (June).

1968   Tet Offensive (January).
        End of escalation. Start of Vietnamization (March).
        Nuclear Non-Proliferation Treaty (July).

1969   Nixon becomes President (January).
        Secret bombing of Cambodia starts (February).
        American troops start to leave Vietnam (April).

1970   Invasion of Cambodia (April).

1971   Invasion of Laos (February).

1972   Nixon visits Communist China (February).
        SALT I signed (June).

1973   Paris Peace Treaty ends American fighting in Vietnam
        (January).
        C.I.A. organises military coup in Chile (September).
        Arab–Israeli War. Oil embargo (October).

1974   Ford takes over from Nixon (August).
        North Vietnamese advance on Saigon.

1975	Communist victories in Cambodia, Vietnam and Laos (April and May).
	Helsinki Agreements (September).
1977	Carter becomes President (January).
1978	Camp David Agreements (September).
1979	Iranian Revolution (January).
	United States recognises Communist China (January).
	Israel–Egypt Peace Treaty (March).
	SALT II signed but not ratified (June).
	Sandinista Revolution in Nicaragua (July).
	U.S. Embassy staff taken hostage in Iran (November).
	Russian invasion of Afghanistan (December).
1980	Economic sanctions against Russia (January).
1981	Reagan becomes President (January).
	Iranian hostages released (January).
	Martial law in Poland (December).

'counter-insurgency' forces such as the Green Berets were trained to act against guerrilla armies in countries like Vietnam.

Khrushchev had not been planning to create a 'first strike capability' in 1961, but in response to what appeared to be aggressive moves by the United States, the Soviet Union joined a renewed arms race which has continued to this day. McNamara later admitted, 'if we had had more accurate information about planned Soviet strategic forces (in 1961) we simply would not have needed to build as large a nuclear arsenal as we have today'.

Rivalry between the superpowers accelerated in the related area of space travel. In 1961 Yuri Gagarin was the first man to go into space, and provided further evidence of the Soviet Union's technical advance. Kennedy responded by starting the Apollo programme which succeeded in putting a man on the moon in 1969. This decision was not applauded by all Americans. Eisenhower thought that 'anybody who could spend $40 billion in a race to the moon for national prestige is nuts.' Under Kennedy over half of all the federal budget went on space or defence.

The Berlin Wall

Berlin remained the major cause of East–West disagreement in 1961. East Germany's economy was being constantly undermined by the steady flow of her most talented and valued workers to the West by the way of West Berlin. Despite rigorous security, about 3 million people had left for the higher wages and greater freedom on the other side of the 'iron curtain'. Khrushchev demanded again at the Vienna summit that West Berlin should be handed over to East Germany. Kennedy responded with increased military preparations.

The East German government, with Soviet consent, acted on their own to solve the problem. In the early hours of 13 August, 1961 the authorities started to build a totally secure wall around West Berlin to

13.2 The Berlin Wall showing watchtower, floodlights and graffiti.

13.3 An aerial view of the Berlin Wall. In the centre is the Brandenburg Gate, a major landmark in the centre of the once united city.

prevent any more defections. Over the years this has been strengthened with mine fields, automatic firing devices, tank traps and continual armed patrols. The immediate Western reaction was indignant. The wall symbolised to Western critics the inhumanity of Communist rule. Great personal unhappiness resulted as families were split up. Kennedy visited the city in 1963 and expressed his sympathy with its people: 'Ich bin ein Berliner.' It may have been a somewhat crude device, but the wall did manage to reduce tension in the long term. The West remained in Berlin and the East German economy was able to thrive, so the superpowers no longer had to make warlike gestures to get their way. The only losers were the citizens of East Germany, but the United States had long ago abandoned them to their fate under Communist rule.

Latin America since 1945

Kennedy faced his most severe challenge from the Soviet Union in Latin America, where previously Communist involvement had been insignificant. The United States continued to dominate this poverty-stricken region and exclude outside interference.

In 1947 the Rio Pact was signed by most states on the American continent. This defensive agreement stated that an attack on one should be treated as an attack on all. In 1948 the Organisation of American States was founded to enable members to discuss matters of common interest. Its rules did, in fact, outlaw interference by any state in the internal affairs of another. This was obviously directed at the United States.

When she received American criticism of her policies in Eastern Europe, the Soviet Union was eager to point out that the United States also had a sphere of influence in Latin America. A member of Truman's administration remained firm: 'We ought to have our cake and eat it too; ... we ought to be free to operate under this regional arrangement in South America, and at the same time intervene promptly in Europe; ...

we oughtn't to give away either asset.'

Aid was offered to the region, but this rarely attempted to tackle the crushing social and economic problems which were the major causes of political unrest. Most money was spent on American-made arms. When economic development was encouraged it was mainly through American firms and the profits left the region for the United States. Some advances were made with the establishment in 1959 of the Inter-American Development Bank with a capital of $1 billion. Kennedy was particularly concerned by Latin American problems and in 1961 formed the Alliance for Progress to provide loans. Little real progress was achieved, however, and there were always strings attached. For example, the money had to be spent on American goods which were often more expensive than their European or Japanese competitors.

Despite OAS rules, the United States was still prepared to intervene in her smaller neighbours' affairs when she felt her interests were threatened. For example, in 1954 the CIA organised a successful military coup in Guatemala to overthrow the radical government of Jacobo Arbenz Guzman. He had displeased Eisenhower's administration by nationalising the American owned United Fruit Company which dominated his country, and refused to pay compensation.

Castro and Cuba

A more formidable challenge to American interests developed in Cuba. This country had effectively been ruled by the United States since 1898. Americans owned 90% of the island's mining wealth and 40% of the vital sugar industry. In addition, there was a United States naval base at Guantanamo Bay to remind Cubans where real power lay.

After 1952 the island was ruled, with American backing, by the corrupt and unpopular Batista. He was challenged by a left-wing guerrilla movement led by Castro, and was forced to flee in 1959. Castro was cautiously welcomed by some American liberals who recognised the injustices

13.4 The Cuban leader, Fidel Castro.

supported by Batista's regime. Eisenhower's administration became concerned when the new government took its revenge on supporters of Batista, and then started a programme of social and economic reforms. This included the nationalisation of many American businesses in an attempt to make the country truly independent of foreign control. Castro still wanted to remain on good terms with the United States, but a request for aid was turned down. When Cuba signed a trade agreement with the Soviet Union, American suspicions about Communist involvement in Castro's revolution appeared to be confirmed. The United States ended Cuban sugar imports, a move which could cripple the island's economy, and the C.I.A. started to train an army of anti-Castro exiles based in America. In January 1961 diplomatic relations were broken off.

The Bay of Pigs invasion

When Kennedy took over power Senator Fulbright told him: 'The Castro regime is a thorn in the flesh; but it is not a dagger in the heart.' Nevertheless, Kennedy agreed to the C.I.A.'s plans to help the Cuban exiles overthrow Castro so long as direct American involvement was limited to air support. The planners believed the Cuban population would immediately rebel against what was assumed to be an unpopular tyranny and help the invaders. This was a complete miscalculation. The landing on the Bay of Pigs on 17 April, 1961 was a fiasco as it was clumsily planned and executed, and was convincingly defeated by Cuban forces.

Kennedy took the blame for this embarrassing defeat but did nothing to improve relations with Castro, who drew closer to the Soviet Union because of this

Study this cartoon and answer the questions which follow:

Why Theese Excitement? Eet's Just a Wooden Horse!

Source
William Sanders, *Greensboro Daily News,* 1962. Reprinted by permission of *The News.*

Questions
(1) a Identify the man
   (i) pulling the wooden horse;
   (ii) talking to O.A.S.
   When had each come to power in his country?

    b What does (ii) fear (i) will do?
    c Why does the cartoonist see similarities between
       'Communism in Cuba' and a 'wooden horse'?
    d What happened in 1962 to justify this comparison?
 (2) a What do the initials O.A.S. represent?
    b Explain why O.A.S. might have good reason to fear the
       horse.
 (3) (These questions can only be answered after studying Chapter
    18).
    a How did events in the late 1970s and early 1980s provide
       further evidence of the threat from the wooden horse?
    b What did the United States do about this situation?

---

attack. He even instructed the C.I.A. to assassinate Castro, although the attempt failed.

The Cuban Missile Crisis

On 14 October, 1962 a U-2 plane over Cuba photographed launchpads capable of firing nuclear missiles at most major American cities. Kennedy reacted strongly and on 22 October ordered a naval blockade to prevent any more ships bringing offensive military equipment to Cuba. Plans were also made for a bombing raid and invasion of the island. United States forces were placed on alert as Khrushchev was told to dismantle the missile sites or risk war. There was no response and Russian ships continued to head for Cuba. After the world held its

---

The Cuban Missile Crisis

Khrushchev was very keen to point out on 27 October that the United States was using double standards:

1   'You are worried over Cuba. You say that it worries you because it lies at a distance of ninety miles across the sea from the shore of the United States. However, Turkey lies next to us ... you have stationed devastating rocket weapons ... in Turkey literally right
5   next to us.'

Kennedy's younger brother Robert, the Attorney-General, was one of the President's most important advisers in this crisis. Here he gives his account of a conversation with the Soviet ambassador, Dobrynin, in response to Khrushchev's complaints about missiles in Turkey:

'I said that there could be no quid pro quo or any arrangement made under this kind of pressure, and that in the last analysis this was a decision that would have to be made by NATO. However, I said, President Kennedy had been anxious to remove those missiles
10 from Turkey and Italy for a long period of time. He had ordered their removal some time ago, and it was our judgement that, within a short time after the crisis was over, those missiles would be gone.'

Sources

Kennedy, R. F., *Thirteen Days: A Memoir of The Cuban Missile Crisis* (1969). Both quoted in Ambrose, S. E., *Rise to Globalism,* Penguin, 1980, pp. 265 and 267.

Questions

(1) Describe the United States' relations with Cuba in the years 1959–62.

(2) What measures did the United States take to try to force the Soviet Union to give way in 1962?

(3) What was Khrushchev demanding that Kennedy should do in return for the removal of Soviet missiles from Cuba?

(4) Why was Kennedy not prepared to agree to a 'quid pro quo or any arrangement made under this kind of pressure' (lines 6–7)?

(5) What was the outcome of Robert Kennedy's conversation with Dobrynin?

13.5 This photo taken on 5 November 1962 shows Russian military equipment being reloaded onto ships for transportation back to the Soviet Union.

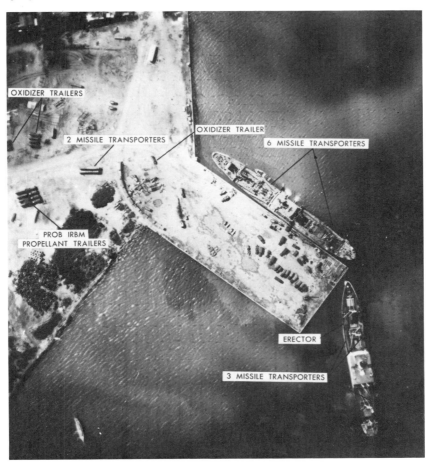

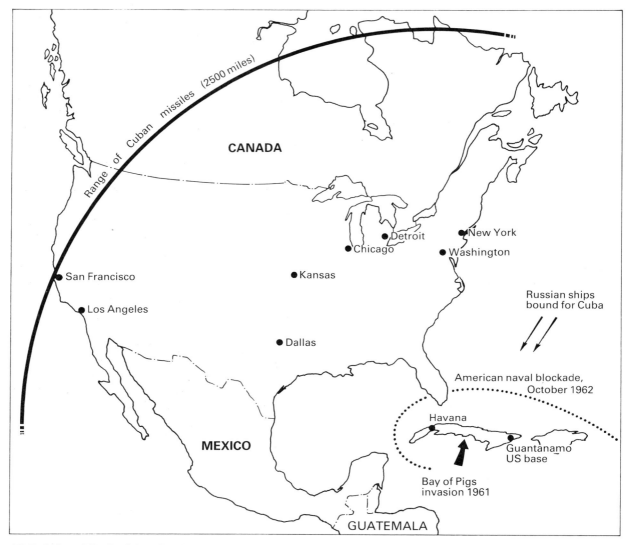

13.6 Cuban Missile Crisis October 1962.

breath for several days, on 28 October Khrushchev agreed to the dismantling of the missile sites, but this was on the understanding that the United States would promise never to invade Cuba, and that her missiles in Turkey and Italy would also be withdrawn. This latter agreement was to remain secret, because although Kennedy had ordered the removal of these obsolete weapons before the crisis even developed, he refused publicly to appear to be giving way to Soviet pressure. Prestige was at stake.

Before this crisis Kennedy had not been an outstandingly successful or popular President, but his bold tactics improved his image considerably. However, it has been questioned whether his willingness to risk nuclear war on this issue was actually justified. For a while the negotiations depended entirely on whether the United States should lose face and publicly agree to remove missiles which it no longer even wanted. Kennedy was fortunate that it was Khrushchev who agreed to make the difficult and embarrassing decision to lose face and make the order that in 1964 contributed to his own downfall.

Relations between the superpowers improved after this as they both appreciated how near they had come to catastrophe. In 1963 the 'hotline' was installed between the White House and the Kremlin so that both leaders could swiftly communicate with each other in emergencies. They also agreed to a Test Ban Treaty outlawing nuclear tests in the atmosphere. In future Kennedy was less willing to confront the Soviet Union. Instead he hoped that both superpowers could 'help make the world safe for diversity. For in the final analysis, our most common link is that we all inhabit this small planet. We all breathe the same air. We all cherish our children's future. And we are all mortal.'

The New Frontier at home

Kennedy hoped to be able to make the first important series of reforms to America's society and economy since 1938. He was ambitious, proposing a system of state health insurance known as Medicare, considerable improvements to the education service, an attack on poverty, and most radical and controversial of all, laws to ensure that blacks benefited from genuinely equal civil rights. (These issues are dealt with more fully in Chapters 14 and 15.) The conservative-dominated Congress was able to obstruct and delay nearly all of his most cherished reforms while he lived. Kennedy should still be given the credit for putting topics like civil rights and Medicare at the top of the list of priorities, thus preparing the ground for his successor Johnson to push them through Congress.

The most urgent domestic issue facing America in 1961 was the economic slump which had produced 8% unemployment. Kennedy wanted to stimulate the economy to achieve much higher rates of growth, not only to keep the population at work, but also to outstrip the Soviet Union which appeared to be catching up. He took the apparently bold step of deliberately ignoring the idea of a balanced budget (althsough in reality no

Timeline

America at home since 1961

1961	Kennedy becomes President (January). 'Freedom Rides' organised by CORE (May).
1963	Violence at Birmingham (April). Kennedy assassinated and is succeeded by Johnson (November).
1964	Civil Rights Act (July). Economic Opportunity Act. Johnson re-elected as President (November).
1965	Medicare and Education Acts (April). Voting Rights Act (August). Major rioting at Watts is first of many others 1965–68 (August).

1968	King assassinated (April). Civil Rights Act. Robert Kennedy assassinated (June). Riots at Chicago Democratic Convention.
1969	Nixon becomes President (January).
1972	Watergate burglary (June). Nixon re-elected (November).
1973	Watergate revelations start (March). Agnew resigns. Ford becomes Vice-President (October). Energy crisis begins to affect America (October).
1974	Nixon resigns. Ford becomes President (August). Ford pardons Nixon (September).
1977	Carter becomes President (January).
1978	National Energy Act (November).
1981	Reagan becomes President (January).
1985	Reagan starts his second term as President.

government had seriously attempted this since the 1920s) and increased spending on a variety of projects. In 1963 he also persuaded Congress to cut income taxes substantially. These policies, known as the New Economics, enabled people to spend more money on goods and therefore create jobs. This was an outstanding success: by 1964 the Gross National Product (GNP) was increasing at a rate of 5% per year; in 1966 unemployment was down to 4%. The American economy went through its longest-ever continuous boom.

The assassination of Kennedy

On 22 November, 1963 the world was stunned when Kennedy was shot dead as he took part in a motorcade through the streets of Dallas, Texas. Soon afterwards Lee Harvey Oswald was arrested for the crime. No truly satisfactory explanation for this deed has ever been obtained, partly because, incredibly, Oswald himself was shot two days later, in full view of television cameras, by strip club owner Jack Ruby. Oswald had lived in the Soviet Union, had a Russian wife and was a member of the 'Fair Play for Cuba' committee, but no political motive has been proved. Some researchers claim it was more likely that right wing conspirators organised it because they objected to his liberal civil rights policies. Chief Justice Earl Warren conducted an official inquiry and reported in 1964 that Oswald acted entirely alone. Detailed investigation of the report reveals that all the evidence does not necessarily fit this conclusion.

Regardless of the identity or motives of the culprits, Kennedy's death was a deeply shocking experience for the nation. Very soon a legend had been created around his name. He was suddenly discovered to have been a great President in the making, an inspiring leader, a formidable statesman and

13.7 President Kennedy slain.

The verdict on Kennedy

There have been wildly different opinions about Kennedy's performance as President. Two journalists give their verdicts:

'What was killed in Dallas was ... the death of youth and the hope of youth, of the beauty and grace and the touch of magic.... He never reached his meridian: we saw him only as a rising sun.'

James Reston in New York Times

'In the administration of John F. Kennedy, activity was mistaken for action ... toughness was mistaken for strength, articulacy was mistaken for clarity, self-confidence was mistaken for character.'

Fairlie, H., The Kennedy Promise (1974)

Questions
(1) Produce evidence to justify both of these opinions of Kennedy.
(2) What is your assessment of his record?

---

spokesman for the West. His White House was likened to 'Camelot'. As time has passed other judgements have been less flattering: Kennedy took the world needlessly to the edge of war; he failed to handle Congress well enough for it to pass his reform programme; he took the United States into the Vietnam War (see Chapter 16); he promised too much and achieved very little. The contrasting views of two well-respected journalists can be seen on page 145.

In the short term, the new President, Lyndon B. Johnson, was able to take advantage of a nation temporarily united by grief and horror, when during Kennedy's Presidency it had often been deeply divided. This unity enabled Johnson to turn Kennedy's ideas and hopes into laws within months of taking office. The topic to which Kennedy was most passionately committed at the time of his death was civil rights.

14 The black revolt

The negro in American society before 1945

In theory the Constitution of the United States is committed to the idea that all American citizens are born equal and should have equal rights and opportunities to lead a full life. Throughout most of American history these civil rights have certainly not been applied to the black population.

At the end of the First World War blacks were most numerous in the former slave states of the South. In many places they were actually the majority, but whites had always managed to control the government and economy of the area. The 'federal' system of government means that each individual state is able to run its own internal affairs without much outside interference. After the Civil War (1861–65) Southern states made 'Jim Crow' laws to maintain white supremacy and defeat the North's attempts to control their affairs. Blacks were prevented from registering to vote by 'poll taxes' imposed on any voter or literacy tests which discriminated against poorly educated people. Most public facilities, including schools, were segregated on the basis of race. In 1896 the Supreme Court had declared that this was legal provided that the facilities were 'separate but equal'. If blacks wanted to prove that the education given in their schools was inferior to that in white schools, they would have to prove it in the white-controlled courts. The chances of such a case being heard at all were very slender. The result was that inequality was the rule. Very little protection

---

Segregation of the races

The Fifteenth Amendment to the Constitution (1870):

1   'The right of citizens of the United States to vote shall not be denied or abridged by the United States or by any State on account of race, color, or previous condition of servitude.'

Carter Glass at the Virginia Convention in 1900 was not going to be deterred by the Constitution:

'We are here to discriminate to the very extremity of permissable

5   action under the limitations of the federal constitution, with a view to the elimination of every Negro voter who can be gotten rid of, legally, without materially impairing the numerical strength of the white electorate.'

Source
Quoted in Lomax, L. E., *The Negro Revolt*, Hamish Hamilton, 1962

In 1956 the city council of Montgomery, Alabama, issued this statement:

The council 'will not yield one inch, but will do all in its power to

10   oppose the integration of the Negro race with the white race in

147

Montgomery, and will for ever stand like a rock against social equality, intermarriage, and mixing of the races under God's creation and plan.'

Source
Quoted in Lewis, D. L., *Martin Luther King,* Allen Lane, 1970

Questions
(1) a   In what ways were many states able to evade the Fifteenth Amendment and cause 'the elimination of every Negro voter who can be gotten rid of, legally' (line 6)?
    b   In which region of America were these practices most common? Why?
(2) a   What dispute brought Montgomery to national attention during 1955–56?
    b   Name the leader of this civil rights campaign in Montgomery. Describe the tactics he advocated in this and other campaigns.
    c   How was this conflict ended?

Consult rest of chapter

14.1 Segregated drinking fountain in use in the American South.

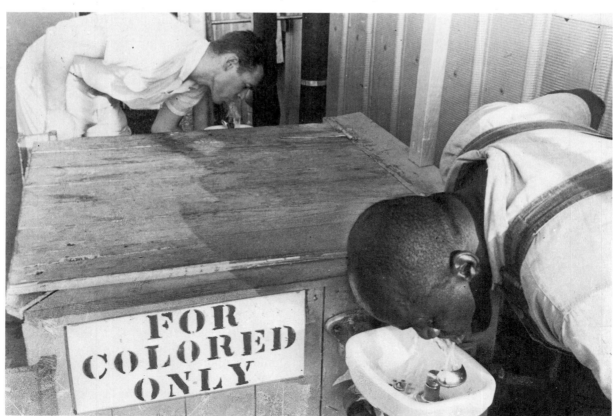

was given by the forces of law and order. Dozens of lynchings occurred each year, but the culprits were rarely brought to trial because it was not an offence in federal (as opposed to state) law.

Even in matters where laws were not so important, for example the quality of housing and obtaining a job or promotion, the wealthy white community ensured that blacks were kept in conditions which were often little better than in the days of slavery before 1865. The majority of negroes had to accept this position with resignation. One of their most important early leaders, Booker T. Washington, believed that segregation was unalterable, and said the races should try to be 'separate as the fingers, yet one as the hand'.

In times of economic prosperity, particularly during the World Wars and since 1945, many Southern blacks migrated to the industrial cities of the North and West in search of better paid jobs, but they did not find that the quality of life was substantially better. Jim Crow laws might not exist, but wages for blacks rarely matched those for whites, housing was generally shoddy and education substandard. When unemployment has increased, the first to suffer have always been the blacks. Competition for scarce jobs has frequently sparked off race riots. In 1919 alone 120 died as a result.

The New Deal brought some improvements for the negro, but no changes in the law were made. Blacks were helped because they were poor, not because of their race. In 1941 Roosevelt did end discrimination in defence industries, and established the Fair Employment Practices Commission (FEPC) to enforce this, but the armed forces remained segregated.

A Fair Deal for blacks

Truman was one of the first Presidents to give serious attention to civil rights. His Missouri background was strongly racist, but he managed to break away from this tradition. Nonetheless, he was more interested in equality than integration of the races. He believed that 'separate but equal' was the ideal solution if applied properly. In 1946 he set up the President's Committee on Civil Rights which the following year made proposals for extensive reforms, including a

Lynching

'The Negro was taken to a grove, where each one of more than five hundred people, in Ku Klux ceremonial, had placed a pine knot around a stump, making a pyramid to the height of ten feet. The Negro was chained to the stump and asked if he had anything to say. Castrated and in indescribable torture, the Negro asked for a cigarette, lit it and blew the smoke in the face of his tormentors.

The pyre was lit and a hundred men and women, old and young, grandmothers among them, joined hands and danced around while the Negro burned. A big dance was held in a barn nearby that evening in celebration of the burning, many people coming by automobile from nearby cities to the gala event.'

Source
The Washington Eagle 1920 in Snowman, D., *America Since 1920*, Heinemann Educational Books Ltd, 1980, p. 28

14.2 A lynching in a Southern state in the 1930s.

permanent FEPC to replace the wartime version, anti-lynching laws, the banning of the poll tax and an end to segregation. Congress did not accept any of these proposals. Truman's most important achievement was to integrate the races in the armed forces, an action which did not require Congressional approval.

The civil rights movement

In the 1950s the issue of civil rights started to gain national attention for the first time. The movement had for years been dominated by the highly respectable National Association for the Advancement of Colored People (NAACP). It aimed to work towards equality and integration by challenging racist laws in the courts in the hope that they would be declared unconstitutional. It had some important victories but many blacks felt that progress was too slow. This contributed to the growth of a large number of organisations, mainly in the South, who preferred to take more direct and dramatic action. These included the Student Nonviolent Co-ordinating Committee (SNCC), the Southern Christian Leadership Conference (SCLC) and the Congress for Racial Equality (CORE).

Christian ministers, who were often the most important members of Southern black society, played a leading role in the

Nonviolence

King started to develop his philosophy of nonviolence in Montgomery in 1955–56. This circular was distributed by the bus boycott's organisers:

'If cursed, do not curse back. If struck do not strike back, but evidence love and goodwill at all times. If another person is being molested, do not arise to go to his defense, but pray for the oppressor.'

In 1963 King explained the strength of the philosophy:

'We've come to see that this method is not a weak method. For it's the strong man who can stand up amid opposition.... You see, this method has a way of disarming the opponent. It exposes his moral defenses ... and he just doesn't know what to do. If he doesn't beat you, wonderful! But if he beats you, you develop the quiet courage of accepting blows without retaliating. If he doesn't put you in jail, wonderful! Nobody with any sense likes to go to jail. But if he puts you in jail, you go in that jail and transform it from a dungeon of shame to a haven of freedom and unity. And I submit to you that if a man hasn't discovered something that he will die for, he isn't fit to live.'

Source
Both quoted in Lewis, D. L., *Martin Luther King*, Allen Lane, 1970

'I Have a Dream'

On 28 August, 1963 King addressed an audience beside the Lincoln Memorial, Washington D.C.:

'I say to you today, my friends, even though we face the difficulties of today and tomorrow, I still have a dream. It is a dream deeply rooted in the American dream.

I have a dream that one day this nation will rise up and live out the true meaning of its creed: "We hold these truths to be self-evident; that all men are created equal".

I have a dream that one day on the red hills of Georgia the sons of former slaves and the sons of former slaveowners will be able to sit down together at the table of brotherhood.

I have a dream that one day even the state of Mississippi, a state sweltering with the heat of injustice, sweltering with the heat of oppression, will be transformed into an oasis of freedom and justice.

I have a dream that my four little children will one day live in a nation where they will not be judged by the color of their skin but by the content of their character.

I have a dream today.

I have a dream that one day down in Alabama with its vicious racists, ... little black boys and black girls will be able to join hands with little white boys and white girls as sisters and brothers.

I have a dream today.'

Source

Quoted in Hacker, G., Learmouth, J., Robinson, R., *Conflict 2,* Nelson, 1969, p. 93

---

movement. The most influential and inspiring campaigner was the Reverend Martin Luther King, whose oratory and philosophy stirred the conscience of America. He was committed to the philosophy of 'nonviolence' used to good effect by Gandhi in India. Nonviolence was to be combined with civil disobedience, a refusal to obey unjust laws and co-operate with the oppressors. King explains the reasoning behind these tactics on page 151. In the South at least, nonviolence dominated the civil rights movement until about 1963.

Desegregating the education system

The NAACP's greatest triumph came in 1954 with the *Brown* v. *Board of Education of Topeka* case. The Supreme Court declared

14.3 Martin Luther King addressing a college audience.

that 'separate but equal' was unconstitutional and ordered schools to be desegregated 'with all deliberate speed'. The court's failure to demand 'immediate' changes gave individual states the opportunity to delay obeying the law as long as possible. If the process was to be speeded up the President was the only man able to do it. Eisenhower privately disagreed with the court, and believed 'you cannot change people's hearts merely by laws'. He was not a racist, but he was not willing to force people to change their traditions.

Events forced him to act. In 1957 the federal courts ordered the school board of Little Rock, Arkansas, to integrate. The state governor resisted the decision, not only because he disapproved of integration, but also he believed, like most Southern whites, that individual states should be left to decide such matters for themselves. This idea is referred to as States Rights. He did nothing to prevent a mob of thousands threatening the handful of black children who tried to enter a previously white school. Reluctantly Eisenhower sent 10 000 national guardsmen and 1000 paratroopers to keep order and enable these children to be educated. Similar obstruction of the law occurred elsewhere and by 1963 only 30 798 out of 2 901 671 black children in the South attended mixed schools. In Mississippi the first school did not integrate until 1964.

There was a similar struggle in the universities. When James Meredith tried to enter Mississippi University in 1961, he was greeted by a riot. Kennedy sent the national guard, but two died, hundreds were wounded, and 23 000 troops were needed to keep order in the following months. There was almost a repetition at the University of Alabama in 1963, where Governor George Wallace personally blocked the doors to black students.

Buses, lunch counters and restrooms

King first became involved in the civil rights movement in 1955. He led a boycott of the buses in Montgomery, Alabama, in protest at the prosecution of a black woman who dared to sit on a seat reserved for whites. As blacks were 75% of the passengers this sudden loss of customers was very expensive for the bus company. Victory was achieved, after the boycott had lasted a year, when the Supreme Court condemned segregation of buses. This example of the success of nonviolent protest inspired others to use the same tactics.

There was direct action in 1960 in Greensboro, North Carolina, when groups of students asked to be served at 'whites only' Woolworth's lunch counters. On being refused service they staged a 'sit in'. The SNCC co-ordinated similar demonstrations all over the South. Many people were arrested but lunch counters started to abandon their restrictions.

In 1961 CORE organised 'Freedom Riders' to travel all over the South to challenge segregated restrooms and other

---

The Freedom Rides

This is a small selection of the incidents which occurred during the 1961 'Freedom Rides':
'May 8   Arrival in Charlotte (N.C.); arrest of one Rider for trespass while demanding shoeshine at Union bus terminal. . . .
May 13   Travelling through Athens (Ga.), where all facilities are used, and arrival in Atlanta; restaurant closed at Greyhound station. . . .
May 14   . . . Department of Justice advises Birmingham police it has

received warnings of planned violence when buses reach their city. Greyhound bus met by mob in Anniston; passengers prevented from getting off. Tires slit and go flat six miles out of Anniston. ... An incendiary device thrown through a window sets fire to the bus which is completely destroyed. All passengers are removed, and 12 admitted to hospital . . . .

May 20   . . . At 8.30 a.m., after 18 hours of waiting, the Riders are taken on a Greyhound bus for Montgomery. The F.B.I. advises local police in Montgomery of probability of violence; are assured that local authority sufficient. On arrival, a "race riot involving hundreds broke out". At least 6 Riders are beaten, 3 severely. The mob attacks Negroes who have no connection with the Riders, and whites who appear sympathetic'.

Source
Lomax, L. E., *The Negro Revolt*, Hamish Hamilton, 1962, pp. 135–138.

facilities in bus terminals. An account of their well publicised and often violent journeys appears on page 153. They won their case when Kennedy's administration ordered the desegregation of all inter-state transport facilities. The instruction was obeyed with great reluctance.

Birmingham, Alabama

Birmingham was probably the most segregated city in the South. It had successfully resisted pressure to integrate, so King mounted a campaign in the spring of 1963 to force the authorities to change. The nonviolent protestors came into conflict with Police Commissioner Eugene 'Bull' Connor. His men broke up demonstrations with water cannon, dogs and baton charges, and made arrests at the rate of 500 per day. These events were fully reported by the national press and television, and many whites who had previously been indifferent to the campaign, were now sickened by this brutality. Kennedy privately said: 'The civil rights movement should thank God for Bull Connor. He's helped it as much as Abraham Lincoln.' Again, troops had to be sent to

restore order. Kennedy forced the city authorities to give way and desegregation started slowly.

The Kennedys and civil rights

In 1960 the majority of blacks voted with enthusiasm for Kennedy as he promised to work for civil rights. When in power his record was unimpressive. He failed to propose new laws, partly because he knew that Southerners in Congress who supported States Rights would obstruct their passage, just as they had done for decades. His response to the widespread violence directed at civil rights workers was often delayed, and appeared to be more concerned with keeping the peace than helping their cause.

Progress was made on the question of voting qualifications. Eisenhower's major contributions to civil rights were the 1957 and 1960 Acts which provided some protection for blacks who wished to register. A division in the Justice Department was founded to take action in the courts on behalf of those whose rights were being denied. From 1961 Attorney-General Robert Kennedy was forceful in the use of this

14.4 Martin Luther King being interviewed during a civil rights march in Alabama.

power. In 1964 an important advance was made when the Twenty-fourth Amendment banned the poll tax. Civil rights campaigners were also active in this work. The Voter Education Project from 1962 and the Mississippi Summer Freedom Project in 1964 fought against white hostility to help blacks take advantage of their rights. They hoped that if negroes did vote in state and federal elections all other problems could be solved.

By 1963 John Kennedy was finally convinced that a major Civil Rights Act was necessary if real gains were to be made. Although he was unable to turn his proposals into law, he did make a crucial contribution by putting the full weight of presidential authority behind the movement. His closeness to the cause was cruelly demonstrated when it was reported that white Southern schoolpupils cheered at the news of Kennedy's assassination.

The 1964 Civil Rights Act

To the surprise of many of his former Texan colleagues, Johnson committed himself to the passage of Kennedy's civil rights programme. The 1964 Act made segregated education and public accommodation illegal. All races were to be entitled to have equal employment opportunities. Most important was the demand that when the Federal Government financed a project, racial integration must occur. This affected most areas of public life. The results were impressive and desegregation proceeded at an accelerated rate, although discrimination in employment was largely untouched.

The civil rights movement's success was highlighted by the award of the Nobel Peace Prize in December 1964 to King 'for the furtherance of brotherhood among men'. But five days after receiving this award he was in prison in Selma, Alabama, for his involvement in a voter registration campaign. In this city 57% of the population were black but only 335 were on the voting register, compared with 9543 whites. The demonstrations drew national attention, but Sheriff James Clark failed to understand it: '...all this nigger fuss here of late. We always git along. You just have to know how to handle them.' His special techniques included the use of an electric cattle prod.

After some of the most brutal violence seen in the South, Johnson obtained the passage of the 1965 Voting Rights Act. This outlawed such devices as literacy tests and resulted in a rush to register. By 1968 there were a million new black voters.

The end of nonviolence

After 1964 the focus of attention moved from the rural South to the cities of the North and West. Since 1945 these cities had attracted large numbers of blacks in search of work. They could only afford to live in the often dilapidated and overcrowded inner city areas, whose former white residents had drifted to the more pleasant suburbs. The result was racially segregated housing caused not by laws, but by economic necessity. Inevitably, inner city schools were overwhelmingly black; public facilities were often of a deplorable quality; unemployment for blacks was usually at twice the rate for whites; crime rates were alarming; one parent families were common; illegitimacy was frequent. A fact of life for ghetto residents was a frequently unsympathetic, alien and often brutal police force which was more likely to clamp down on black offenders than white ones.

Kennedy had ordered all federal housing projects to be integrated, but it was easier to move blacks into an area than to keep the whites living there. The 1968 Civil Rights Act, among other things, forbad racial discrimination in the sale of housing. Such laws are very difficult to enforce, and there was little improvement in the situation.

The problems of the ghettos started to erupt into violence in the summers of the mid-1960s. The first major riot was in 1965 in the Watts area of Los Angeles. Others followed. In 1966 serious disturbances occurred in Chicago, New York, Philadelphia, Cleveland and other cities. 1967 was the worst year of all, and America seemed to be in a state of civil war which no-one could control.

The Federal Government was helpless. Civil rights leaders condemned the rioting but sympathised with the problems which were totally different from those of the South. As King said: 'Jobs are harder and costlier to create than voting rolls. The eradication of slums housing millions is complex far beyond integrating buses and lunch counters'. A backlash started amongst whites who had supported earlier civil rights protests in the South. They now feared for their jobs, their homes and their schools. City authorities tried to clamp down hard on the rioters, but this probably made the situation even worse. As white gangs started to involve themselves in the riots there was a real danger of a 'race war'.

Black Power

To the ghetto blacks the doctrine of nonviolence was meaningless. They had lost faith in its ability to solve their social and economic problems and there appeared to be no prospect of racial integration. A rival philosophy, Black Power, argued that there should instead be racial separation. Blacks should run their own society without white interference. If necessary they should achieve their objectives by the use of force. The slogan 'Black is Beautiful' was coined as a reaction to centuries of whites indoctrinating negroes to be ashamed of their colour. Some Black Power leaders argue their case on page 157.

The Black Panthers, advocating a race war, were the most extreme members of this movement. The Black Muslims totally rejected white society together with its religion. Its most famous convert was boxer Cassius Clay, who changed his name to Mohammed Ali. Malcolm X, the most

Black Power

Malcolm X of the Black Muslims in his autobiography describes his treatment by the whites who ran the detention home to which he was sent:

1   '...it just never dawned upon them that I could understand, that I wasn't a pet, but a human being. They didn't give me credit for having the same sensitivity, intellect, and understanding that they would have been ready and willing to recognize in a white boy in
5   my position. But it has historically been the case with white people, in their regard for black people, that even though we might be *with* them, we weren't considered *of* them. Even though they appeared to have opened the door, it was still closed. Thus they never did really see *me*.
10   This is the sort of kindly condescension which I try to clarify today, to these integration-hungry Negroes, about their "liberal" white friends, these so-called "good white people"....'

Source
Malcolm X, Haley, A., *The Autobiography of Malcolm X.* Quoted in Hacker G., Learmouth, J., Robinson, R., *Conflict 2,* Nelson, 1969, p. 89

Stokely Carmichael was one of the most talented and forceful Black Power leaders:
'If we are to proceed towards true liberation, we must cut ourselves off from white people. We must form our own institutions,
15   credit unions, co-ops, political parties, write our own histories'.
Carmichael was succeeded as leader of SNCC by H. Rapp Brown:
'The white man won't get off our backs, so we're going to knock him off.... If it comes the the point that black people must have guns, we will have means and ways to obtain those arms.'

Source
Quoted in Muse, B., *The American Negro Revolution 1963–68,* Indiana University Press, 1968

Questions
(1) In what ways did whites appear to open the door (line 8) in the 1960s?
(2) Which people and groups are being criticised when Malcolm X writes of 'integration-hungry Negroes' and 'their "liberal" white friends' (lines 11–12)?
(3) a Where in America was Black Power most popular?
     b Why were blacks already 'cut-off from white people' in these areas?
     c How did the ideas of Carmichael differ from those of Martin Luther King?
(4) When and where did blacks appear to attempt to knock the whites off their backs (line 16)?

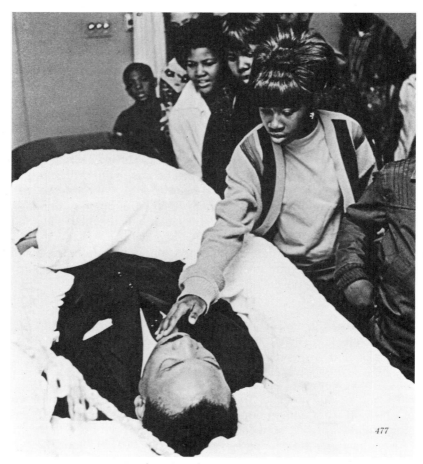

14.5 Martin Luther King's body lying in state.

impressive leader of this cult, was shot dead in 1965. Even formerly nonviolent groups adopted Black Power, much to King's distress. SNCC was transformed by Stokely Carmichael. One historian wrote: 'King was content to march with dignity into the lion's den; Carmichael sought to twist the lion's tail.'

The final defeat for nonviolence came in Memphis, Tennessee, when King was assassinated in April 1968 by a white extremist.

The end of the revolt

Since 1968 much of the heat has gone out of the issue of race relations, but the problems have certainly not disappeared. Although Johnson's Poverty Program did much to help blacks, the ghettos still exist, as do the difficulties which go with them.

The issues have altered in recent years. The white backlash was directed in the 1970s at the question of 'bussing' children long distances in order to create racially balanced schools. This was in effect an admission that integrated housing was not likely to be obtained in the foreseeable future. Bussing, it was hoped, could lessen the damage done by ghettos. Nixon avoided taking a clear stand on this, but in 1971 the Supreme Court gave its approval to the practice.

Blacks have been able to play a more equal part in society. Visible evidence of this is the

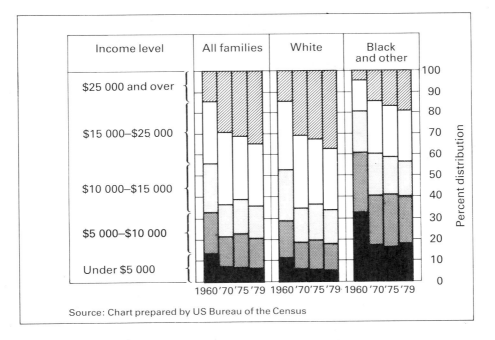

14.6 Money income of families in Constant (1979) Dollars – Percent distribution by income level and by race: 1960 to 1979.

Source
U.S. Bureau of the Census

	Black Male Unemployment (%)	National Unemployment (%)
1960	10.7	5.5
1965	7.4	4.5
1970	7.3	4.9
1975	13.7	8.5
1980	13.3	7.1

greater frequency with which they now appear on television, and the fact that they are elected to office in city, state and federal governments. The Federal Government has deliberately appointed blacks to positions of importance. For example, President Carter appointed Andrew Young as ambassador to the UNO. Prejudice remains strong, however. This was demonstrated in Chicago in 1983 when most white Democrats voted Republican rather than back the party's black candidate for mayor. Although the Reverend Jesse Jackson attempted to obtain the Democratic nomination for the 1984 presidential election, the day when America will have her first black President is still a long way off.

15 Lyndon Johnson's Great Society

Johnson takes over

Five days after the assassination of Kennedy the new President, Lyndon B. Johnson, addressed Congress: 'All I have, I would have given gladly not to be standing here today.' He went on to ask Congress to pass Kennedy's programme which had been endlessly delayed by its opponents. The most important matters, tax cuts and civil rights, were completed the next year by a Congress anxious to pay tribute to the dead President's name.

The Poverty Program

Although much of Johnson's programme was started by his predecessor, he also had ideas of his own. He said he wanted to move America 'upward to the Great Society' which 'rests on abundance and liberty for all'. Central to this dream was an attack on poverty. America was the wealthiest society in history, but there was an increasing awareness of pockets of long-term poverty which earlier governments had ignored. It is impossible to give precise figures for those in

---

Lifeline

Lyndon B. Johnson (1908–73)

Lyndon Johnson came from a Texan family, whose poverty he liked to refer to in later years. After a short teaching career he entered local politics and worked on various New Deal projects. He was elected to the House of Representatives in 1937 and the Senate in 1948. As a Senator he had a remarkably successful career, soon rising to the rank of Democratic leader. In this position he was able to bargain with unrivalled skill, cunning and ruthlessness in order to pass those bills he favoured, and block those he opposed. He rarely needed to speak in a debate to get what he wanted.

He managed to offend large numbers of people with his vulgar and outrageous behaviour: he took a party of female journalists on a 90 m.p.h. car ride through Texas, drinking beer and providing graphic descriptions of the sex life of a bull; he lifted his pet beagle up by its ears, deeply offending animal lovers; at a press conference he decided to display the scar from his gall bladder operation. He was very secretive and unforgiving to those who crossed or disagreed with him. On the other hand, he was generous, immensely hard-working, and genuinely committed to helping the more unfortunate members of society. Henry Cabot Lodge observed: 'His virtues seem huge and his vices seem like monstrous warts ...'

15.1 President Lyndon B. Johnson speaking after he had signed the new Immigration Bill at the foot of the Statue of Liberty in 1965

need, but Johnson estimated that over 20% of the population, some 40 million people, were unable to supply themselves with the basic necessities of life. Kennedy's attention had been drawn to the depressed Appalachian mountain region and the blacks, but there was also great distress amongst the elderly, single mothers and the unskilled. Their problems were all the more difficult to tolerate because they lived in the midst of such an affluent society.

In 1964 the Economic Opportunity Act was passed to tackle some of these problems. The Federal Government started, amongst other things, to train unskilled youths, create programmes to rebuild run down communities, and to loan money to poor families. The achievements were impressive: by 1972 poverty had been reduced to about 25 million people. However, the Vietnam

'The abdominal showman'

Study this cartoon and answer the questions which follow:

Source
David Levine 1966 in Morison, Commager, Leuchtenberg, *A Concise History of the American Republic,* OUP, 1977, p. 739

This caricature takes advantage of the episode when Johnson displayed his fresh operation scar to journalists. The scar here is seen to resemble a map of Vietnam.

Questions
(1) What point is the artist trying to make about the effect Vietnam was having on Johnson's administration?

(2) Show how, and explain the reasons why this prediction came true by 1968.

Poverty in the Affluent Society

Official government statistics on poverty give the following picture:

		Millions	
1960	Total poor	**39.9**	22% total population
	White poor	**28.3**	18% white population
	Nonwhite poor	**11.6**	56% nonwhite population
1972	Total poor	**25.4**	13% total population
	White poor	**17.5**	10% white population
	Nonwhite poor	**7.9**	32% nonwhite population

War, accompanied by inflation and tax increases in the late 1960s, destroyed much of the Poverty Program's good work.

The 1964 presidential election

Johnson, riding on the tide of sympathy for Kennedy, was in a very strong position to be elected President in his own right. When the Republicans nominated Senator Barry Goldwater of Arizona to challenge him, the result became a foregone conclusion. Goldwater was a sincere, likeable man of limited ability, who stood on a platform which criticised civil rights legislation, supported States Rights, strongly opposed Communism and disapproved of social security. He frightened moderate Republicans and helped Johnson to an overwhelming victory by 43 129 000 to 27 178 000. The Democrats won heavy majorities in Congress and for the first time since 1938 there was a real chance of progress on reform. Johnson gloated: 'It could be better but not this side of Heaven.'

Building the Great Society

The combination of large Democratic majorities and Johnson's unique skill in manipulating Congress (described on page 6) resulted in a series of reforms of major and lasting importance. In 1965 Medicare was approved, despite much hostility from doctors. This provided for insurance schemes and government subsidies to pay some medical bills for the poor and elderly. This was a great advance towards a caring society, but it stopped deliberately short of a welfare state.

As a former teacher in a poor area of Texas, he took particular interest in education. The 1965 Act enabled the Federal Government to give $1 billion to the individual states to help those schools in the greatest need. About 90% of the nation's schools received some assistance. This was followed by $2.4 billion aid to higher education, laws to attack the growing problem of environmental pollution, and an extensive house-building programme. Johnson's 'Great Society' reforms amounted to the most important burst of domestic reforms since Roosevelt's Hundred Days, and have been of lasting benefit to the nation.

Coming apart

In 1964 Johnson appeared to lead a nation strongly committed to his Great Society. By 1966 this unity was beginning to disintegrate as conservatives started to have doubts about the growth of the power of Federal Government, together with welfare and civil rights legislation. The mid-term elections brought heavy defeats for many Democrats and an end to the majority in favour of continuing the Great Society programme.

Away from Washington, America was in the middle of serious social and political unrest. At the root of the discontent was the Vietnam War. In the mid-1960s the United States was sending ever increasing numbers to take part in what critics saw as a costly, futile and immoral conflict. Many young people, especially white, middle class students, were starting to rebel against traditional American values and policies which had apparently led to Vietnam. There were frequent anti-war demonstrations and violence was commonplace. Students also found much to criticise in their universities. In 1964 the University of California at Berkeley was closed down by a 'sit in', and others followed.

By 1968 this protest movement was directed clearly at Johnson, and such was its force, that he almost became a prisoner in the White House. His prospects for the forthcoming elections appeared poor.

Foreign policy

Johnson's foreign policies were overwhelmingly dominated by Vietnam, and this is dealt with fully in Chapter 16. The war had a crippling effect on not only his domestic policies but also his dealings with the rest of the world, especially the Soviet Union. He would have preferred to continue to improve East–West relations, but this was difficult because the Russians gave their Communist allies support, both diplomatically and in terms of military and economic aid.

While the United States wasted her vast resources in South East Asia, the Soviet

15.2 Anti-war demonstrators.

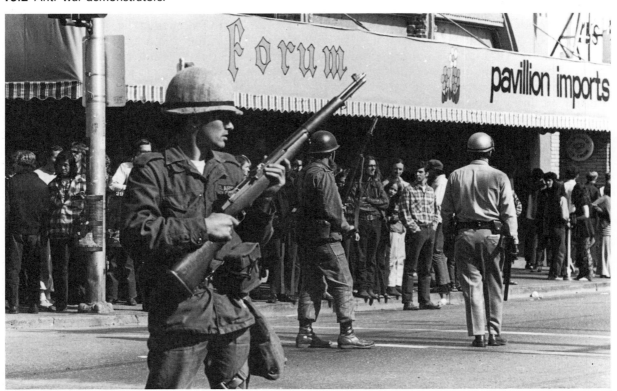

Union built up her armed forces so that her nuclear power nearly matched America's. This was an expensive process and the Communists were becoming interested in ending this arms race. Vietnam, rivalry in the Middle East and the Warsaw Pact's invasion of Czechoslovakia in 1968 did not make negotiations easy, but a Non-Proliferation Treaty was signed in 1968 by the superpowers and Britain (but not by France or Communist China). This banned the spread of nuclear weapons technology to 'non-nuclear' nations. Further improvements in relations came during Nixon's Presidency.

Latin America

Hopes of an Alliance for Progress were largely disappointed in the later 1960s. The United States generally preferred stability to reform, and took every opportunity to make aid dependent on trade deals with American companies. This made economic development unnecessarily slow and costly. The President of Colombia said in 1968 that his country had 'received two program loans under the Alliance. I don't know if we can survive a third.'

The Dominican Republic

The Dominican Republic was ruled after 1940 by the ruthlessly efficient dictator, Trujillo, who was tolerated by the United States. In 1961 he was assassinated. The following year elections brought Juan Bosch to power with 60% of the votes. He was left wing, but non-Communist, and was committed to radical reforms in his backward country. In 1963 Reid Cabral overthrew him in a coup backed by conservative businessmen, landowners and the Catholic Church. The new regime was welcomed only by the United States who gave it economic aid. In 1965, when supporters of Bosch attempted to bring down Cabral, the United States decided to intervene, despite this being against OAS rules. She claimed American lives were in

danger and there was a risk of a Cuban or Communist take over. It was later proved that these excuses were deliberate lies.

In April 23 000 troops landed, restored order and prevented Bosch from regaining power. In May an OAS peace-keeping force replaced the Americans. In 1966 the moderately conservative Joaquin Belaguer won an election which meant that American interests in the area were safeguarded. Bosch saw it differently: 'This was a democratic revolution smashed by the leading democracy in the world.'

The 1968 elections

In 1967 Senator Eugene McCarthy announced that he would run for President and promised to take America out of Vietnam. In early 1968 Robert Kennedy, who intensely disliked Johnson, joined the race and promised to be a formidable opponent. Faced with this mounting opposition within his own party, Johnson decided in March not to try for another term. Further tragedy struck the Kennedys when Robert too was assassinated in June by an Arab extremist who disliked America's support of Israel. This left the field clear for Vice-President Hubert H. Humphrey to win the Democratic nomination. McCarthy's youthful campaigners attracted widespread attention but were never likely to convince the majority of moderate voters. Anti-war demonstrators turned up in force at the Democratic Convention in Chicago where they clashed with police under orders from the hard-line Mayor Daly. The official report described these appalling scenes as a 'police riot'. Humphrey's cause was further damaged by George Wallace who stood as a candidate supporting States Rights, and strongly opposing civil rights reforms. He attracted many Southern Democratic votes away from the official candidate.

The Republicans inevitably benefited from the Democrats' ineffectiveness. Nixon was nominated and, compared with the extremism of Goldwater in 1964, presented himself as a moderate who could heal the

Johnson as President

The journalist Louis Heren gives his view of Johnson's suitability for the role of President:

'The natural gifts which made him the most successful Senate majority leader in history rendered him unfit to lead the nation in times of crisis. National leadership could not be exercised from a back room, with cajolery, fixing, and the rest of his tricks, and Johnson knew no other way.'

Source
Heren, L., *No Hail, No Farewell* (1970).

Question
After studying Chapters 14, 15 and 16, produce evidence to back up this verdict on Johnson. Is it fair in your opinion?

self-inflicted wounds of American society. In addition to making vague statements about ending the war, he promised to deal with the problems of law and order. He appealed to 'Middle America', the millions who were 'unpoor, unyoung and unblack', and believed their way of life was being threatened after a decade of upheaval. Nixon was harmed by his reputation which was still somewhat unsavoury and his far from warm personality. The result was very close, with Nixon just ahead by 31 720 000 to 31 271 000. Wallace received an impressive vote of nearly 10 million. For the first time ever the new President did not have a majority in either House of Congress. This would make life very difficult for him in the future.

16 Vietnam

Colonial War 1945–54

In September 1945 Ho Chi Minh announced in Hanoi the creation of the Democratic Republic of Vietnam (DRV). Ho was leader of the Viet Minh, a Communist led alliance of many groups committed to obtaining Vietnam's independence from France. The Viet Minh were able to take control because following the defeat of Japan there was no other power in the area to stop them.

At Potsdam it had been agreed that France should be allowed to reoccupy her former colonies of Vietnam, Cambodia and Laos (collectively known as Indochina). The Viet Minh had little choice but to accept this until its army could build up its strength to challenge the well equipped French forces.

Open warfare began in November 1946. The French easily controlled all major towns, industries and communications. They drove the Viet Minh to their strongholds in the mountains and North where a guerrilla campaign was started. Ho describes these tactics on page 170. Despite their considerable advantages the French were unable to overcome the enemy and were eventually obliged to commit half a million

---

Timeline

The Vietnam war

1945   Ho Chi Minh announces the creation of the Democratic Republic of Vietnam (September).

1946   War breaks out between the French and Viet Minh (November).

1949   Communists take power in China (October).

1950   United States starts aid to the French in Vietnam.

1954   Battle of Dien Bien Phu.
Geneva Agreements divide Vietnam into a Communist North and non-Communist South.
Diem takes control in South.
United States provides aid to Diem.

1957   Violent opposition to Diem starts in South Vietnam.

1959   North Vietnam starts to encourage the rebels.

1960   NLF formed.

1961   Kennedy increases number of American advisers in South Vietnam.

1963   Buddhist monks burn themselves to death (May).
        Diem overthrown by ARVN (November).
        Johnson succeeds Kennedy (November).

1964   *Maddox* attacked in Gulf of Tonkin.
        Gulf of Tonkin Resolution (August).

1965   'Rolling Thunder' starts (February).
        United States ground forces start to increase rapidly.

1966   More Buddhist suicides by fire.

1968   Tet Offensive (January).
        Johnson temporarily halts bombing of the North, and stops the escalation of United States forces in Vietnam (March).
        Paris Peace Talks start (May).
        Anti-war movement at its peak.

1969   Nixon becomes President (January).
        Vietnamization starts: United States forces reach a peak of 543 000 (April) and then start to be reduced.

1970   Sihanouk overthrown by Lon Nol in Cambodia (March).

        United States forces attack Communist bases in Cambodia (April).

1971   ARVN and United States forces attack Communist bases in Laos (February).

1973   Paris Peace Treaty signed (January).
        All United States combat troops leave (March).

1975   Communists victorious in Cambodia, Vietnam and Laos (April and May).

French and Vietnamese soldiers against the Viet Minh. Their enemy still managed to dominate about half the countryside.

France tried to save her position by attempting to gain the support of those Vietnamese nationalists who opposed the Viet Minh. In 1949 she established an 'independent' government led by the Emperor Bao Dai. Her war effort was not substantially helped, but it did improve her relations with the United States.

United States policy towards Vietnam

Ho asked the United States to recognise the DRV in 1945, but the request was ignored

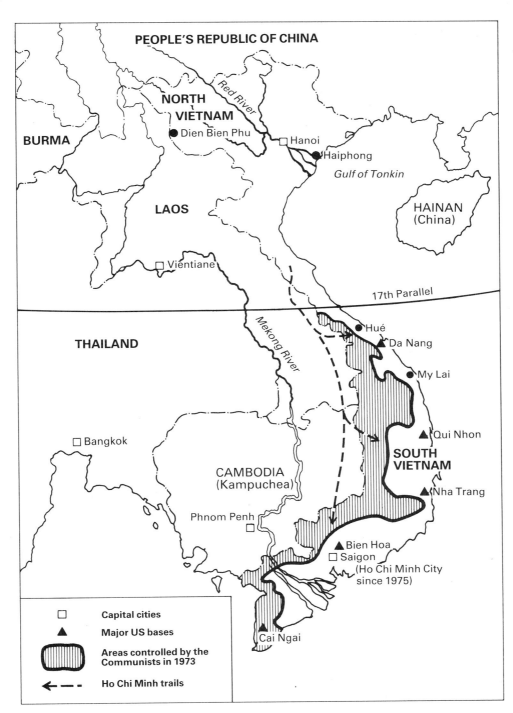

16.1 The war in Vietnam.

even though Truman had no sympathy for France's attempts to restore colonial rule. The United States gave no encouragement to either side before the Cold War in Asia was transformed by the Communist victory in China. France was now seen to be fighting

The guerrillas and the peasants

The tactics described here by Ho Chi Minh in 1952 were used with great success for the next two decades by Communist guerrillas in Vietnam:

1   'When fighting in an enemy-occupied area, we must use guerrilla tactics.... We must absolutely not go in for large-scale battles and big victories, unless we are 100% certain of success.

    The aim of guerrilla warfare is not to win large-scale battles and
5   win big victories, but to nibble at the enemy, harass him in such a way that he can neither eat nor sleep in peace, to give him no respite, to wear him out physically and mentally, and finally to annihilate him. Wherever he goes, he should be attacked by our guerrillas, stumble on land mines or be greeted by sniper fire. Here
10 is what French soldiers say in their letters: "In Vietnam, death is lying in wait for us in every cave, every bush, every pond...."'

Source
Ho Chi Minh, *Selected Writings,* Foreign Languages Publishing House, Hanoi, 1977, pp. 150–151

The NLF aimed to work closely with the peasants:
    'The Party is like a plant. The people are like the soil that nourishes the plant.... If the roots of the plant go deeply and firmly into the ground, only then will the plant grow well and steadily.'

The guerrillas were given these instructions:
    'Be fair and honest in business with the people.... Never take even a needle from the people. When staying in civilian houses, maintain it as if it is one's own.... Be polite with the people and love the people.... Be respected and loved by the people.'

Source
Quoted in Fitzgerald, F., *Fire in the Lake,* Boston: Little, Brown, 1972.

Questions
(1) a Who were the 'enemy' (line 1) in 1952?
    b In what sort of places were the enemy strongest at this time?
    c How did Ho Chi Minh come to face a different enemy within ten years?

(2) a Explain why Ho Chi Minh opposed 'large-scale battles and big victories' (line 2).
    b What military strategies were used against the guerrillas in the 1960s? Why did they not succeed?

(3) Find out which other Communist leader's ideas strongly influenced Ho Chi Minh's tactics and words.

not against nationalists but against Communists. The United States was starting to accept the 'Domino Theory' which has dominated her policy in South East Asia ever since. This describes the countries of the region as a row of dominoes placed on end. When one is pushed over the rest inevitably topple as well. (This is explained on this page.) The theory appeared to be proved when the Viet Minh received aid from China. Although Chinese help was important the Viet Minh mainly fought the war on their own resources.

In an attempt to prevent the dominoes from falling and to contain Communism the United States recognised Bao Dai's government and started to send substantial military aid. By 1954 she paid for 78% of the cost of the war against the Viet Minh.

The Geneva Agreements 1954

Despite American help the French came no nearer to victory and by 1953 were prepared to negotiate. The United States agreed, but was determined to prevent a total Communist triumph. The Viet Minh too

---

The Domino Theory

This statement by the National Security Council in 1952 expresses the 'Domino Theory' which dominated United States policy in South East Asia:

1   'Communist domination, by whatever means, of all South East Asia would seriously endanger in the short term, and critically endanger in the longer term, United States security interests.

    The loss of any of the countries of South East Asia to communist
5   aggression would have critical psychological, political and economic consequences. In the absence of effective and timely counteraction, the loss of any single country would probably lead to the relatively swift submission to or an alignment with communism by the remaining countries of this group. Furthermore, an alignment with
10   communism of the rest of South East Asia and India, and in the longer term, of the Middle East ... would in all probability follow: such widespread alignment would endanger the stability and security of Europe.

    Communist control of all of South East Asia would render the
15   U.S. position in the Pacific offshore island chain precarious and would seriously jeopardise fundamental U.S. security interests in the Far East.

    South East Asia ... is the principal world source of natural rubber and tin, and a producer of petroleum and other strategically
20   important commodities....

    The danger of an overt military attack against South East Asia is inherent in the existence of a hostile and aggressive Communist China, but such an attack is less probable than continued communist efforts to achieve domination through subversion.'

Source
Ellsberg, D., *The Pentagon Papers,* Quadrangle, Chicago, 1971

(1) How serious was the threat of 'Communist domination ... of all South East Asia' (line 1) in 1952?

(2) Explain the likely processes by which 'the loss of any single country would probably lead to the relatively swift submission to or alignment with communism by the remaining countries in the group' (lines 7–9).

(3) Name the parts of 'the Pacific offshore island chain' (line 15) which the United States considered strategically vital.

(4) What events convinced the United States that Communist China was 'hostile and aggressive' (line 22) at this time?

---

realised that they were unlikely to totally defeat their opponents and accepted the need to compromise. China, prompted by the Soviet Union, encouraged this attitude.

As the peace talks at Geneva drew near in 1954 the French were humiliatingly defeated at Dien Bien Phu. This made their bargaining position very weak so the United States actively considered directly intervening with air attacks. It was decided that this would achieve nothing.

The complex Geneva Agreements were a victory for no-one. Laos and Cambodia, where France had been involved in similar struggles, were made independent. Vietnam was temporarily divided at 17°N, with the Viet Minh to control the North, and their opponents the South. Elections were planned for 1956 after which the nation would be reunited. The United States did not sign these agreements but said she would accept them.

Diem's South Vietnam

The United States found herself supporting the weaker part of Vietnam. The country was in economic chaos and there was no effective government. By 1955 Ngo Dinh Diem had surprisingly taken control. He was a dedicated nationalist, strongly anti-Communist and reasonably honest. The United States believed he would be able to create a strong, democratic state to resist further Communist expansion. Neither Diem nor the Americans had any intention of allowing Vietnam to be reunited because they were in no doubt that Ho would win any election.

The United States gave the South considerable aid, the majority of which went to build up the Army of the Republic of Vietnam (ARVN). American advisers trained the ARVN to deal with a conventional assault on the model of North Korea in 1950. This became a severe liability when a guerrilla war developed. Much attention was also paid to building railways, hospitals and schools, and training civil servants. In the cities consumer goods were abundantly available. At first sight Diem's South Vietnam appeared to be a showcase for American aid to the Third World, but there were serious problems.

The United States' pleading for democratic reforms was constantly ignored. There was no democratic tradition in Vietnam and Diem did nothing to develop one. Typical of his attitude was the referendum in 1957 when he obtained 98.2% support including 605 000 votes in Saigon where only 405 000 were registered. In later elections most opponents were arrested. Nor was there any serious attempt to introduce overdue reforms to give land to the peasants

16.2 French troops captured at Dien Bien Phu, 1954.

and so the poverty of the majority of Vietnamese was unaffected.

Violent opposition to Diem developed in 1957 when former Viet Minh supporters started a terror campaign against government officials. In 1960 the National Liberation Front was formed. It was led by Communists, the Viet Cong (VC), and declared its aims to be 'peace, national independence, democratic freedoms, improvement of the people's living conditions, and peaceful national reunification'. The first encouragement from Ho Chi Minh's DRV did not come until

1959, and although some practical aid came after that, the NLF was mainly organised and recruited in the South.

Kennedy and South East Asia

Although South Vietnam was at grave risk in 1961 the situation in Laos was more disturbing. The pro-American government, formed after a coup planned by Eisenhower's administration, was under threat from the Communist Pathet Lao forces and needed urgent aid. In 1962 Kennedy made a strategic retreat by agreeing to the formation of a neutral government led by Souvanna Phouma, and thus lost an ally.

In Vietnam he decided that firmer action was needed to prevent further Communist gains. He believed the South was the object of aggression from the North, organised by China and the Soviet Union, and so the United States had a duty to help her. The number of American troops was increased to 15 000 by 1963. They were officially not to enter combat, but to train the ARVN in new counterinsurgency techniques. In return Diem was to start a serious programme of land reform.

Again Diem disappointed the Americans and the military position deteriorated alarmingly. The failure of Kennedy's hopes came in 1963 when seven Buddhist monks publicly burned themselves to death in protest at the war. They appeared to represent the feelings of a large proportion of the population (80% were Buddhist) and finally convinced the United States that Diem must go, as he had created neither a democratic nor a strong South Vietnam. The C.I.A. gave its approval when a coup overthrew and murdered Diem in November 1963. He was succeeded by a series of short-lived military governments. Stability did not return until 1965 when Air Vice-Marshall Ky and General Thieu took over, but none of these military men had any solutions for the country's problems.

16.3 Buddhist monk burning to death in South Vietnam.

Johnson escalates the war

Johnson decided to continue his predecessor's policies. He genuinely wanted reforms and had no desire to increase the number of American troops in the country. However, he believed the threat came from outside South Vietnam and the United States had a duty to resist it to contain Communism.

The turning point for American involvement came in 1964. In February she started secret attacks on the DRV which in August provoked retaliation against the destroyer *Maddox* in the Gulf of Tonkin. In response to this Johnson obtained from Congress a resolution which gave him virtually unlimited powers to react against armed attack. In later years it was admitted that he had deliberately lied about the alleged aggression. This resolution meant that Congress had almost no control over events in this war.

Rolling Thunder

In February 1965 Johnson ordered the start of a massive bombing campaign code-named Rolling Thunder. This was intended to halt the supply of men and munitions along the Ho Chi Minh trails. As help to the VC increased the bombing became heavier and more widespread. By the end of the war most cities and military targets in the North had been devastated causing about a thousand civilian casualties per week. Enemy positions in the South too were heavily bombed, and resulted in about half a million dead or wounded.

All this achieved little. The resilience and adaptability of the Communists constantly amazed the United States. As cities were destroyed the population was scattered throughout the countryside where small-scale munitions industries were set up. Over 30 000 miles of tunnels were dug as air raid shelters. There were full time squads of workers to repair roads and bridges, and provide human muscle when mechanical transport was no longer possible. Aid was sent from China and, increasingly, the Soviet Union. The DRV's will to continue with the war was not reduced.

The State Department justifies Rolling Thunder

In February 1965 the State Department made the following statement:

1   '... the war in Vietnam is not a spontaneous and local rebellion against the established government.... In Vietnam a Communist government has set out deliberately to conquer a sovereign people in a neighboring state.... North Vietnam's commitment to seize
5   control of the South is no less total than was the commitment of the regime in North Korea in 1950.'

Questions

(1) How accurate is the view that 'the war in Vietnam is not a spontaneous and local rebellion' (line 1)?

(2) a What is meant by the term 'sovereign people' (line 3)?
     b Why would North Vietnam not agree with this description of the South?

(3) In what ways were the wars in Korea and Vietnam (a) similar to, and (b) different from each other?

16.4 American B52 bomber in the air above North Vietnam.

The ground war

The failure of the bombing campaign to check the supplies from the North made it necessary to increase rapidly the number of American ground forces after 1965. South Korea, Australia and New Zealand also sent men. This mainly conscripted army was officially committed to enter combat and soon started to take over the role of the ARVN which then became demoralised and ineffective.

Their major problem in action was to identify and isolate the guerrillas who infiltrated the villages where most had originally lived. The VC were usually indistinguishable from the peasants who sheltered them. Many Americans developed a contempt or hatred for the Vietnamese whom they were supposedly defending, but who appeared to be helping snipers or laying mines and booby traps. Sophisticated technology such as herbicides like 'agent orange' which wiped out half of the South's

timberlands in an attempt to expose the enemy, and 'people sniffers' to detect human urine, were also employed. Napalm was used indiscriminately to destroy buildings, jungle and people alike.

As it was impossible effectively to police the whole country 'search and destroy' operations were used to clear an area. A typical large scale example was 'Cedar Falls' in 1967. When the population in this VC stronghold had been told to leave and their homes heavily bombed, 30 000 troops surrounded and searched for the enemy. Afterwards all shelter and tunnels were destroyed by fire and further bombing. Only 700 VC were killed and within weeks of the operation the enemy were back in control.

Although American troops rarely lost an encounter with the VC they did not get any nearer to victory. One journalist described their attacks as a 'sledgehammer on a floating cork. Somehow the cork refused to stay down'. The NFL's cause was helped by the fact that no matter how much the United

States escalated the war the North could always keep pace because every year 200 000 youths became of age for military service. The Americans tried to mark their progress by 'body counts' but all corpses, VC and peasant alike, were generally identified as enemy, and thus presented a totally misleading impression to the generals and public. Nonetheless, the VC throughout the war suffered much heavier casualties than the American and ARVN forces.

The strain of fighting in this dirty and demoralising war was too much for many servicemen. Philip Caputo writes about his own experiences on page 178. Drug taking was a common way out of the misery: by 1971 about 5% of American soldiers in Vietnam were addicted to heroin. Many atrocities were committed by both sides.

Most civilians at home refused to believe the details of the My Lai massacre in which 400 civilians died in an orgy of mindless brutality. Many similar episodes went unreported.

Winning over hearts and minds

Most of the United States and South Vietnamese governments' policies did more to repel the majority of peasants than to attract them. Most emphasis was on military strategy with little awareness of the effect on the Vietnamese way of life. Where land reform was tried (which was rarely) the results were usually disastrous, with peasants losing their land and alien, corrupt officials making ill-informed decisions. As the often

16.5 A U.S. Navy UH-1E Iroquois helicopter patrols overhead as boats of the Vietnamese Navy 22 wind their way up a narrow canal in search of enemy soldiers attempting to escape from the operational area 13 miles south of East Saigon, 1967.

'A Rumor of War'

Philip Caputo volunteered to go to Vietnam and describes the war he fought in:

'War is always attractive to young men who know nothing about it, but we have also been seduced into uniform by Kennedy's challenge to "ask what you can do for your country" and by the missionary idealism he had awakened in us. America seemed omnipotent then: the country could still claim it had never lost a war, and we believed we were ordained to play cop to the Communists' robber and spread our political faith around the world.

... The rare instances when the VC chose to fight a setpiece battle provided the only excitement; not ordinary excitement, but the manic ecstacy of contact. Weeks of bottled up tensions would be released in a few minutes of orgiastic violence....

Beyond adding a few more corpses to the weekly body count, none of these encounters achieved anything....

... Our mission was not to win terrain or seize possessions, but simply to kill.... The pressure on unit commanders to produce enemy corpses was intense and they in turn communicated it to their troops.... It is not surprising, therefore, that some men acquired a contempt for human life and a predilection for taking it.'

Source
Caputo, P., *A Rumor of War,* Macmillan, 1977, pp. 12–18

16.6 South Vietnam's Chief of Police summarily executing a Viet Cong officer captured in Saigon in February 1968. The head of South Vietnam's National Police said after the shooting, 'They killed many Americans and many of my people.'

insensitive military pursued the VC, villages were frequently destroyed and the peasants fled. The result was that by 1972 about 5 million people had become refugees and were separated from their ancestral lands. The whole Vietnamese culture is firmly rooted in the sacred, ancestral land of the village: to be driven away from it is a shattering blow. The Americans and the South Vietnamese government received most of the blame even though it was the presence of the VC in the villages which usually provoked the destruction.

In the cities, too, normal life had broken down; the armies employed virtually all able-bodied men; bars and brothels prospered; corruption was normal; inflation soared. The whole country was totally dependent on American money. Any Vietnamese nationalist would find this an unbearable situation and make the NLF seem an attractive alternative. In 1966 a further outbreak of Buddhist suicides by fire served to emphasise this feeling of despair.

In contrast, the NLF was highly sensitive to the needs of the peasantry. If they had to make the choice they would literally rather send their men to the villages without weapons than without attractive political philosophies. They tried to help the people and work with them to earn their trust and loyalty. (See page 170). It was the VC who were often welcomed as liberators, not the ARVN. Their Communist philosophy was adapted clearly to meet the needs of the Vietnamese, but this usually took second place to their Nationalism. They were therefore able to attract those who knew nothing of Communism but wanted a united nation free of foreign domination.

The American anti-war movement

In 1964 most American voters believed the war in Vietnam was just. As death tolls mounted, draft calls reached 30 000 per month and still no victory was in sight, a vocal section of society started to attack Johnson's policies. Influential people joined the movement including Jane Fonda,

Mohammed Ali, Martin Luther King and Dr Spock. Doubts even spread to Johnson's administration yet no acceptable alternative strategy was proposed. Most Americans still thought that Communism should be resisted but felt others should take over the burden of dying. 'I want to get out but I don't want to give up' was the typical attitude.

The Tet Offensive

While the government continued to issue a stream of confident forecasts about the war the exhaustive coverage on television revealed an alarming 'credibility gap'. The optimists were rudely awakened during the Tet holiday in January 1968, when the VC caught the United States' forces completely unawares by attacking nearly every town and city in the South. Most embarrassing of all, enemy soldiers actually invaded the United States Embassy in Saigon. They were soon beaten back with 40 000 men killed, but they had convincingly proved that for all her sacrifices the American army was still not in control of the country. It was a military defeat but a psychological victory.

General Westmoreland, the United States commander, asked for even more men to add to the half million already there. Johnson finally decided to call a halt to this futile escalation and instead started a process which later, under Nixon, came to be known as Vietnamization. This led to a disengagement of American forces from the war. He also temporarily reduced, and for a while stopped, the bombing of the North to persuade the Communists to begin talks.

Vietnamization and disengagement

In 1968 Nixon promised to end the war but without allowing the Communists to win. His strategy of Vietnamization was to make the ARVN take over most of the fighting, with the United States concentrating its efforts on an increasingly destructive bombing campaign and the supply of arms. By inflicting unbearable suffering on the

'It don't fit'

Study this cartoon and answer the questions which follow:

Source
Dallas Notes/LNS 1969 in Bullock, A., *History of the 20th Century*, Octopus, 1976, p. 477

Questions
(1) Who do the two figures represent?

(2) a What sort of things are being offered to the smaller person?
     b Why is the gift being made? What might be expected in return?
     c Explain in what ways the gift 'don't fit'.
     d What might the receiver of the gift prefer instead?

(3) Choose three different countries where this type of relationship could be said to have been attempted in the years since 1945 but without any of the successes expected by the figure on the left. Explain in each case how and why these relationships failed.

16.7 Military police and State Troopers, out in force with gas-masks, guns and truncheons, to tackle an anti-war demonstration at Fort Dix.

enemy he hoped to force them to make concessions at the Paris Peace Talks which had made no progress since they started in May 1968. Nixon wanted to convince the North that although the United States might not win, she would certainly not be defeated.

Vietnamization occurred swiftly. American forces reached a peak of 543 000 in April 1969 but by July 1972 there were only 45 600 left. In the meantime the ARVN grew substantially to over a million strong and undertook nearly all combat missions. This policy appeared to be successful as after 1968 the South was probably more secure than it had been for many years. This was because the VC had been severely weakened by the Tet Offensive and became heavily dependent on North Vietnam.

Extending the war

Vietnamese Communists had for years infiltrated neighbouring Cambodia and Laos to send supplies to the South. They also established sanctuaries out of American reach but only thirty miles from Saigon. In Cambodia the insignificant Communist Khmer Rouge had been fighting for many years against Prince Sihanouk's government which had always tried to be neutral in all superpower conflicts. In February 1969 Nixon ordered the secret bombing of the Communist sanctuaries. Sihanouk was overthrown by the pro-American Lon Nol in March 1970. In April, without consulting the new government, Nixon authorised an American invasion of Cambodia to destroy

Communist bases. The operation failed and the troops left in June. Considerable damage was done to Lon Nol's regime: by 1971 the Khmer Rouge had attracted much support and controlled half of the country. A similar attack was made on bases in Laos in 1971, but the mainly ARVN force met with fierce resistance and hastily retreated.

These extensions of the fighting brought a revival in the anti-war movement at home. The protestors became even more indignant after frequently shocking details of American policy were leaked by the *New York Times* in the *Pentagon Papers,* and Lieutenant Calley was convicted for twenty-two murders at My Lai. By 1971 opinion polls reported that 71% of Americans believed it had been a mistake to send troops to Vietnam and 58% thought the war was immoral. Nixon was under great pressure to end the war.

The Paris Peace Treaty of 1973

By 1972 all parties in the conflict were exhausted and anxious for peace. The DRV made a major conventional assault early in the year and had only been halted by some of the heaviest bombing of the war. Her economy and people could stand no more.

In January 1973 after exhaustive negotiations a treaty was signed. This was in effect a 'cease-fire in place': Thieu's government was preserved; the Communists were allowed to remain in control of those areas which they held in the South; United States forces were to leave Vietnam; prisoners of war were to be returned. The future of Vietnam was left ominously vague and few doubted that there would be an early resumption of fighting.

The last United States troops left in March 1973. Over 56 000 Americans had died since 1965 and the cost had been $146 billion. The suffering of the Vietnamese people was immeasurably greater.

The damage done to the United States' position in the world is still being felt: the Soviet Union had been allowed to reach nuclear equality; several of her Allies were extremely critical of American actions; her self-declared moral superiority over the Communists was put in doubt by a

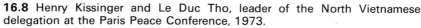
16.8 Henry Kissinger and Le Duc Tho, leader of the North Vietnamese delegation at the Paris Peace Conference, 1973.

brutalising conflict in which Americans often seemed to be the most inhuman. At home the nation was divided and the economy severely weakened. The cost of containment was devastating.

The dominoes fall

The United States continued to bomb the Khmer Rouge and send reduced aid to Thieu's regime, but the Communists were soon victorious all over Indochina. In Vietnam the superbly equipped ARVN collapsed when the DRV advanced in 1974. The United States refused to intervene so the South unconditionally surrendered in May 1975 and Vietnam was officially reunited in 1976. The Khmer Rouge took over Cambodia (renamed Kampuchea) in April 1975 and the Pathet Lao had a complete victory in December.

Since 1975 the United States relations with these states have been strained. In 1976 the pro-Chinese Pol Pot came to power in Kampuchea and started the most extreme revolution ever attempted, resulting in at least 2 million deaths from mass murder or starvation. Vietnam, backed by the Soviet Union, became increasingly hostile, invaded Kampuchea in 1978 and set up a friendly regime. The United States saw this as evidence of Soviet expansionism, refused to recognise this new government and blocked UNO aid to the hard-pressed Kampucheans. China and her new-found friend the United States now recognise a coalition, which includes the Khmer Rouge and Prince Sihanouk's supporters, as the legal government. These events have less to do with Indochina than with superpower rivalry as the United States and China try to weaken the Soviet Union.

17 The crisis of the Presidency 1969–76

Foreign policy

Nixon appointed as his National Security Advisor the prominent academic Henry A. Kissinger. Together they conducted a flamboyant foreign policy which marked a considerable break with the past. They started a policy of détente, a lessening of tension between East and West.

By 1969 the power of the United States had declined relative to the rest of the world. Although her military might was still growing, the Vietnam War had proved that she was unable to dominate other nations as she had once done. Inflation and severe competition from European and Japanese industry were causing economic problems. The Soviet Union's economy too was stagnating and unable to pay for the cripplingly expensive arms race. The Russians were also disturbed by the threat from China which in 1969 brought the two Communist powers near to war. It was this international situation which Nixon and

---

Lifeline

Richard M. Nixon (1913–   )

Richard Nixon came from a poor Californian family but acquired wealth and power through relentless hard work. His early political reputation was as an anti-Communist witch hunter and enemy of Communist China. This makes his policy as President of détente all the more remarkable. During the election campaign for the Senate in 1950 he described his liberal Democratic opponent, Helen Douglas, as 'pink right down to her underwear'. In 1952 he was Eisenhower's running mate and nearly brought him great embarrassment when allegations of financial irregularities were levelled at him. He successfully denied the charges. He became a national figure as Vice-President, but his reputation as 'Tricky Dicky' was hard to live down.

In 1960 his cold, aloof, unglamorous style was in sharp contrast to the debonair Kennedy, and perhaps tipped the balance against him. He was surprisingly defeated for the Governorship of California in 1962. Relations with the press had always been bad, and he told reporters, 'You won't have Nixon to kick around any more.' After this humiliation he strove to improve his image, including his 'five o'clock shadow', and succeeded in reappearing in 1968 as a moderate statesman able to lead the West. When he became President, however, he had made enough enemies to ensure that he would not have an easy time.

Kissinger skilfully exploited. They hoped to 'link' matters such as trade or arms control with agreement on Vietnam or the Middle East. They largely failed in this respect, partly because the Soviet Union was unable to influence North Vietnam or the Arabs, but also the Soviet Union was unwilling to work in this way.

Relations with Communist China since 1969

Both the United States and China were distrustful of the Soviet Union and were now prepared to use each other to strengthen their own security. A relaxation of restrictions on contacts with China was started in 1969. After Kissinger made a secret visit, Nixon undertook a well publicised journey to Peking in February 1972. The United States was now moving towards a 'Two China' policy – recognition of both Taiwan and Communist China. However, little was achieved by the visit apart from goodwill and an opening up of trade. Later that year, despite American opposition, Taiwan was replaced by Communist China at the UNO.

Contacts between the former enemies continued to develop throughout the 1970s, but the United States did not recognise the

Nixon's China policy

1 'The meeting between the leaders of China and the United States is to seek the normalization of relations between the two countries and also to exchange views on questions of concern to the two sides.

5   In anticipation of the inevitable speculation which will follow this announcement, I want to put our policy in the clearest possible context. Our action in seeking a new relationship with the People's Republic of China will not be at the expense of our old friends.

It is not directed against any other nation. We seek friendly
10 relations with all nations. Any nation can be our friend without being any other nation's enemy.

I have taken this action because of my profound conviction that all nations will gain from a reduction of tensions and a better relationship between the United States and the People's Republic of
15 China.

It is in this spirit that I will undertake what I deeply hope will become a journey for peace – peace not just for our generation but for future generations on this earth we share together.'

Source
Department of State Bulletin, August 2, 1971. Quoted in Commager, H. S., *Documents of American History,* Meredith Corporation 1973, pp. 752–753

Questions
(1) a Describe briefly the state of relations between the United States and the People's Republic of China in the years 1949–71.
  b What is probably meant by 'the normalization of relations between the two countries' (line 2)?

(2) Which 'other nation' (line 9) might feel threatened by this meeting? Why should this be so?

(3) a What word is usually used to describe the policy of seeking 'a reduction of tensions' (line 13) between the United States and her rivals?

   b Apart from a desire to avoid war, why were the United States and her major rival both very keen to reduce tension at this time?

   c In what other ways did Nixon put this policy into practice in his years as President?

(4) Why was Nixon's policy towards the United States' rivals abandoned after 1975? (Also consult Chapter 18.)

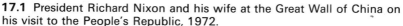

17.1 President Richard Nixon and his wife at the Great Wall of China on his visit to the People's Republic, 1972.

Communist government until 1979, when she also abandoned her 1954 mutual defence treaty with Taiwan. The Soviet intervention in Afghanistan in 1979 concerned both China and the United States and brought them closer together. President Reagan, however, has given more encouragement to Taiwan in the form of arms, and relations with the Communists have deteriorated to some extent.

Détente with the Soviet Union

The Soviet Union was very disturbed by this flirtation between her two major opponents and feared an attempt to encircle her. In 1970 there was the start of negotiations with the United States which led to the signing of the first Strategic Arms Limitation Treaty (SALT I) in 1972. SALT I placed limitations on the increase in nuclear weapons but did nothing actually to reduce stockpiles. Nixon succeeded in his aim of keeping the United States ahead in the race, but was prepared to accept sufficiency rather than superiority.

The improvement in relations between the superpowers was further signalled by Nixon's visits to Moscow, a trade agreement and the recognition by the United States in 1972 of the East German Government. In 1975 at the European Security Conference in Helsinki the United States recognised the Soviet Union's domination of Eastern Europe, but this was linked to a promise by all countries to respect human rights. This was probably the high water mark of détente. However, since 1975 the Helsinki Agreements have been severely criticised for giving too much to the Soviet Union, and not adequately protecting human rights in Communist countries.

Injustice and order?

Kissinger was fond of these words of Goethe: 'If I had to choose between justice and disorder on the one hand, and injustice and order on the other, I would always choose the latter.' Following this policy the United States after 1969 increased its aid to many friendly governments in unstable areas of the world. By 1974 arms sales were about $10 billion compared with an average of $2.5 billion in the mid-1960s. Relations became much closer with countries such as Portugal, South Africa, Zaire and Iran, all of whom could best be described as right-wing authoritarian regimes.

In 1970 Salvador Allende, a nationalist and Marxist, was elected President of Chile. His policies of nationalisation of American assets particularly upset the United States. In response the C.I.A. and the Chilean armed forces organised a coup in September 1973. Allende was killed and replaced by General Pinochet, whose government was soon notorious for its total disregard of human rights, but was loyal to the United States.

Southern Africa was a region of considerable unrest in the early 1970s. Kissinger improved relations with the Portuguese dictatorship in the hope of obtaining NATO bases in the Azores. After the Portuguese revolution in 1974, her African colony of Angola was made independent. The United States and South Africa tried to influence the immediate struggle for power by giving aid to the FNLA and UNITA against the MPLA, which was backed by the Soviet Union and 15 000 Cuban troops. The MPLA was victorious by 1976.

Building a majority for 1972

Throughout Nixon's first term as President his main objective was to obtain a landslide victory in the 1972 elections. The Democratic majorities in Congress were able to prevent him acting as he would have liked, and the Senate even took the unusual step of rejecting two of his nominations to the Supreme Court. Outside Congress the news media, which he had long detested, appeared to him to be unfairly critical of his policies, particularly in South East Asia, and to give encouragement to the anti-war movement. He felt that he was not being given the credit his achievements deserved, especially in détente and the withdrawal from Vietnam. In his mind there was a liberal-radical conspiracy to attack him.

His response to this criticism was to appeal to the 'great silent majority' of conservative Americans by speaking strongly on topics such as 'law and order', drugs, pornography and sexual permissiveness. He described student demonstrators as 'bums'. He was particularly tough on the anti-war movement by having large numbers of protestors arrested with only a scant regard for their legal rights. When four students at Kent State University, Ohio, were shot dead by national guardsmen, he took no action.

His respect for 'law and order' was somewhat inconsistent. His administration was always noted for being secretive and conspiratorial. Policy was decided by a small group of aides in the White House who shared Nixon's distaste for criticism. From 1970 some took it upon themselves, probably with the President's approval, to attack his opponents. A prominent Nixon man, John Dean, looked for ways to 'use the available Federal machinery to screw our political enemies'. An 'enemies list' was drawn up, including journalists, Congressmen and academics. These people were subjected to phone tapping, interference with mail, law suits and surprise tax inspections. A particular target was Daniel Ellsberg who leaked the *Pentagon Papers* to the press. In order to prevent further leaks a group known as 'the plumbers' was formed. One of its first tasks was to break in to Ellsberg's psychiatrist's home to try to find any embarrassing information. The attempt failed.

Nixon approached the 1972 election in an almost unbeatable position largely because of his enormously popular foreign policy successes. Despite the fact that the Democrats were in disarray and their candidate George McGovern was too 'left-wing' to have wide appeal, the Campaign to Re-Elect the President (known outside the White House as CREEP) was formed to make sure no chances were taken. In addition to normal electioneering, CREEP organised 'dirty tricks' to disrupt the rival campaign. For example, misleading press releases were forged, fights were started at meetings and candidates received unrequested public support from homosexuals. Nixon was sent thousands of letters supporting his policies which in reality were produced by CREEP. In June 1972 the Democratic headquarters in the Watergate complex in Washington were burgled. Five men were arrested, but no-one was able to prove that they were associated with the White House. The electorate showed no concern, while Nixon's campaign proceeded smoothly.

As he had hoped Nixon won by 47 170 000 to 29 170 000, one of the most convincing margins ever, but yet again the Democrats remained firmly in control of Congress. His strategy had failed. The hostility of Democrats in Congress became a crucial factor when the Watergate scandals were drawn to the public's attention.

The Watergate revelations

When the Watergate burglars came to trial in March 1973 it soon was apparent that they were closely connected to the White House. Nixon denied any personal knowledge of misdeeds and ordered an enquiry. In May, Congress established its own investigating committee, chaired by Sam Ervin, with the authority to summon witnesses and demand evidence. Over the next few months its proceedings were televised to an astounded nation. A stream of witnesses, who worked closely with Nixon, revealed that there had been an attempt to obstruct justice and cover up the burglary. As the Senators probed further more was discovered about CREEP, dirty tricks, secret intelligence investigations, perjury and other abuses of Presidential power. No-one could prove that Nixon was directly involved until it became known that he taped all of his conversations. The Ervin Committee demanded the tapes but Nixon at first refused. Under mounting pressure from public opinion, and eventually the Supreme

17.2 Nixon resigns.

Court, he was at last forced to give way. Although there were unaccountable gaps, frequently labelled 'expletive deleted', the tapes showed that Nixon was clearly aware of what was going on.

In October, Vice-President Spiro T. Agnew also came under fire and was forced to resign after accusations of corruption, tax evasion and conspiracy. He was succeeded by Gerald R. Ford, Republican leader in the House of Representatives. Allegations of tax evasion were also levelled at Nixon.

By 1974 the government of the United States was being paralysed as Nixon was overwhelmed by the problem of satisfying or evading his accusers. Many of Nixon's

17.3 President Ford being assisted to his feet after falling down aircraft steps in Salzburg, 1975. He was in Austria to have talks with President Sadat of Egypt.

colleagues were forced to resign and several went to prison. The House of Representatives was starting to prepare charges for the President's impeachment (trial by the Senate which is the only way a President can be removed). It seemed almost certain that the Senate would convict Nixon in the autumn.

On 8 August 1974, he stopped fighting and became the first President to resign from office. He never admitted he was guilty of abuse of power or any illegal acts, and only confessed to 'misjudgement'. The following day Gerald Ford was sworn in as President without ever having been elected even as Vice-President.

The aftermath of the Watergate Affair

In the 1960s American Presidents were able to increase their power at the expense of Congress, particularly in the field of foreign affairs. Nixon was not the first President to misuse his authority but the Watergate Affair, coming as it did so soon after the traumatic Vietnam War, made most Americans believe that future Presidents should be more tightly controlled by Congress. Ford and Carter's administrations were never given the freedom which Johnson and Nixon had exercised, and this may partly explain the uncertainty of policy in the years since 1973. It is an open question as to whether a newly confident Congress has used its power more wisely than an overbearing President.

Perhaps the only consolation which Americans could gain from Watergate was that their democratic system had been able to expose the criminals and remove them from authority. Few other countries allow such open criticism and inquiry into the processes of government.

'A Ford not a Lincoln'

The new President was very modest about his own abilities and reminded the world that he was 'a Ford, not a Lincoln'. He had had an unspectacular career to date and was the object of many unkind jokes (Johnson claimed Ford 'is so dumb that he can't fart and chew gum at the same time'). On taking office Ford promised to 'heal the wounds' created by Watergate. He wanted an 'open, candid Administration' but did not start very convincingly by keeping most of Nixon's cabinet. In September he was severely criticised for pardoning Nixon, who would probably soon have been convicted for obstructing justice. It looked like the prime culprit was not to be punished while a host of lesser offenders were serving prison sentences. However, the pardon did serve to end Watergate and allow the nation to turn to other critical problems.

In the early 1970s the American economy began to be affected badly by inflation, low productivity, foreign competition, increasing unemployment and rising oil prices. Nixon and Ford's limited success in coping with this recession is dealt with in Chapter 18.

18 The end of Détente

The reaction to Watergate

The 1976 presidential election aroused so little interest that barely half of all Americans bothered to vote. Ford was challenged by Governor James E. Carter of Georgia who presented himself as an eager, honest outsider, uncorrupted by the intrigue and double-dealing of Washington. At home he wanted an end to 'big government'. In foreign affairs he promised a concern for human rights and reduced arms expenditures. Above all he wanted honesty in Washington. His lack of experience of government was a disadvantage so despite the disasters which had plagued the Republicans in recent years, Ford ran Carter very close, only losing by 38 498 000 to 40 250 000.

The energy crisis

Jimmy Carter believed the energy crisis was 'the greatest challenge that our country will face during our lifetimes'. Since 1971 the demand for oil had started to exceed supply, enabling the Organisation of Petroleum Exporting Countries (OPEC) to raise its prices. Following the 1973 Arab-Israeli War, OPEC for a while had used oil as a political weapon by refusing supplies to those countries, including the United States, which backed Israel. They also took the opportunity of increasing their income further, for reasons explained by the Shah of Iran on page 193. Between 1971–74 crude oil prices rose by about ten times. Americans, who were 6% of the world's population yet consumed 33% of the world's energy, were badly affected. After years of deliberately low oil prices, America's own reserves were being rapidly exhausted, so she was becoming dependent on imports from the Middle East.

The economic consequences were very damaging. Inflation, already at worrying levels, was made considerably worse. The balance of payments (the difference between the cost of exports and imports) started to show a deficit, and the value of the dollar began to fall. This increased the price of imports and further boosted inflation. America was entering an economic recession. More visible signs of the crisis were much higher prices of gasoline for motorists and filling stations forced to close through lack of supplies.

Nixon and Ford had called for Americans to conserve energy by turning down thermostats and driving more slowly in more economical vehicles. When Ford sought tougher restrictions Congress weakened them.

Carter's Energy Bill aimed to discourage consumption by increasing prices through taxation, combined with financial benefits for those who used solar power or insulated their homes. Consumer groups, and oil and natural gas producers were hostile to this. They wanted Carter to encourage more production at home by reducing taxes and restrictions on their businesses, combined with furthering the development of alternative sources of energy such as nuclear power. Despite much intensive pressure by Carter, the Bill was drastically altered by a Congress unwilling to upset the electorate by agreeing to higher prices. The 1978 National Energy Act produced only half the savings for which Carter had hoped. This was a major defeat. Concern about the energy crisis diminished in the 1980s as the world economic recession reduced demand for oil and kept prices stable. A return to prosperity would renew the fears of the 1970s.

18.1 President Jimmy Carter in 1977.

OPEC's price rises

The Shah of Iran, a strong supporter of the United States on most issues, explained in December 1973 why OPEC increased its prices:

'You increased the price of wheat you sell us by 300%, and the same for sugar and cement.... You buy our crude oil and sell it back to us, refined as petrochemicals, at a hundred times the price you've paid us.... It's only fair that, from now on, you should pay more for oil. Let's say ... 10 times more.'

Questions
(1) For what (a) economic and (b) political reasons did OPEC increase its prices in the early 1970s?

(2) What was the effect on (a) the American economy, and (b) United States foreign policy of these rises?

The economic recession

Throughout the 1970s the American economy had been afflicted by high levels of inflation, rates of interest and unemployment, accompanied by the inability of business to compete with Western European and Japanese manufacturers. Most attention was paid to inflation. Nixon had some temporary success in bringing it under control by a series of wage and price restrictions, but the 1973 oil price rises renewed the upward spiral. Ford preferred voluntary action by employers and workers together with cuts in the federal budget. His hope was to 'Whip Inflation Now' (WIN) but he had limited success. He later used tax cuts to increase consumer spending. Although this made prices rise faster, unemployment was reduced and the recession was stopped from getting worse.

Carter originally was more concerned by

The American Economy 1972–80

	Gross National Product (billions of dollars)	Unemployment (%)
1972	1186	5.6
1973	1326	4.9
1974	1434	5.6
1975	1549	8.5
1976	1718	7.7
1977	1918	7.0
1978	2156	6.0
1979	2414	5.8
1980	2626	7.1

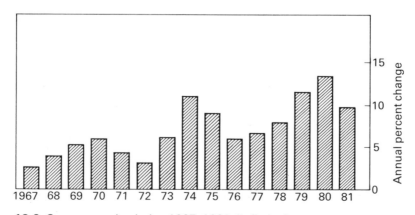

18.2 Consumer price index 1967–1981 (Inflation).

Source:
U.S. Bureau of the Census

high unemployment and aimed to create jobs with more federal spending and reduced taxes. In 1978 the economic situation deteriorated sharply, with inflation in 1979–80 reaching an alarming 18%. He was forced to reverse his policies. He now tried to halt price rises by cutting the federal budget, delaying tax reductions and increasing interest rates, all of which led to higher unemployment. By the time Carter left the White House in 1981 America had moved from 'recession' into 'depression'.

Human rights and détente

Carter believed that the 'soul of our foreign policy' should be human rights. The United States ought only to deal with nations prepared to protect basic rights, such as freedom of speech, conscience, religion and organisation. In his campaign he was very critical of détente because he claimed nothing was really being done to look after the interests of dissidents within the Communist bloc. In particular the Helsinki Agreements were criticised. He wanted to continue arms reductions talks, but any future agreement must be linked to this issue.

In his early months in office he made bold statements condemning oppression in countries as varied as Chile, Ethiopia, Brazil and El Salvador. Several of these states resented his meddling and rejected American aid rather than change their policies. When Carter wrote to the prominent Russian dissident Andrei Sakharov, and strongly attacked the Soviet Union's behaviour, the response was hostile. It was interpreted as interference in her internal affairs and resulted in a worsening of relations.

Negotiations leading towards SALT II had started under Ford but made little headway. Carter's insistence on linkage to human rights, combined with the United States' development of the neutron bomb and production of Cruise missiles intended to be deployed in Europe, made progress even slower. SALT II was eventually signed in June 1979 but could not come into effect until the Senate ratified it.

Afghanistan

In 1978 the non-aligned Afghan government was overthrown in a violent coup and replaced by a pro-Soviet Marxist regime. There was considerable internal unrest as Moslem rebels fought against this atheist government. Relations with the United States were poor, especially after February 1979 when the American Ambassador in Kabul was murdered.

In December 1979 an internal feud brought Babrak Karmal to power backed by the Soviet Union. A heavily armoured force of nearly 100 000 men was 'invited' in to help keep the Marxist regime in control, but found itself bogged down in a struggle with the rebels.

The United States' reaction was immediate. Carter said it led to a change in his opinion of what the goals of the Soviet Union were. It was seen as expansionism which presented a threat to Pakistan, Iran and the Indian Ocean. Carter asked the Senate to delay ratifying SALT II and imposed economic sanctions on the Soviet Union: the sale of grain was banned (Reagan reversed this in 1981) and the trade in high technology was restricted. He tried to organise an international boycott of the Olympics due to start in Moscow in June 1980, but this was only a partial success as eighty-five nations were eventually represented.

In January 1980 the United States announced the creation of a Rapid Deployment Force to take action at short notice throughout the Third World. Her military strength in the Indian Ocean was also to be reinforced by extending her base at Diego Garcia, and the acquisition of new facilities in Oman, Kenya and Somalia. This restored the balance in the Horn of Africa which had long caused the United States concern. Since 1977 the Soviet Union, helped by Cuban troops, had strongly backed Ethiopia in her war with Somalia. As she had another base in South Yemen the Soviet Union was in a strong position to interfere with the vital Red Sea shipping lanes.

By the end of Carter's Presidency East–West relations were worse than they had been at any time since the early 1960s: détente was at an end.

The Middle East

In the 1960s the United States was firmly committed to the preservation of Israel while the Soviet Union backed the Arab cause. In 1967 Israel won an overwhelming victory against the Arabs and made large territorial gains. She refused to return these lands, despite American pressure, and this intensified the conflict in later years.

Further warfare occurred in October 1973. Israel again defeated her neighbours but lost a large proportion of her armaments in the process. She needed urgent replacements from the United States before she could continue her campaign against Egypt. Arab oil producers imposed an embargo on Israel's supporters and the Egyptian leader, Anwar Sadat, appealed to the Soviet Union to intervene. The United States warned her

18.3 The Near East in the early 1980s.

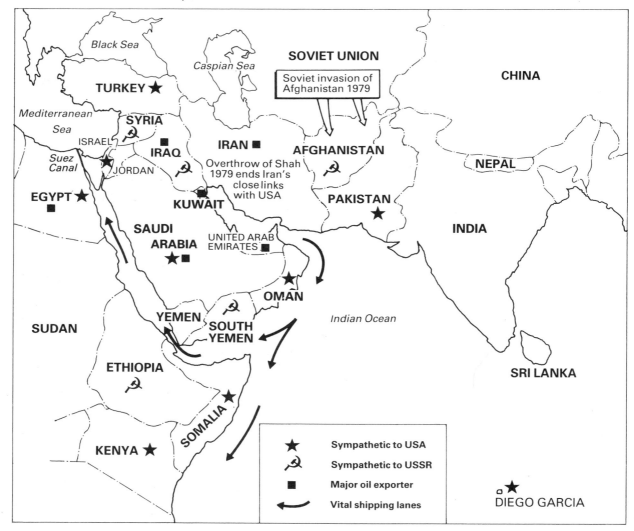

18.4 Soviet-made tanks of the People's Army of Afghanistan parade through Kabul in 1979.

18.5 Israel and her Arab neighbours.

off with a high level nuclear alert.

Kissinger was determined to use this situation to produce a long-term solution to the problem, but also to exclude the Soviet Union. He wanted to prevent either side from winning and keep both dependent on the United States for aid and security. As Kissinger observed: 'The Arabs can get guns from the Russians but they can get their territory back only from us.'

Over the next months he embarked on an exhausting programme of 'shuttle diplomacy', flying between the various embattled nations. Using the bait of aid he was able to obtain disengagement of the armies, cease-fire agreements, and an end to the oil embargo in March 1974. No permanent solution was reached but it was obvious that America's need for Arab oil had made her more willing to put pressure on Israel to make concessions.

The Camp David Agreements

Sadat's attitude changed after the 1973 defeat. He expelled the Soviet Union's advisers in 1976 and decided to take the initiative to seek a peaceful settlement. Sadat and his opposite number Begin visited each other's countries in 1977, and with the active encouragement of Carter, started negotiations. In 1978 agreement was reached at Camp David, Maryland, which led to the

18.6 President Carter with Prime Minister Begin of Israel and President Sadat of Egypt at Camp David, Maryland, in 1978.

1979 Peace Treaty. In return for considerable American aid to both sides, Egypt recognised the existence of Israel and the Israeli occupied territory in Sinai was restored to her. Israel, however, would not give way on other major differences with the Arabs. The United States was particularly critical of Israel's determination to continue building Jewish settlements in the occupied West Bank of Jordan. Egypt became isolated from the Arab world and clearly aligned with the United States. The relationship has not altered since Sadat's assassination in 1981. Although Carter made substantial progress he was unable to achieve the permanent solution he had hoped for.

Lebanon

In the early 1980s the most troubled nation in the Middle East was the Lebanon. Following the civil war in 1975–76, her government had very little real power

because her territory was divided amongst several warring factions. The Palestine Liberation Organisation (PLO) controlled large areas of southern Lebanon from which it launched attacks on Israel. The PLO was supported by the Moslem Druse forces, and by the Syrians who entered Lebanon in 1976 in their defence. In opposition to this generally left-wing grouping were the right-wing Christian Phalangists who were backed by Israel.

In response to repeated PLO attacks the Israelis invaded Lebanon in 1978 to destroy its bases. After considerable international pressure, the Israelis withdrew. The United States was particularly angered by this invasion as it came at a critical time in the Camp David peace negotiations.

A further, even more determined invasion by Israel came in June 1982. Israeli forces besieged Beirut and refused to withdraw until PLO and Syrian forces left the city. The United States severely criticised Israel for her ruthless attacks on the defenceless

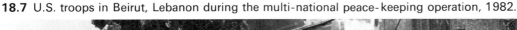

18.7 U.S. troops in Beirut, Lebanon during the multi-national peace-keeping operation, 1982.

capital city which caused considerable civilian casualties. The PLO and Syrian forces agreed to leave in September under the supervision of a new International Peacekeeping Force composed of French, Italian, British and predominantly United States forces.

The United States came into increasing conflict with the Israelis as she sought a settlement in the region. In September 1982 Reagan proposed a bold plan to set up a Palestinian state in the West Bank and Gaza to be linked to Jordan. Israel rejected this totally. Israel also resisted American pressure to leave Lebanon and allow the Lebanese government to restore its own authority. In May 1985 Israeli troops withdrew from much of Lebanon but still occupied a security zone along the Israeli-Lebanese border.

Events in Lebanon took on an alarming appearance following a massive bomb attack on a United States base in Lebanon. Moslem extremists were held responsible. With the intention of demonstrating his support for the Lebanese government, in November 1983 Reagan sent a powerful fleet to the area

equipped to repel any challenge by Moslem forces. This situation threatened to bring the United States into direct confrontation with the militant Syrians, who have close links with the Soviet Union. A superpower conflict appeared to be in the offing.

Reagan's Lebanese policy suffered severe setbacks early in 1984 when it became obvious that the Lebanese government had little chance of regaining military or political control over the whole country. The International Peacekeeping Force appeared to be fighting for a lost cause. United States troops were withdrawn in February and all other members of the Force were evacuated from Lebanon by March. The United States fleet remained off-shore awaiting developments. This was a major defeat for Reagan as he began his campaign for re-election in November 1984.

The Iranian Revolution

In 1953 the CIA had organised a coup to make Mohammed Riza Pahlavi Shah of Iran.

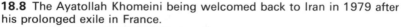

18.8 The Ayatollah Khomeini being welcomed back to Iran in 1979 after his prolonged exile in France.

His government was strongly pro-Western, allowing American companies to dominate the oil fields and the United States to install listening devices along the Soviet border. In 1977 Carter visited the Shah and praised him for creating 'an island of stability' and for 'deserving the respect and the admiration and love' of the Iranian people.

This was wishful thinking as in January 1979 the Shah was forced to leave Iran by radical Moslem revolutionaries opposed to his 'Western' reforms and oppressive regime. The religious leader Ayatollah Khomeini returned from exile to take charge, but the country degenerated into chaos as rival groups struggled violently for power.

The revolutionaries were equally opposed to the Soviet Union and United States. They were particularly anti-American because of the support the Shah had received in pursuing his repressive policies. Iran left CENTO and became aggressively anti-Israeli. When the Shah went to America for medical treatment, Khomeini urged all Moslems to gather at his hospital to 'dismember him'. In November 1979 students occupied the United States Embassy in Teheran and took its staff of about sixty hostage. They demanded the return of the Shah to face criminal charges. The Iranian authorities did nothing to obtain the hostages' release.

18.9 The American hostages arrive in West Germany after their release from Iran. Their release came half an hour after Carter's term as President ended.

The United States responded with economic sanctions and gained the UNO's support, but the Iranians were determined to humiliate her. In desperation on 24 April 1980 Carter ordered a military expedition to release them by force, but mechanical failure brought disaster to the mission. Carter was severely criticised at home for this move which may have endangered the hostages' lives. The Shah's death in July did little to improve the position.

By the end of the year Iran was prepared to compromise, with Algeria acting as mediator in the negotiations. The United States agreed to restore Iranian property frozen in America, and promised never to interfere in Iran again. The hostages were released on 20 January 1981, but not before Carter had handed over power to Reagan.

The hostage dispute succeeded in destroying Carter's prestige, which had already suffered severe setbacks over energy, the economy and relations with the Soviet Union. Occasional naivety and lack of experience contributed to his disappointments, but his high ideals were also frustrated by a short-sighted Congress, world recession and unforeseeable crises abroad.

The Republicans nominated Ronald Reagan to oppose Carter in 1980. He was a former Hollywood star of such films as 'Bedtime for Bonzo', who had made a successful career in politics. His performance as Governor of California had made him the hero of the newly confident conservatives in America. The decisive victory for Reagan by 43 219 000 to 34 917 000 was no surprise.

18.10 'The twentieth century Adonis', 1940. Ronald Reagan posing for a sculpture class having been selected as having 'the most nearly perfect male figure'.

Reaganomics

The most urgent problem Reagan had to face at home was the depression. He was a follower of the 'monetarist' school of economists which believes that inflation must be defeated by controlling the supply of money in the economy. This is mainly achieved by balancing the government's budget through reducing expenditure, combined with increasing interest rates to stop individuals and businesses living beyond their means. At the same time Reagan hoped to increase production by removing restrictions on the economy, and reducing taxes to encourage higher earnings by individuals and business. This was really just a more extreme version of the policies Carter had been forced to adopt. By 1983 inflation was down to 4% but unemployment had risen rapidly to over 10%. Even Reagan's critics agreed that there were signs of recovery appearing, although at a high social cost.

Despite his efforts difficulties remained as he was unable to balance the budget: he refused to cut expenditure on arms, and as unemployment rose there was little choice but to increase welfare spending. He was reluctantly forced to pay out more on food relief than Carter ever did. Many economists predicted grave dangers for the American and world economies if the huge budget deficit and high interest rates were not reduced.

A new Cold War

Reagan was very suspicious of détente and believed that the United States should adopt a much tougher attitude to prevent more 'aggression' by the Soviet Union which he described as an 'empire of evil'. He therefore abandoned SALT II and started to strengthen the American arsenal. The B-1 bomber and neutron bomb were ordered after Carter had halted their production, and the enormously expensive MX missile system was planned. In 1984 he ordered a research programme on 'Star Wars' weapons designed to attack enemy satellites and missiles in space.

At the same time Reagan was prepared to negotiate with the Soviet Union, but only from a position of strength. Talks started at Geneva aimed at reducing nuclear weapons. As these took place NATO decided to stick to the decision made under Carter to deploy the new Cruise and Pershing II missiles in Europe if agreement was not reached. These weapons were intended to counter the Soviet Union's newly deployed medium range SS-20s. Progress was hampered by accusations of bad faith on both sides and the tense international atmosphere produced by the situations in Afghanistan, Poland and Central America. When Cruise missiles were deployed in November 1983 the Soviet Union walked out of the Geneva talks in protest.

The Madrid Conference in September 1983 to revise the Helsinki Agreements also met with no success. The existing tension in this case was made worse by the shooting down by the Soviet Union in September of a South Korean airliner which had strayed, somewhat mysteriously, over Soviet territory.

Martial law in Poland

Throughout the 1970s, Poland had been beset by economic problems. This had led to demands by workers to be allowed to form an independent trade union, Solidarity, to protect their interests. The government was forced to accept this in 1980. As Solidarity's influence grew throughout 1981 the Soviet Union became concerned that Communist rule, and her own security, were at risk. In December martial law was declared by the Polish government, Solidarity was banned and its leaders arrested.

Reagan imposed economic sanctions on the Soviet Union and Poland in retaliation for this repressive action. He tried to obtain support from his European allies but they

were reluctant to follow suit, mainly because they were being asked to make large financial sacrifices. Considerable bad feeling resulted from this disagreement. Even though martial law was suspended in December 1982, Solidarity was still outlawed and East–West relations remained poor.

Central America

The region where the United States felt her interests were most at risk in the early 1980s was Central America. The area was dominated by pro-American right-wing dictatorships which had largely failed to make vital social and economic reforms. The impoverished peasants gave substantial support to the various left-wing guerrilla movements who despaired of the possibility of peaceful change. The United States believed these revolutionaries were being encouraged and armed by Cuba. In several of these states law and order had broken down as death squads, often acting on government orders, took revenge on their opponents and terrorised the population. In El Salvador alone it is estimated that 25 000 people died between January 1980 and September 1981 as a result of political violence.

In 1979 the brutal Somoza regime in Nicaragua was overthrown by the Sandinista guerrillas. Carter recognised the new government and provided aid to rebuild the devastated country. Reagan reversed this policy because he thought a Communist system, reliant on Cuba and the Soviet Union, was being created. His critics argued that Reagan was in fact helping to produce the situation he feared most: as the Sandinistas were deprived of American aid they turned to the Soviet Union. Nicaragua was also accused of spreading revolution to neighbouring countries, particularly El Salvador. Reagan financed anti-Sandinista guerrillas, and sent aid and advisors to El Salvador, Guatemala and other threatened governments. He was determined to prevent more dominoes in Central America from falling to Communism. His opponents were

18.11 Central America and the Caribbean.

afraid that he might even send American troops to the region and repeat the disastrous mistakes of Vietnam.

Cuba and Grenada

The Cuban influence in the Caribbean continued to cause the United States some concern. In 1979, when it became clear that the Soviet Union had a combat brigade based on Cuba, Carter demanded its immediate removal. The Soviet Union refused, and unlike 1962, the United States was powerless to force her troops to leave. This clearly showed how the balance of power had changed.

A new problem emerged on the small island of Grenada. In 1979 the pro-American government of Sir Eric Gairy was overthrown in a peaceful coup by Maurice Bishop, a left winger committed to a radical programme of reform. When it was clear that the new regime had friendly relations

with Cuba, the United States started to put economic pressure on the island with the intention of bringing about a change of government.

In October 1983 Bishop was overthrown and murdered by a more extreme, pro-Cuban faction inside his own armed forces. The United States saw this as yet another attempt by Cuba to spread revolution in the region. It was claimed that Cuba already had a large number of troops on the island. Reagan quickly ordered an invasion of Grenada intended to prevent Cuban domination and to return the island to democracy. Following an easy military victory most of the troops were withdrawn by the end of 1983. Elections were held in 1984.

The 1984 presidential election

Reagan approached the 1984 election as he appeared to approach all obstacles, with the utmost self-confidence. He had every reason to do so. The American economy was in the middle of a remarkable recovery which was producing impressive growth rates and falling unemployment. Interest rates were very high, but drifting downwards. The value of the dollar in relation to most other currencies was steadily rising. This apparently satisfactory situation was largely brought about by an enormous government deficit, something Reagan had been committed to eradicate in the 1980 election campaign. Voters did not seem to worry about this potentially disastrous problem so long as their standards of living continued to improve. Abroad, the United States was widely believed to be in a much stronger position than it had been four years earlier. Reagan had been 'tough on the Russians' by adopting a hard line in nuclear arms negotiations, deploying Cruise missiles, increasing military spending, and resisting the Cubans and Sandinistas in America's backyard. Most Americans felt a renewed pride in their nation which even the humiliating failure of Reagan's policies in the Lebanon could not dispel. The fact that far more Americans had been killed abroad serving their country under Reagan than under Carter did not appear to concern the electorate. Reagan made them feel strong, proud and prosperous, and millions were won over to his side.

Reagan's cause was made even easier, however, by the weakness of the opposition. In their search for an effective candidate to confront Reagan, the Democrats underwent a bitter primary election campaign which left the party deeply divided, and the winner significantly discredited. The sincere but unimaginative former Vice-President Walter Mondale had started the campaign soon after the 1980 election and was always the front runner. He faced a surprisingly serious challenge from the almost unknown Senator Gary Hart, who claimed to want a new, youthful and dynamic image for the Democrats. In many ways the most impressive candidate was the Reverend Jesse Jackson, the first black ever to attempt to obtain a party nomination. He challenged the complacency of a white dominated party,

especially when he encouraged large numbers of blacks and Hispanics (Latin Americans) to register as voters for the first time. In the past these groups had often chosen not to participate in politics. If they did use their votes they could have considerable influence on elections. Mondale was able to win his party's nomination largely due to the support provided by traditional-minded party activists and interest groups such as trade unions. At an early stage in the campaign it was quite clear that Mondale would need much wider backing than this if he were to defeat Reagan.

He made a bold attempt to attract new support by selecting Geraldine Ferraro as his running mate. She attracted a great deal of attention as the first woman ever to be nominated for the Vice-Presidency, but she was unable to help Mondale weaken Reagan's position.

The contest was to a large extent fought on television with presentation of the candidates in the hands of advertising agencies. Reagan's campaign was chiefly in the hands of two men whose earlier creations had included a singing cat, and Michael Jackson selling Pepsi Cola. This style of campaigning was widely criticised for its concentration on images rather than issues. It certainly favoured Reagan who was completely at home in front of the camera, and who concentrated on generalised statements rather than details of policy. By contrast Mondale was ill at ease and unattractive to the viewers.

When issues were debated Mondale often had the better of the argument, although this fact failed to alter voting behaviour. Reagan was able to draw strength from the increasingly conservative mood of many sections of society. He stressed his commitment to traditional American values and a 'society which lets each person's dreams unfold into a life of unending hope'. Free enterprise must be safeguarded and unnecessary spending on welfare projects should be cut. He received enthusiastic backing from the 'Moral Majority', a vociferous, militant fundamentalist Christian pressure group, for many of his policies, such as opposition to abortion and support for compulsory prayer in schools. Many liberals, feminists, nuclear disarmers, blacks and non-Christians were alarmed by Reagan but Mondale was unable to inspire them, or to convince waverers that he would make a better President. Even when it was pointed out that Reagan would be a record seventy-seven years old, and with declining physical and mental abilities if he completed a second term in the White House, few electors were concerned. The truth was that for most voters, including a third of registered Democrats, their great liking for Ronald Reagan as a man overcame any reservations they might have for his policies. This was borne out in the results.

Reagan won overwhelmingly with 53 million votes (59%) to 37 million (41%). He won in every state except Mondale's own Minnesota, and in the District of Columbia. The electoral college margin was a record 525 to 13.

Reagan was able to win more votes than Mondale from all age groups, and most national minorities and religious groups. Even though Ferraro was an Italian-American, Roman Catholic woman, these sections of society all favoured Reagan. Mondale was more attractive than Reagan only to blacks, Jews, the unemployed, the poor and trade unionists, but even with these sections of society support for him was only lukewarm.

The performance of the Republicans in the Congressional elections, however, was much weaker. They lost ground in the Senate, where their majority was reduced by two to 53 to 47. In the House of Representatives they reduced the Democratic majority slightly but still trailed 181 to 254. This confusing result occurred because one-fifth of the electorate voted for a Democrat for Congress but backed the Republican Reagan for President. Reagan was faced with a Congress which was very likely to attack much of his legislative programme.

'You ain't seen nothing yet'

As Reagan started his second, and final four years as President, political observers inevitably speculated about the future. At the time of writing it seems probable that with such convincing electoral support he will have the prestige to persuade even a critical Congress to accept many of his proposals. However, as the 1988 elections approach the less influence he will have because Congress will be fully aware that soon it will have to bargain with another President. Reagan will have little to offer in return for support and will become a 'lame duck'. The chances of seeing what Reagan has termed a 'second American revolution' are slim.

Economists believe his most important task will be to attempt to reduce the budget deficit. Since he has rejected the idea of tax increases the other main option open to him will be to reduce spending. He is certainly enthusiastic about cutting many domestic spending programmes, but this is unlikely to be sufficient to balance the budget. Defence spending will also need to be brought under control. There seems very little likelihood of this happening since his foreign policies are based on strengthening the United States' military power.

Towards the end of 1984 both superpowers seemed to be more willing to resume détente. The Soviet Union's foreign minister, Gromyko, visited the United States in September, and Reagan more frequently expressed his determination to reach an agreement on limiting nuclear armaments. In March 1985 arms talks restarted in Geneva. On the other hand, there was no relaxation in the United States' hard line in Central America. On the day after Reagan was re-elected there were strongly worded American allegations that Nicaragua was receiving a shipment of Soviet MiG fighters. Nicaragua protested to the United Nations, and claimed the United States was about to invade her territory to overthrow the Sandinistas.

18.12

Perhaps significantly, it was the Soviet Union which tried to reduce the tension between the two countries.

Only time can tell whether Reagan will be able to lead the United States back to her former pre-eminence in the American continent and elsewhere in the world. In the forty years since the end of the Second World War there have been major changes in the nature of international politics. Once, the United States had been to a certain extent able to impose her wishes on most parts of the world. By the 1980s her power and prestige had been successfully challenged or ignored by countries as 'insignificant' as Vietnam, Cuba, Nicaragua, Iran and Lebanon. Even some of her NATO allies were becoming less willing to follow automatically America's policies. This was seen clearly with regard to the decision to deploy Cruise missiles. The United States could undoubtedly annihilate all life on earth and deter any acts of aggression by the Soviet Union. But could she succeed in the more difficult and delicate task of persuading the governments of the non-Communist world to adopt acceptable policies without taking the politically risky step of using military force?

It has been perhaps Reagan's greatest achievement that he has managed to convince Americans that the state of the nation is healthier than it had been in 1980, and that the prospects are even brighter. This view of the United States' position at home and abroad is disturbingly over simple and ignores many significant problems. Both Reagan and the electorate prefer to play down these difficulties and argue that the solution to them is to remain firm and loyal to traditional American values. Reagan's optimism and self-confidence are irresistible: 'America's best days lie ahead and you ain't seen nothing yet.'

Glossary

AAA
The Agricultural Adjustment Administration was established in 1933 as part of Roosevelt's New Deal programme. It was intended to help increase farm incomes and improve production methods.

Administration
This term is usually used to describe a President's team of assistants, advisers and civil servants. In Britain the word 'government' would generally be used.

Alliance for Progress
Formed in 1961, the Alliance for Progress was designed to provide loans to Latin American countries for economic development. It achieved little of lasting benefit.

Amendment
There have been twenty-six amendments (changes) to the United States Constitution. These affect, sometimes drastically, the way America is governed. An amendment can only be made with the approval of three-quarters of all the individual states.

Americanism
See pages 5–6.

Anarchist
Someone who supports the idea of a society with no government.

Annex
A territory is annexed when it is taken over by a more powerful state, frequently by force.

Armistice
An agreement to stop fighting.

ARVN
The Army of the Republic of Vietnam (South Vietnam).

Autonomy
The right of self-government.

Axis
The 'Rome-Berlin Axis' of 1936 was designed to provide joint military assistance for Franco in the Spanish Civil War. It developed into a firm alliance between Hitler's Germany and Mussolini's Italy by 1939.

Back Yard
This term is frequently used to describe the Caribbean, Central and South America, areas where the United States feels she has a special interest, and a right to intervene where necessary.

BEF
The Bonus Expeditionary Force was a demonstration of unemployed ex-servicemen who marched on Washington D.C. in 1932 to demand early payment of veterans' bonuses promised at the end of the First World War.

Bill of Rights
The first ten amendments, ratified in 1791, are usually known as the Bill of Rights. They concern themselves with the protection of individual liberties such as freedom of speech, the right of peaceful assembly, the right to bear arms, and the right to a fair trial.

Bizonia
In 1946 the British and American occupied zones of Germany united to form Bizonia.

Budget
The annual estimate of the money the Federal Government will raise (mainly by taxation) and the amount it will spend. When more money is collected than spent the budget is in 'surplus'. When more is spent than collected, the budget is in

'deficit'. When the two sums are equal the budget is 'balanced'.

Capitalism
This economic system is favoured by the United States. The means of production (land, factories, etc.) are owned by a relatively small number of people and are managed mainly for reasons of private profit.

CCC
The Civilian Conservation Corps was founded in 1933 as part of Roosevelt's New Deal. It gave employment to young men on projects to help conserve the countryside.

Cede
When a territory is given by one country to another it is ceded. This is frequently done under pressure.

CENTO
Known from 1955 as the Baghdad Pact, this alliance was renamed the Central Treaty Organisation (CENTO) when Iraq left. The remaining members were Britain, Turkey, Iran and Pakistan. Its aim was to contain Communism. It collapsed after the 1979 Iranian Revolution.

CIA
The Central Intelligence Agency supervises American intelligence activities (spying) throughout the world. It has also been active in influencing the affairs of other countries to help American interests.

Civil rights
In the 1950s and 1960s civil rights campaigners tried to obtain for blacks the same opportunities as whites in all walks of life. Particular emphasis was placed on the right to vote, and desegregation of education and all public facilities.

Cold War
The period of tension and confrontation, but not open warfare, between the United States and Soviet Union since 1945.

Collective security
A system for maintaining international peace whereby all nations act together against any aggressor. The League of Nations and United Nations Organisation were formed in part to put this principle into practice.

COMECON
The Council for Mutal Economic Assistance (COMECON) was founded by the Soviet Union in 1949 in response to Marshall Aid. It aimed to help East European economies to recover and to tie them closely to the Soviet Union.

COMINFORM
The Communist Information Bureau (COMINFORM) was formed in 1947 as a means of strengthening the control by the Soviet Union over other European Communist Parties.

Communist
A member of the political party which believes all the means of production (land, factories, etc.) should be owned by the state or community. The Soviet Union's version of Communism also involves a one-party state with considerable restrictions on individual liberties. The philosophy of this party was first developed by Marx and Engels in the nineteenth century.

Congress
The part of the Federal Government which makes laws. It has two sections, the Senate and House of Representatives. The Senate has 100 members, two from each state regardless of size. The House has 435 members elected by constituencies with similar populations.

Conservatives
Those people who prefer to maintain existing conditions and values rather than agree to change.

Constitution
The American Constitution (rules by which the United States is governed) is a written document dating back to 1787. Any disputes

arising from the meaning of this Constitution are decided by the Supreme Court. The court has the power to declare 'unconstitutional' any actions which are forbidden by the Constitution.

Containment
The policy of preventing the spread of Communism beyond the territory already controlled by the Soviet Union. It was first proclaimed in the Truman Doctrine in 1947 and has dominated American foreign policy since then.

Convention
Once every four years each political party meets to choose its candidate for the forthcoming presidential election. Attending these conventions are delegates representing party organisations from each state. They are selected by a variety of processes, the most common of which are elections by party activists (caucuses), or primary elections when all party supporters are able to express their preference amongst the rival candidates. Delegates are usually committed to support one candidate for the presidential nomination.

CORE
The Congress for Racial Equality (CORE) was one of many groups campaigning for civil rights in the 1950s and 1960s. It is particularly associated with the 'Freedom Riders'.

Coup d'état
A violent or illegal change of government.

Conventional forces
Armed forces which rely on non-nuclear weapons.

CREEP
Nixon formed the Campaign to Re-Elect the President in 1972. Opponents referred to it as CREEP. It later became notorious for its use of 'dirty tricks' to undermine opponents' campaigns.

CWA
The Civil Works Administration was formed in 1933 as part of Roosevelt's New Deal to provide emergency, short-term jobs for the unemployed. It ceased to exist in 1934.

Deficit
See 'Budget'.

Democracy
A political system where the government is chosen by the whole adult population exercising a free and secret choice amongst several alternatives. For a democratic system to work properly there must be freedom of speech and the press, and the liberty to demonstrate and assemble peacefully. The Soviet Union claims to be a democracy and believes the American and West European versions are fraudulent.

Democratic Party
The Democratic Party in the twentieth century has been more liberal than the Republicans. Democrats are usually prepared to accept reforms where necessary and often support high spending by an active Federal Government.

Depression
In an economic depression there will be a sharp decrease in the amount of trade and a resulting increase in bankruptcies and unemployment. The term 'depression' is frequently alternated with 'recession'. The latter is a more short-lived and less severe version of a depression. Which word is chosen largely depends on individual opinion.

Détente
A relaxation of tension between the superpowers. This usually refers to the early 1970s.

Domino Theory
This theory dominated United States policy in South-East Asia from the early 1950s. It compares the countries of this region with a row of dominoes placed on end. When one falls over the rest inevitably topple as well.

The United States saw Communists attempting to push over first North Vietnam, then South Vietnam, Cambodia, Thailand and so on. In recent years this theory has also been applied to Central America.

Draft
Compulsory military service (conscription).

DRV
The Democratic Republic of Vietnam was founded in 1945 by Ho Chi Minh. It soon came into conflict with the French who wished to return Vietnam to colonial rule. From 1954 it had a more secure existence and was more frequently known as North Vietnam. After 1975 the Communist DRV reunited with the Republic of Vietnam (South Vietnam).

Dry
Those who supported prohibition of alcohol were frequently known as 'drys'.

Fair Deal
Truman's programme of liberal reforms in the years 1945–53 was usually known as the 'Fair Deal'. He hoped for improvements in the social security system, housing provision and civil rights. The achievements were very limited.

Fascism
Fascists are violently opposed to Communism and democracy. They are extreme nationalists, and are frequently racist. They believe in the rule of a dictator and idealise the use of armed force. Individual human rights are generally ignored in the supposed interests of the state. The most important fascist states have been Mussolini's Italy and Hitler's Germany.

Federal Government
This is based in Washington D.C. and is concerned with matters affecting all the United States. Other affairs are left to the fifty individual state governments.

FEPC
The Fair Employment Practices Commission was founded in 1941 to end racial discrimination by Federal Government employers.

FERA
The Federal Emergency Relief Administration was set up in 1933 as part of Roosevelt's New Deal to provide help, through the states, for the needy.

FNLA
The American and South African backed National Front for the Liberation of Angola was one of several groups involved in a struggle for power after 1975.

Founding Fathers
The group of men who devised the Constitution of the United States and so helped to create one nation out of the thirteen separate states. Most influential were George Washington, Benjamin Franklin, James Madison and Alexander Hamilton.

Free enterprise
The economic system whereby anyone with initiative, skill or wealth, may own a business and receive the profits it produces. In a free enterprise economy government interference is reduced to a minimum.

Free French
The French government-in-exile 1940–44 led by Charles de Gaulle. It claimed to be the genuine French government in opposition to the German dominated Vichy French regime.

Free trade
The absence of restrictions, usually tariffs, on international trade.

GNP
The Gross National Product (GNP) is a calculation of the amount of wealth a country produces. It is the most frequently used indicator of prosperity.

Great Society
Johnson hoped to move towards a 'Great Society' with an extensive programme of liberal reforms in the 1960s. These dealt with health, education, poverty and civil rights. The achievements were considerable.

Guerrilla
Guerrilla warfare is conducted by small groups of soldiers aiming to harass enemy troops and to lower their morale. These tactics are usually used against a powerful army when a large scale confrontation would bring defeat.

HOLC
The Home Owners Loan Corporation was set up in 1933 as part of Roosevelt's New Deal. It aimed to help with the repayment of loans taken out to buy homes.

Hoovervilles
Ironically named after President Hoover, these shanty towns appeared all over America during the 1930s to house those who were migrating in search of work.

House of Representatives
See Congress.

Human rights
It is generally accepted that these rights should belong to all human beings. They include the right to life, a fair trial, freedom of speech, conscience and religion. Most people in reality lack all or some of these.

Hyphenates
A term frequently used to describe the many national groups within American society. These include Irish-Americans, German-Americans and Polish-Americans.

Impeachment
The President and Supreme Court Justices can only be forcibly removed by impeachment. This means a trial, on criminal charges, conducted by Congress.

Imperialism
This imprecise term is frequently a term of abuse. It means the control by one country of other weaker ones. The methods of control vary considerably and include military conquest and economic influence. The Soviet Union claims that the United States is an imperialist power because she has military bases throughout the world, and is able to exert considerable influence over a large number of smaller countries. The Soviet Union is seen as an imperialist power because of her control over Eastern Europe and influence elsewhere.

Integration
The policy of ending separation between the races especially in education and public facilities. This particularly applied to the Southern States in the period up to the 1960s.

Internationalist
A supporter of close relations between states. See Isolationist.

Iron Curtain
This term, first coined by Winston Churchill in 1946, describes the heavily guarded frontier between the Russian dominated Eastern Europe and the West European democracies.

Isolationist
Someone who believes that entanglements with other nations should be minimised. This term is usually used to describe the United States' foreign policy in the 1920s and 1930s.

Jim Crow laws
These were designed to ensure that blacks were kept in a disadvantaged position, mainly in Southern States. Devices employed included poll taxes, literacy tests to qualify to vote and segregated schools. The Supreme Court and Civil Rights legislation have largely abolished these laws since the 1960s.

Khmer Rouge
The political party and guerrilla army which gained power in Cambodia in 1975. It was strongly influenced by Chinese Communist ideas.

KKK
The Ku Klux Klan is the extreme racist organisation dedicated to preserving what it believes to be the true American way of life. In its campaign against blacks, Jews, Catholics and others, many violent acts have been committed.

Laissez-faire
The policy of no government interference in the running of business or other matters of supposedly private concern. This is often associated with free enterprise.

Latin America
Central and South America and the Caribbean are often loosely described as Latin America.

League of Nations
The league was established by the peace treaties of 1919 and was intended to help keep the peace and solve problems of international concern. Although the league was originally President Wilson's idea, the United States failed to join when the Senate rejected the idea in 1920.

Lend-Lease
In 1940 the United States agreed to provide Britain with unlimited supplies of armaments and raw materials and allow her to pay for them after the war. This 'Lend-Lease' scheme was later extended to other countries in the war against Germany, Italy and Japan.

Liberals
Those people who tend to support reforms to produce greater equality of opportunity and personal freedom.

Liberation
This policy is associated with Eisenhower and Dulles in the 1950s who argued that the United States should 'liberate' countries controlled by the Soviet Union. This is in contrast with Truman's policy of containment.

Marshall Plan
As part of the policy of containment, and to help their economies to recover from the disruption of war, the United States started in 1948 to provide substantial amounts of economic aid to many European countries. When the scheme ended in 1952 $13 billion were spent and the results were impressive. The plan was originally proposed by Secretary of State, General George C. Marshall.

Medicare
This system of insurance schemes and government subsidies for medical care for the poor and elderly was started in 1965 as part of Johnson's 'Great Society'. It is the nearest that the United States comes to Britain's National Health Service.

Middle America
This loose term is perhaps best defined by a series of negatives: those who are 'unpoor, unyoung and unblack'. 'Middle Americans' have become more vociferous since the 1960s and have strongly supported conservative Republicans like Nixon and Reagan.

Mid-term elections
These elections for all members of the House of Representatives and a third of the Senate come half way through a President's term of office.

Mid-West
The vast prairie region of the United States noted for cereal farming. It includes states such as Iowa, Nebraska and the Dakotas.

Monetarism
The economic theory which has strongly influenced the policies of Presidents Carter and Reagan. See page 202.

MPLA
The Popular Movement for the Liberation of Angola was backed by the Soviet Union and Cuba in its victorious campaign in the civil war 1975–76.

NAACP
The National Association for the Advancement of Colored People worked for racial equality and integration by challenging racist laws in the courts. Its greatest victory was the 1954 *Brown* v. *Board of Education of Topeka* decision that 'separate but equal' facilities were unconstitutional.

Nationalise
The taking-over by the state of privately owned property.

Nationalist
A nationalist is usually eager to strengthen his own country and to make it totally independent of control by other nations.

NATO
The North Atlantic Treaty Organisation was founded in 1949 as an alliance of nations in Western Europe, Canada and the United States committed to contain Communism.

NEI
The Netherlands (or Dutch) East Indies gained independence in 1949 and is now known as Indonesia.

Neutrality Acts
This series of laws after 1935 was designed to ensure that the United States was not drawn into other nations' wars by economic contacts with belligerents. They had little effect.

Neutral Rights
Before the Second World War the United States claimed that as a neutral power she had a right to trade with any nation. Any interference with these neutral rights was considered to be a hostile act.

New Deal
In 1933 Roosevelt promised a 'New Deal' for the American people in order to bring the nation out of economic depression. It involved a considerable amount of government spending and activity in areas previously thought to be beyond its concern.

New Frontier
Kennedy believed it was necessary to create a 'New Frontier' in 1961 in order to revive the United States after what he saw as a period of stagnation. He started a programme of military expansion, active foreign policies, space exploration, economic and social reforms and civil rights legislation.

NIRA
The National Industrial Recovery Act was passed in 1933 as part of Roosevelt's New Deal. See page 51.

NLF
The National Liberation Front, formed in 1960, was an alliance of nationalist groups led by Communists, which aimed to reunite North and South Vietnam. It fought an increasingly destructive war against the South Vietnamese government and the United States until 1975. It was originally organised entirely in the South but received large amounts of aid from the North as the war intensified.

Non-aligned
A non-aligned state tries to remain neutral in the rivalry between the Soviet Union and United States.

NRA
The National Recovery Administration was created by the NIRA in 1933. See pages 51–52.

OAS
The Organisation of American States (OAS) was founded in 1948 to enable members to discuss matters of common interest.

OEEC
The Organisation for European Economic Co-operation was formed in 1948 to administer aid under the Marshall Plan.

Okies
Although they were supposedly from Oklahoma, this term was used to describe any farming families who were forced off their land during the Depression. They usually moved to areas like California in search of work.

OPA
The Office of Price Administration was formed in 1941 to prevent the inflation which was likely to be produced by wartime shortages and full employment.

OPEC
The Organisation of Petroleum Exporting Countries was formed in 1959 to control the supply of oil in the world and to keep prices high for the benefit of the producers. Its power was at its height during the early 1970s.

Open World
After 1945 the United States hoped the world could be reorganised to allow complete freedom for all nations to trade and invest wherever they chose. In this 'open world' no state should be allowed to control a sphere of influence where outside interests could be excluded.

OVERLORD
The codename for the Allied invasion of Normandy, France, in June 1944.

Override
See Veto.

Pathet Lao
The Communist, nationalist guerrilla army which fought throughout the period since 1945 and finally obtained power in Laos in 1975.

PLO
The Palestine Liberation Organisation is committed to the re-establishment of a Palestinian state. It has fought a guerrilla campaign against Israel since 1948.

Poll tax
This tax was imposed on any voter, but as blacks were usually poor, it hurt them most. Blacks were therefore discouraged from voting. This 'Jim Crow' law was banned in 1964.

Poverty Program
This was an important part of Johnson's 'Great Society' programme after 1964. It involved job training, urban renewal schemes and loans to poor families.

Prohibition
From 1920 it was illegal to make, sell or transport alcoholic beverages. This prohibition was never successfully enforced and was ended in 1933.

PWA
The Public Works Administration was established in 1933 by the NIRA as part of Roosevelt's New Deal. See page 53.

Radical
Someone who supports drastic reforms (literally from the 'roots').

Ratify
Congress must ratify (approve) many Presidential decisions and appointments. This applies to treaties and cabinet appointments.

Recession
See Depression.

Relief
Emergency financial help for the poor is commonly referred to as 'relief'.

Reparations
Following both world wars there were strong demands from the victors for reparations, repayment by the defeated 'aggressors' for the damage caused by the conflict.

Republican Party
The Republicans tend to appeal to the more conservative American voters. They are reluctant to accept a strong Federal Government and are usually anxious to cut the federal budget.

RVN
The Republic of Vietnam, created by the Geneva Agreements of 1954, is also known as South Vietnam.

SALT
The United States and Soviet Union signed Strategic Arms Limitation Treaties in 1972 and 1975, although SALT II was never ratified. They were designed to limit the growth in some kinds of nuclear weapons.

Sanctions
Sanctions (punishments) are applied when one country has acted against the wishes of another. Economic sanctions can include a partial or total ban on trade in order to weaken the opponent. Military sanctions usually mean war, and are often used when economic sanctions have failed to have the desired effect.

SCLC
The Southern Christian Leadership Conference, led by Martin Luther King, worked for civil rights using nonviolent methods.

SEATO
The South East Asia Treaty Organisation was formed in 1954 to help contain Communism. Its members were the United States, Britain, Australia, New Zealand, France, Thailand, Pakistan and the Philippines.

Secretary of State
The government official in charge of American foreign policy.

Segregation
Until the 1960s, in most Southern States blacks and whites were deliberately segregated (kept separate) in as many ways as possible. See Integration.

Self-determination
See Autonomy.

Senate
See Congress.

SNCC
The Student Nonviolent Co-ordinating Committee worked for civil rights, and is particularly associated with the 'sit in' campaign after 1960.

Socialism
Socialists share very similar aims to Communists, but are not necessarily members of the Communist Party, which believes in the inevitability of a revolution to achieve its objectives.

Social Security
Government payments to the unemployed and needy.

Speculation
See pages 34–37.

Sphere of Influence
A region of the world dominated by a great power. The countries of such a region are only able to act with the approval of the great power concerned.

States Rights
The belief that individual states should not be subjected to interference in their own way of life by the Federal Government. Southern whites have frequently used 'states rights' to resist attempts to end racial segregation.

Supreme Court
The highest court in America. Its power to interpret the meaning of the Constitution can have great importance. Acts of Congress (laws) may be brought to the court for a judgement on whether they obey the Constitution's rules. If the court declares an Act to be 'unconstitutional' it is immediately repealed.

Surplus
See 'Budget'.

Tariff
A tax on goods entering a country. It is usually imposed to protect home producers by making foreign goods more expensive.

This encourages home consumers to buy home produced goods.

Third World
Nations which are developing economically, but are at present very poor.

Truman Doctrine
See 'Containment'.

TVA
The Tennessee Valley Authority was established in 1933 as part of Roosevelt's New Deal. See page 56.

U-2
U-2 spy planes were capable of flying at altitudes beyond the reach of Soviet planes. From the late 1950s they provided the United States with important information about Soviet activities.

Un-Americanism
See pages 121–3.

Unconstitutional
See Supreme Court.

UNITA
The National Union for the Total Independence of Angola was backed by the United States and South Africa in the civil war 1975–76.

UNO
Nearly all countries belong to the United Nations Organisation, which was founded in 1945 and is based in New York. Its purpose is to preserve world peace and encourage cooperation in the solution of problems of international concern. Its success to date has been limited.

Veto
The President has the power to veto (reject) any law approved by Congress. If this happens Congress may override it by a two-thirds vote in both the Senate and House and thus force the President to accept it.

VC
The Viet Cong (the Vietnamese Communist Party) took the leading role in the NLF's guerrilla war against South Vietnam.

Vichy France
When Germany defeated France in 1940 the French government moved to Vichy and continued to administer part of France. In reality the Vichy regime was a puppet of the Germans, whose army occupied all but the South-West of France.

Viet Minh
This was a coalition of many groups committed to obtaining the independence of Vietnam from France. It was founded in 1941 and led by the Communist, Ho Chi Minh. The Viet Minh fought a successful war against the French which ended in the partitioning of Vietnam in 1954. The Viet Minh was later replaced by the NLF.

Vietnamization
This was the policy, adopted after 1968, of replacing American with Vietnamese troops. The United States continued to provide aid. The process was completed when the United States withdrew her forces in 1973.

Washington D.C.
The District of Columbia (D.C.) is the site of the federal capital city, Washington. It is not a part of any of the individual states so that the capital cannot be dominated by any state.

WASPs
White Anglo-Saxon Protestants are regarded by some as the 'ideal Americans'.

Watergate
President Nixon was forced to resign in 1974 as a result of revelations about misuse of Presidential power. These scandals, usually known as the Watergate affair, emerged after it became clear that the burglars of the Democratic Party headquarters at the Watergate complex were connected with the White House.

Welfare state
A country where the government ensures
that all its citizens have the basic means to
live a decent life. This usually includes
sickness and unemployment insurance, a
national health service, old age pensions and
free education.

Wets
Those who opposed the prohibition of
alcohol were known as 'wets'.

Whites
The opponents of the Communists in the
Russian civil war were known as Whites.

WPA
The Works Progress Administration was
formed in 1935 as part of Roosevelt's New
Deal. See page 54.

Yellow Dog Contracts
Before they were made illegal in 1933, many
employers refused to hire workers unless
they signed 'Yellow Dog Contracts'. These
contracts banned workers from joining a
union.

Index

'G' before a page number indicates a reference to the Glossary